Legalism Unmasked

Dirk Waren

Soaring Eagle Press

Legalism Unmasked (New Revised Edition)

Copyright © 2018 by Dirk Waren

Unless otherwise indicated, all scripture quotations are taken from the Holy Bible, New International Version®. NIV®. Copyright © 1973, 1978, 1984 by the International Bible Society. Used by permission of Zondervan Bible Publishers.

Many NIV citations are from the 2011 Revised edition.

Other versions of the Bible cited are listed in the **Bibliography**.

All underlining and italics in scriptural citations are added by the author.

Pronominal references to Deity in this work are generally not capitalized.

Edited by J. Altieri and KEEII.

Illustrations by KEEII.

ISBN: 978-0692064351
PUBLISHED BY SOARING EAGLE PRESS
Youngstown

Printed in the United States of America

"For the Letter Kills,
But the Spirit Gives Life"

CONTENTS

Chapter 1

Unmasking Legalism

I ran into someone on the internet the other day and he denounced Christianity on the grounds that it had "hypocritical teachings" and its followers were "enslaved to rules." He also referred to God as an "invisible sky daddy."

These are fairly typical criticisms of Christianity but it's ironic that not one of them is legitimate. All three criticisms refer to **legalism**, which is *counterfeit* **Christianity**. It's easy for people to mistake the counterfeit for the genuine because the counterfeit *looks* like the genuine. Just as a counterfeit $50 bill looks like the real thing so someone thoroughly infected by legalism *looks* like a genuine Christian. You can only tell the difference upon close inspection, as long as you know for what to look.

Let's consider this man's three criticisms in light of what the Bible actually teaches:

As far as "hypocritical teachings" go, 'hypocrisy' literally means to put on an act. I explained to the man that the Bible outright denounces hypocrisy (1 Peter 2:1) and blatantly states that God's wisdom is

"WITHOUT HYPOCRISY" (James 3:17[1]). This guy might have run into some professing believers who were hypocrites, but this doesn't mean that Christianity itself is hypocritical or that it advocates hypocrisy. How foolish to discount *all* Christianity simply because of a bad experience with *some* people who propose to be Christians. It's throwing the baby out with the bathwater.

Concerning his criticism that believers are "enslaved to rules," I told him I didn't know what version of Christianity he was exposed to but it certainly wasn't REAL Christianity because authentic Christianity outright denies enslavement to religious rules, as seen here:

> **It is for <u>freedom</u> that Christ has set us <u>free</u>. Stand firm, then, and <u>do not</u> let yourselves be burdened again by a yoke of Slavery.**
>
> **Galatians 5:1**

The "yoke of slavery" Paul was referring to was the YOKE OF RELIGIOUS LAW, which—in this case—included the Old Testament Torah and its hundreds of laws, like circumcision, as well as traditional fasts and observing various holy-days.[2] While Paul adamantly declared elsewhere that the Law was "holy, righteous and good" (Romans 7:12) it was actually a yoke of slavery if the Law was pursued as a means of reconciliation with God and the all-and-end-all of faith. What then was the purpose of the Law? To *prove* the need of a Savior. In fact, the Law pointed to the Savior (John 5:39). New Testament believers are set free from the yoke of slavery to the Law through spiritual regeneration, which is made available through the Good News of Christ.

To all intents and purposes, there are only two laws in Christianity with three applications: **Love God** and **love people** as you **love yourself**. When believers fulfill these two simple laws, they automatically fulfill *all* the moral law (Matthew 22:36-40). All believers have to do is learn to put off the "old self" and put on the "new self," meaning live out of their new spiritual nature and not the flesh. This

---

[1] New King James Version.
[2] Circumcision was an issue as confirmed by Galatians 2:3 and 5:2-3 whereas the others are addressed in 4:10.

enables them to be "like God" and walk in "true righteousness" (Ephesians 4:22-24). Do you find this incredulous? Keep reading.

I then explained to the man that what he referred to as "enslavement to rules" was actually legal-ism, because legalism focuses on religious rules rather than what Christianity is really about. Christianity is not a set of rules, like every *religion* on Earth, but rather a dynamic *relationship* with the Creator of the universe through spiritual rebirth. True believers aren't "enslaved to rules" like prune-faced religionists because we simply live according to our new nature, which is who we ARE. Remember, the gospel literally means "good news." Why? Because Jesus Christ came to give us ABUNDANT LIFE (John 10:10), not enslave us to some system of rules. Like the world needs another impotent religion with its dos and don'ts!

As for the man's final criticism, that God was an "invisible sky daddy," this is also a misconception that can be attributed to legalism. I explained that the LORD isn't only in Heaven; he's *everywhere* because he's omnipresent. More than that, he's *within me*, just as he's in all believers (Luke 17:21). Legalists, on the other hand, can't handle this concept because their entire focus is on the outward forms of Christianity, not its heart. As such, God is "out there" somewhere far away, like some big cop in the sky and we *might* be able to reach Him but only if we conform to the lifeless drudgery of the religious grind, whatever that might be.

It's so sad that this is how many unbelievers picture Christianity because it's simply not true. It's even sadder when professing Christians have this perception. It's a picture of legalism, not real Christianity; an image that's often seen in the popular media. Practically anytime a Christian-type character is featured in a mainstream movie or TV show it's either a sourpuss religionist, like the "Church Lady," or an uninspiring milksop. How often do you see someone as dynamic, bold and inspiring as Jesus Christ, Paul, Peter or John? Rarely.

Is it any wonder that a man I was talking to recently argued that Christianity weakens people and instills fear. He likened God and the devil to forest monsters in fairy tales that Christian leaders use to control and limit people through fear. Such a view may reflect some legalistic groups who propose to be Christian, but it's not supported by the Bible in the least. If Christianity weakens people why did Christ give the Holy

Spirit to *empower* us (Acts 1:8)? Why did Paul say we haven't been given a spirit of fear, but a spirit of *power* (2 Timothy 1:7)? Why did Jesus say he came to give us *"life to the full"* (John 10:10)? If Christianity uses the devil to instill fear why did Jesus give *authority* to believers "to *trample on* snakes and scorpions", which are types of the devil and demons, and "to *overcome all the power of the enemy"* (Luke 10:19)? He even added, "nothing will harm you." If Christianity teaches that believers are to have a negative fear of God why does the Bible say "God is love…There is no fear in love. But *perfect love drives out fear"* (1 John 4:16,18)? The only fear believers are encouraged to have is a healthy, reverent fear of God because it's the "beginning of wisdom" and protects us from foolish paths (Psalm 111:10).

It's stunning how deceived people are about Christianity, all because they confuse it with the counterfeit—legalism.

What is Legalism?

Legalism has always been a major threat to genuine Christianity. What exactly is legalism? It's the belief and practice that eternal salvation can be attained through obedience to religious law or good works. That's the common definition. Most Christians think legalism is limited to this meaning, but they're wrong. Its broader definition has to do with its root word **legal**, which of course refers to law or rules. Legal-ism could just as well be called law-ism or rule-ism. It's an *obsession* with moral or religious laws and therefore legalists primarily judge others based on strict adherence to the rules they deem important, many of them being unbiblical. Furthermore, legal-ism emphasizes the *letter of the law* rather than its spirit.

You could say that legalism is the mentality that godliness is an outward job. As such, legalists focus on the outer at the expense of the inner. A person's outward façade is more important than the inward reality. For instance, as long as an individual goes to every church service throughout the week, and all that goes with that—wearing the "right" dress clothes, carrying the Bible, saying "Amen" at the appropriate moment, putting something in the offering, seeking the favor of the pastor, etc.—it's okay to be a malicious, lying, envious, arrogant, abusive, sexually immoral, gossiping, slanderous, drunken, chattering fool the rest of the time (not that any one person would likely be *all* these things). Simply put, legalism is religious hypocrisy. It's putting on an act. It's *fake* Christianity.

Let me stress here that there's nothing wrong with going to genuine church gatherings and everything that might go along with it just noted; the problem is the *attitude* of legalism, the mindset that faith is a mere garnishment when nothing could be further from the truth. Such an attitude is not only unbiblical, it's corrupting, and it'll slowly corrupt anyone who succumbs to it.

As we shall see, legalism takes on many forms, but each form grows from the same root: **religion without relationship** and **rules above the Savior**.

Contrasting Legalism and Real Christianity

Legalism regularly goes unnoticed because most Christians only perceive it according to the first definition above—focusing on something other than the grace offered in the gospel to attain salvation or have a right-relationship with God. They fail to grasp its broader definition, which is rooted in the word legal-ism. To better understand this wider definition, let's compare legalism with legitimate Christianity; the contrast is glaring:

Legalism is **externally imposed human religion**, which attempts to change a person—or measure their worth—from the outward in. It's a spirit that's obsessed with putting on airs of godliness without the heart of godliness. 'Godliness,' by the way, literally means to be *like* God, which is encouraged in the New Testament; see, for example, Ephesians 5:1 and 1 Peter 4:11.

Biblical Christianity, by contrast, is **internally birthed reality**, which transforms a person and measures their worth from the inside out.

Put more simply, legalism is man's way and true Christianity is God's way. Legalism is religion and religion is the human attempt to connect with God through works, whereas Christianity is God connecting with humanity and giving us the gift of righteousness through spiritual rebirth in Christ. The religious person attempts to produce good works in order to please God whereas the believer *has* a relationship with God through spiritual regeneration, which naturally produces fruit and works.

I've heard it put this way: Religion says "do" while Jesus says "done;" religion says "slave" while Jesus says "son" (or "daughter").

The distinction between these two is as great as the difference between death and life! You see, legalism is essentially a spirit of *dead* religiosity. The best it can do is create robotic *sheeple* or sourpuss totalitarians, whereas true Christianity sets free and produces *unique people* filled with the life of the Lord!

Let that sink in, it's important: Legitimate Christianity sets people free and produces unique, empowered individuals whereas the best legalism can do is morph people into religious automatons or joyless authoritarians.

Furthermore, Christianity is beautiful in its simplicity: Love God and love people as you love yourself; learn to put off the flesh and walk in the spirit and you'll produce the fruit of the spirit. That's Christianity in a nutshell. Legalism, by contrast, is a tangled web of religiosity, a muddy quagmire that bogs you down and slowly takes your life.

This sterile religious spirit is no respecter of persons or church/ministry lines; it's a threat to every Christian, small or great, regardless of sectarian boundaries. Every believer and every ministry will be threatened by legalism at varying points in their spiritual journey so it's important to be able to recognize its many faces or defining characteristics. That's the purpose of this book, to unmask legalism, and set the captives free.

Legalism at the Time of Christ and Early Church

The Pharisees were the conservative religious leaders at the time of Christ, but they were notorious legalists. In fact, they're the quintessential example of legalism in the Bible, along with the Teachers of the Law. As such, Pharisaical behavior is synonymous with legalism. Saying someone is Pharisaical is the same as saying he or she is a rigid legalist.

Unsurprisingly, Jesus conflicted with the Pharisees on numerous occasions, even to the point of calling them names like "sons of hell," "blind fools," "hypocrites" (fakes) and "snakes"! We'll observe these examples and more as we progress.

Paul the apostle also encountered legalists and knew how to recognize them because he used to be one. Notice how he refers to legalists in this passage:

> **Beware of the <u>dogs</u>, beware of the <u>evil workers</u>, beware of those who <u>mutilate the flesh</u>! [3]For it is we who are the circumcision, who worship in the Spirit of God and boast in Christ Jesus and have <u>no confidence in the flesh</u>**
>
> **Philippians 3:2-3** (NRSV)

Paul was warning the Philippian believers of legalists who taught that non-Jews had to be physically circumcised in order to be truly saved; they were obsessed with it. Notice that Paul doesn't mince words here. He blatantly calls these legalists "dogs" and "evil workers"!

Calling someone a "dog" was even more offensive in biblical times than it is today. The term referred to people of low moral character.[3] And how would you like to be called an "evil worker"? That's pretty harsh, don't you agree? This is recorded in God's Word to show that legalism is utter wickedness in the LORD's eyes. It cannot be tolerated; it must be confronted, exposed and corrected; and genuine believers should be warned for their protection.

About a decade earlier Paul had to deal with similar legalists who were trying to corrupt the churches in Galatia, that is, modern central Turkey. Paul called the Galatian believers "bewitched" for tolerating these legalists and allowing them to corrupt the Galatian churches (Galatians 3:1). Notice what he says about the legalists:

---

[3] For instance, "dogs" is used in the Bible in reference to homosexual prostitutes (Deuteronomy 23:18), wicked betrayers (Psalm 59:5-6), corrupt leaders (Isaiah 56:10), heathen (Matthew 15:26-27) and, in this passage, staunch legalists.

> **If anybody is preaching to you a gospel other than**
> **what you accepted, let him be eternally condemned!**
> **Galatians 1:9**

This "different gospel" (Galatians 1:6) was propagated by the Judaizers, a group of Jews who insisted that believers must observe Jewish laws & traditions in addition to the grace of the gospel to attain salvation, like the practice of circumcision. But physical circumcision is unnecessary in the New Covenant because believers are circumcised *inwardly* through spiritual regeneration (Romans 2:29 & Titus 3:5). Notice in the above passage what Paul adamantly said concerning anyone who preached this different gospel: "let him be eternally condemned!" You know what this means in plain English? "Let him **go to hell!**"

Yes, as unbelievable as it may seem, Paul, the greatest figure of Christianity after Jesus Christ, was emphatic that those who unrepentantly preached a different gospel—a "gospel" that soiled the body of Christ with legalism—should go to hell!

As you can see, legalism is a grievous sin in God's eyes and cannot be tolerated, whether in myself, yourself or others. It must be recognized, corrected and purged ASAP.

As noted earlier, legalism is no respecter of persons, denominations or ministries; it can infect anyone anywhere—small or great—regardless of sectarian boundaries.

Levels of Infection

Of course, there are levels of infection and **not everyone tainted by legalism is a modern-day Pharisee frothing at the mouth with iniquitous religiosity**. In other words: While legalism is counterfeit Christianity—and therefore *bogus*—it's possible for a genuine believer who is ignorant of legalism to be partially infected by this spiritual disease. Such a person may indeed be an authentic believer, but his/her legalistic qualities are decidedly counterfeit. Are you with me?

Naturally, those infected by legalism will typically degenerate, some to the point where God will literally pull the plug on them, that is, if they're even believers in the first place. For instance, the Pharisees claimed that God was their father but Jesus squarely told them that the devil was their true spiritual father (John 8:41-44). They were dyed-in-the-wool legalists, you see, but they were blind to it because legalism by its very nature creates a spirit of religious arrogance. In fact, the very thing they claimed (being God's children) was actually the opposite. They were totally deceived.

To be expected, this degenerative tendency of legalism works in a generational sense as well. In other words, the spiritual children of legalists will often be corrupted to an even greater degree than their spiritual parents, which explains Jesus' declaration to the legalists of the 1st century:

> **"Woe to you, teachers of the law and Pharisees, you hypocrites! You travel over land and sea to win a single convert, and when he becomes one, you make him twice as much a son of hell as you are."**
>
> **Matthew 23:15**

The spiritual children of these legalists were twice as bad as they were!

The Hideous "Beast" and its Four Limbs

In my experience I've observed five basic strains of legalism—**general legalism** and **four offshoots** or **pillars**. Picture legalism as a hideous beast with four limbs, like so:

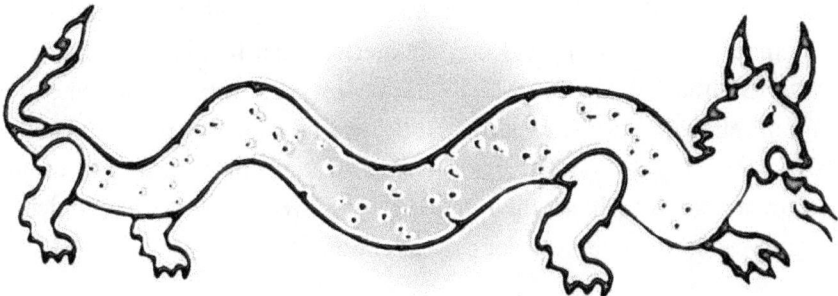

Ugly, ain't he? He's supposed to be. Legalism is a *hideous* beast!

It's possible that legalism could be further segmented, but we'll focus on these five in this book. Since legalism is a colossal beast, separating it into these five categories—**general legalism** and **four limbs**—makes it easier to understand and digest. It also helps in strategizing to purge it since you'll be able to identify the specific form of legalism with which you're dealing. This is important because *you cannot confront and defeat an enemy unless you first recognize the enemy.*

As you go through these various character traits of legalism the first thing you'll want to do is examine yourself to see if *you* are missing it in any of these areas, which I regularly do myself. This is in accordance with Paul's instruction to the Corinthian believers:

> **<u>Examine yourselves</u> to see whether you are in the faith; <u>test yourselves</u>. Do you not realize that Christ Jesus is in you—unless, of course, you fail the test?**
>
> **2 Corinthians 13:5**

Regular self-examination is necessary in order to insure that *you* are freed-up from any flesh issues, in this case legalism or dead religiosity. This is imperative because you can only help others to the degree that you yourself are freed-up, which Jesus illustrated in Matthew 7:3-5. After all, how can you set others free if you're not free yourself? It's just common sense.

The second thing you should do is see if you can identify legalistic qualities in other believers, particularly those who claim to be leaders since they have the most influence, especially those who teach and preach. Before anyone says that this is somehow unChrist-like, remember Jesus himself said that counterfeits can be identified by their fruits (Matthew 7:15-23), which means it's necessary to examine the fruit of fellow believers, in particular those who claim to speak for God.

When you identify legalistic qualities in other believers be sure to do your part to help set them free. How so? We'll go over this in detail in **Chapter 9**, but here's a brief plan of action:

Start with prayer. Intercede for them that God may open their eyes and deliver them. Pray in the spirit for them, which is a powerful spiritual weapon (Ephesians 6:18). You should also find a way to correct from the Scriptures in an indirect sense; as well as set an example of the abundant freedom, life, joy and power true Christianity offers, which you do through your words, attitude and lifestyle. Confront and correct as you have opportunity and are led of the Spirit, as gently as possible (Proverbs 27:5 & 25:15).

If, after a reasonable amount of time, you see no positive change then you may have to take a sterner approach, like Jesus did with the Pharisees and Teachers of the Law. If you fail to see repentance, *leave them*, for they have proven themselves to be counterfeits and this is exactly what Jesus said to do (Matthew 15:12-14). But keep them in prayer and be open to reconciliation since there's always the possibility that they might come to their senses and repent. If they do, be sure to warmly receive them. Christianity isn't some powerless religion or philosophy; it's all about a *real* relationship with God and the *real* positive change that springs from it.

Let's now unmask legalism by looking at its five basic strains. Since legalism is a colossal beast with four ugly limbs (figuratively speaking, of course) we'll spend the most time with the first strain, the "beast" itself, which is **legalism in general**—an overall description of this spiritual disease and its numerous telltale characteristics. We'll spend the next two chapters on this.

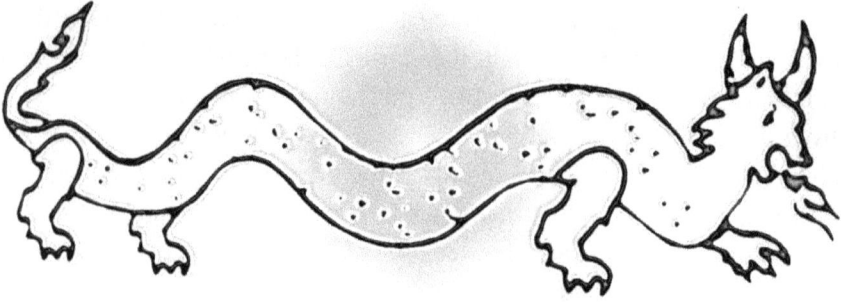

Chapter 2

General Legalism

General legalism is one-and-the-same as Pharisaical-ism. It's the emphasis on external forms of religiosity. In other words, legalists are hell-bent on outward appearances or putting on airs. And I mean "hell-bent" literally.

Notice what Jesus said to this effect:

> "Woe to you, teachers of the law and Pharisees, you hypocrites! <u>You are like whitewashed tombs,</u> which look beautiful on the outside but on the inside are full of dead men's bones and everything unclean. [28] In the same way, <u>on the outside you *appear* to people as righteous</u> but on the inside you <u>are full of hypocrisy and wickedness.</u>"
>
> **Matthew 23:27-28**

This is legalism in a nutshell—putting on appearances so that everything *looks* righteous and godly while being full of wickedness within. This is "hypocrisy," which is **putting on an act**. It's fake Christianity, impure and simple.

Jesus stressed that it's the condition of the heart that's important:

> **"What comes out of a man is what makes him 'unclean.'** [21] **For <u>from within, out of men's hearts,</u> come evil thoughts, sexual immorality, theft, murder, adultery,** [22] **greed, malice, deceit, lewdness, envy, slander, arrogance and folly.** [23] **All these evils come <u>from inside</u> and make a man 'unclean.' "**
>
> **Mark 7:20-23**

As you can see, humanity's sin problem is not an outward matter; it's inward. All outward manifestations of sin are rooted in the condition of the heart, which is why Jesus said: "Make a tree good and its fruit will be good, or make a tree bad and its fruit will be bad, for a tree is recognized by its fruit... For out of the overflow of the heart the mouth speaks" (Matthew 12:33-34). This also explains why human religion always ultimately fails, regardless of its noble intentions. Why? Because human religion cannot give spiritual rebirth and, consequently, cannot reconcile people to their Creator. Christianity can and does—*real* Christianity, not the impotent counterfeit.

True positive change starts within through spiritual regeneration. This is why Jesus stressed that we must be "born again" (John 3:3,6). Genuine change then proceeds by the believer learning to live out of his or her new nature (Ephesians 4:22-24). Only then can we truly be "imitators of God," as instructed in Ephesians 5:1. This means to be like-God or godly. These truths are of the utmost importance in order to walk in newness of life and victory; in fact, they're the antidote to legalism. As such, I'll be stressing them again and again throughout this book.

When I was in my early teens I used to visit a friend's house and even stayed overnight a few times. I was a totally lost kid yet I was still able to discern that something was horribly wrong in that household. Everything *looked* good on the surface. It was a nice modern brick domicile with a fine yard, but there was no love there, no warmth in the relationships, not to mention the parents were serious alcoholics. There was a palpable emptiness there. In short, it was a house, but not a home.

Just the same, legalism is mere window dressing. It can produce a religious person, but it cannot produce a godly believer. It can produce someone who *goes through the motions* of being a godly person, but it cannot produce someone who *is* godly because he or she has a heart of love, life, joy, peace, righteousness and power!

Legalists Create their Own Religion

In a sense, legalists who propose to be Christians create their own religion, a syncretic belief system—part Christianity and part flesh. It's an unholy union of two opposing principles or lifestyles

An excellent example of syncretic religion can be found in 1 Kings 12:28-33. After Solomon's death, his son Rehoboam took over the kingdom of Israel, but he was harsh and the ten northern tribes rebelled, choosing Jeroboam as their king. Jeroboam wasted no time in forging two golden calf idols to be the new "gods" of the Northern Kingdom; one was set up in a southern city and the other in the north. He then appointed "priests" who weren't even Levites and instituted a counterfeit religious festival as well. What Jeroboam did was create a new syncretic religion for the separated northern tribes. It was influenced by Judaism and had some of its trappings, but it left out the most important part— God!

In essence, this is what legalists do with Christianity. They may have the trappings of Christianity, but they don't have the heart. They substitute rules and regulations for God and consequently de-emphasize or forsake the most important part of Christianity—a relationship with the Living LORD. They may know the Bible but they don't know the author of the Bible. Like Jeroboam's non-Levite "priests," legalists ordinate un-anointed men and women as ministers who are mere "yes men" in the cogwheels of the religious grind. They put on the appearances of love while having a heart of hatred and slander. They propose to be genuine while being full of hypocrisy. They claim integrity while living in sin. A good example would be all these "priests" in the Roman Church who molest boys on the side. Unbelievably, the hierarchy has protected them to a large degree. It's absurd. They've created their own religion—proposing to know and represent the LORD while secretly engaging in one of the vilest sins under the sun.

I should add that I'm not talking about believers who miss it and genuinely repent (1 John 1:8-9), but rather a mass problem with no sign of change. It's an ongoing thing because they're *unrepentant*. And, no, this is not a blanket denouncement of all Catholics, so please don't take it that way. The tag people go by isn't important; what's going on **inside** *is*.

The point is that legalists essentially create their own religion. It might look a lot like Christianity, but it's not; it lacks the most important part—God Himself. And because it lacks the LORD it also lacks the life and power that only the Creator can give; the life and power necessary for genuine change. Legalistic Christian religion is fake Christianity.

The Difficulty of Discerning Legalists

Because legalists put on the *appearance* of godliness it can be hard to distinguish them from authentic believers, that is, if you don't know what to look for and you're easily swayed by appearances.

Jesus acknowledged this difficulty when he shared the Parable of the Weeds from Matthew 13:24-30. This story tells of a man who sowed wheat in his field, but his enemy came at night and sowed weeds, possibly darnel, a weed that's hard to distinguish from wheat until the head matures. Both the wheat and the weeds grew together in the field until the workers discovered the weeds. They informed the owner and he deduced that it was the work of an enemy. The workers asked the owner if he wanted them to pull up the weeds but he told them not to because they might accidently root up some of the wheat. He decided to wait until the harvest to separate the two wherein the weeds would be burned and the wheat brought into the barn. Jesus explained this story:

> **"The one who sowed the good seed is the Son of Man. [38] The field is the world, and the good seed stands for the sons of the kingdom. The weeds are the sons of the evil one, [39] and the enemy who sows them**

is the devil. The harvest is the end of the age, and the
harvesters are angels."

[40] "As the weeds are pulled up and burned in
the fire, so it will be at the end of the age. [41] The Son
of Man will send out his angels, and <u>they will weed
out of his kingdom everything that causes sin</u> and <u>all
who do evil</u>. [42] They will throw them into the fiery
furnace, where there will be weeping and gnashing of
teeth. [43] Then the righteous will shine like the sun in
the kingdom of their Father. He who has ears, let him
hear."

Matthew 13:37-43

The "weeds" are children of the devil and they dwell amidst the
"wheat," which are the children of the kingdom of God, meaning the
Church or body of Christ. Remember, Jesus plainly called the Pharisees
children of the devil and they're the ultimate example of legalism in the
Bible (John 8:42-47). At the end of this age Jesus will send out his angels
to weed out of his kingdom all those who do evil and promote sin and
they will be condemned.

This story shows that the devil's children will dwell amongst
God's children in the Church, at least to some extent. In other words, the
counterfeit will function amidst the authentic. Jesus was specifically
talking about dyed-in-the-wool legalists here; people who are stubborn
and unrepentant about their legalism. He wasn't talking about legalists
like Nicodemus who are open to the truth and willing to repent.[4] Christ
was also talking about those in the Church who practice and promote
lawlessness or licentiousness. This is the opposite side of the coin to
legalism, called libertinism, which we'll address in **Chapter 10**. Whether
legalists or libertines, Jesus was referring to those who are *unrepentant*
about their carnality, not to those who realize their sins and humbly
confess (1 John 1:8-9), which *we all* must do on occasion.

The reason I bring up this story is to show that the Bible
acknowledges the difficulty of distinguishing the genuine from the false

---

[4] For evidence of Nicodemus' conversion see John 3:1-10, 7:45-52 and 19:38-
42.

in the Church and any mass attempt to do so would cause collateral damage to believers. The reason it's hard to distinguish legalists is because they put on the *appearances* of godliness while the truth of the heart is quite different.

16 Telltale Signs of Legalism

The Parable of the Weeds shows that most legalists won't be exposed until the day they stand before the Lord to be judged, but this doesn't mean the Church—God's authentic children—should stand idly by and allow legalists to run amok in our fellowships. The best way to keep this spiritual disease to a minimum is to make sure those in leadership positions aren't infected since they have the most influence. How do we do this? The Bible repeatedly shows how to unmask legalists and how to deal with the infection. That's what this book is all about.

Because legalism is merely a surface garnishment it always gives itself away and the New Testament provides numerous telltale signs of this syndrome.

So let's explore 16 traits of general legalism as revealed in the Scriptures:

1. Legalists Focus on Appearances Above all Else

Observe, again, how Jesus bluntly described legalists:

> **"Woe to you, teachers of the law and Pharisees, you hypocrites! <u>You are like whitewashed tombs</u>, which look beautiful on the outside but on the inside are full of dead men's bones and everything unclean. ²⁸ In the same way, <u>on the outside you appear to people as righteous</u> <u>but on the inside you are full of hypocrisy and wickedness</u>."**
>
> **Matthew 23:27-28**

Just as whitewashed tombs look clean and beautiful on the outside so legalists *look* good on the outside. Verse 28 shows that legalists only *appear* to people as righteous, but the inside doesn't reflect their appearance. In fact, they're "full of hypocrisy and wickedness." The root word for 'hypocrisy' is hypocrite, which literally means "actor." Legalists are professing Christians who essentially put on an act; they're not genuine. Does this mean that anyone infected by legalism can't at the same time be a legitimate Christian? As already noted, there are levels of infection and, therefore, it's possible for someone to be a genuine believer and be infected by legalism to some degree. In other words, they may be a legitimate Christian but they've fallen into the practice of putting on an act in one way or another. Such people are in danger of becoming more deeply infected. This is different than someone who's a dyed-in-the-wool legalist, like the Teachers of the Law and Pharisees whom Jesus was addressing in this passage. These were legalists through and through—people who *appear* godly on the outside but are *full* of hypocrisy and wickedness within.

How can you know the difference? Simple: A genuine believer is someone who is born of God and is therefore a child of God (John 1:12-13). As such, he or she will have a natural drive to be godly, that is, to be like God (Ephesians 5:1). Consequently, any genuine believer will be thoroughly repentant upon the realization that he or she is walking in counterfeit Christianity. If you encounter individuals infected by legalism and implement the appropriate techniques relayed in **Chapter 9** and they remain stubbornly unrepentant—after applying much patience and mercy, I should add—you can be sure they're dyed-in-the-wool legalists and not true believers. This doesn't mean there's no hope for them. There's hope for everyone, but change ultimately depends on the will of the individual. Keep implementing the warfare principles and maybe one day they'll come to their senses.

Years ago I came across a minister who showed signs of legalism. We were both involved with a ministry where he was the assistant pastor and I was a regular teacher. He was much older than me so I didn't feel it appropriate to correct him in a face-to-face manner, unless of course I was moved by the Spirit to do so. So I prayed for him, set an example of freedom & abundant life, and simply taught the truths of the Scriptures from the pulpit. Lo and behold one day he was giving a sermon and he admitted his struggle from the pulpit, clearly indicating his repentance and victory. I was so impressed! This was proof that he wasn't a dyed-in-the-wool legalist but rather a true believer who was infected by legalism. How so? He was willing to humbly repent when corrected through the Word and the Holy Spirit.

Getting back to how legalism focusses on appearances, think about it like this: Only one-ninth of an iceberg can be seen above water. The other eight-ninths are unseen. Legalists are people who put all their focus on the one-ninth that can be seen while the other eight-ninths are tainted by hypocrisy and carnality.

I'm not saying that the one-ninth that can be seen means nothing; just that the other eight-ninths are far more important and should be our priority otherwise we'll just be putting on an act, the very definition of hypocrisy. If we concentrate our efforts on the eight-ninths that are unseen it will positively affect the one-ninth that can be seen. This is why Peter encouraged women to not obsess over outward adornments, but rather to focus on the true beauty that proceeds from within (1 Peter 3:3-4). No amount of make-up, expensive jewelry or apparel can compete with the shining beauty of a godly heart. Remember, 'godly' means "to be like God." God is the "fountain of life" who gushes forth life and fullness of joy (Psalm 36:9 & 16:11). Nothing can compare with the radiant glory of a truly godly heart, nothing.

Here's a fairly well-known passage that reveals the tendency of legalists to focus on appearances while the heart is corrupt:

> **But mark this: There will be terrible times in the last days. [2] People will be lovers of themselves, lovers of money, boastful, proud, abusive, disobedient to their parents, ungrateful, unholy, [3] without love, unforgiving, slanderous, without self-control, brutal, not lovers of the good, [4] treacherous, rash, conceited, lovers of pleasure rather than lovers of God— [5]having a form of godliness but denying its power. Have nothing to do with them.**
>
> **2 Timothy 3:1-5**

What a list, huh? Obviously Paul wasn't saying that any *one* person would likely be all these things, but rather that in these "last days"[5] there will be people who have "a form of godliness" but deny the life-changing power of the gospel because they have any number of these fleshly traits active in their lives. By "active" I mean they consistently produce these carnal works with no care of repentance, which indicates a proud, stubborn spirit. Consequently, their supposed godliness is limited to outward *forms*—the mere appearances of righteousness and religious devotion.

Paul was describing hardcore legalists in this passage. In verse 8 he said that these types literally "oppose the truth" or "resist the truth" (NKJV). This is important: *Legalists always resist the truth.* Why? Because it's the truth that sets people (John 8:31-32) and so legalists naturally resist truth because they oppose freedom. They're all about religious bondage, not true freedom. If you see someone who claims to be a Christian who's always opposing or resisting the life-giving truths of God's Word you can be sure he or she is a legalist (or libertine).

Also notice what Paul said at the end of the above passage: "Have nothing to do with them" or, as the New King James Version puts it, "from such people turn away!" When you come across legalists like this—especially legalists in leadership positions—flee for your spiritual health! This is the precise instruction Jesus gave his disciples concerning the legalists of the 1st century: "Leave them; they are blind guides. If a blind man leads a blind man, both will fall into a pit" (Matthew 15:14).

Lastly, what's most important to God is the inside condition of a person, not the outside:

Neither circumcision nor uncircumcision means anything; what counts is a new creation.

Galatians 6:15

The legalists that infiltrated the Galatian churches taught that circumcision was necessary for salvation and spirituality, but Paul denied this religious rule outright. What counts with God is a new creation. This refers to the new birth—the regeneration of one's spirit through Christ. Becoming a new creation and living by your spirit with

---

[5] The "last days" have been in effect since the arrival of the Messiah and extend to his return. See Acts 2:17, Hebrews 1:2, 1 Peter 1:20 and James 5:3.

the help of the indwelling Holy Spirit is what's important, not some outward procedure done to the male reproductive organ! If the latter were true, where would that leave female believers?

2. Legalists are Obsessed with "Putting on Airs"

Since legalists focus on outward appearances they're obsessed with putting on airs. We see this tendency in Jesus' statement:

**<u>"Everything they do is done for men to see</u>:
They make their phylacteries wide and the tassels on their garments long;"**

Matthew 23:5

The real motivation for everything legalists do is to impress others with how supposedly godly they are. As such, they're always "putting on airs" of religiosity.

Jesus said the legalists of 1st century Israel "make their phylacteries wide and the tassels on their garments long". Phylacteries were little leather boxes that contained Scriptures attached to their arms and foreheads.[6] They made sure to make them big enough for people to see, apparently hoping for a reaction like, "Oh, Rabbi Joseph is *so* godly, he walks around with Scriptures on his arm and forehead!"

Tassels were sown to the corners of garments to remind the Israelites to obey God's commandments, as detailed in Numbers 15:38-40 (and also Deuteronomy 22:12). The Pharisees and Teachers of the Law made their tassels longer than normal in order to be noticed. What was their motivation? It had nothing to do with genuine dedication to God, but rather to *impress people!*

Elsewhere Jesus stressed that the legalists of his day liked to walk around in "flowing robes" and "for a show" made lengthy prayers (Mark 12:38-40 & Luke 20:46-47).

---

[6] The parchments in the phylacteries contained these four passages: Exodus 13:1-10, 11-16, Deuteronomy 6:4-9 and 11:13-21.

Christians are guilty of this today when we drape our verbiage with *unnecessary* Christianese. The obvious purpose of this is to be a witness by sending out signals. This is great if our intention is to genuinely reach people and it comes forth naturally, like with Jesus and the woman at the well (John 4:1-42), but discerning people can spot a fake from about twenty paces. I'm talking about when Christian verbiage is mixed into statements in a forced and unnatural manner, which is the case when Christianese is sent out to signal our supposed godliness.

We need to continually ask ourselves if the motivation for what we're wearing, saying or doing is to serve God and love people more effectively or if we're merely putting on airs. This is important because putting airs is the very definition of hypocrisy. Is the main reason we "dress up" for church services to impress others? If so, it's wrong. Why do we carry our Bible or place it on the desk at work or coffee table at home? If it's merely to give the *impression* to others that we're seriously devoted to God's Word then it's wrong. How so? Because it's a lie.

There's a huge problem with putting on airs in the Church today. What do you immediately think of when someone mentions "going to church"? Most people, including unbelievers, think of nice suits, ties, pretty dresses, people carrying their Bibles, droning prayers and sleep-inducing sermons. Why? Because the Church has been putting on airs for decades and centuries. What we *should* immediately think of—if the church in question is spiritually healthy—is loving fellowship, joy, celebration, experiencing the Living God, inspiring teachings from the Scriptures, people getting miraculously healed or supernaturally set free, not to mention the lost seeing the Light and reconciling with their Creator!

Since when did church become all about parading around in fancy dress clothes? Hey, I'm all for dressing up now and then but something is seriously wrong if suits, ties and pretty dresses are the first things people think of when they think of church!

Years ago I was attending an assembly that had a spirit of freedom and lively praise & worship. Sometimes I'd dress up and sometimes I wouldn't, it was about 50/50, but I'd almost always wear dress clothes when teaching. I started to notice that an older worship leader would give me dirty looks whenever I dressed down, particularly Sunday mornings. I naturally caught word of her grumblings, but she wouldn't complain to my face, likely because she knew she had no leg to stand on. James 2:1-4 plainly shows that church gatherings aren't about "dressing up." Rather, they're about *experiencing the LORD* through genuine fellowship, praise & worship, the life-changing power of the Word of God, inspiring ministry and the miraculous moving of the Holy Spirit, not putting on airs to impress others!

Airs of Poverty and Airs of Wealth

We need to address one last thing about putting on airs and it has to do with money and possessions. I've noticed that some Christians believe it's godly to be poor while others think that financial prosperity and expensive possessions indicate the blessing of God and spiritual maturity. As such, the former will sometimes put on airs of poverty to prove their godliness while the latter will show off their wealth and possessions to prove their spirituality. Both attitudes represent the two extremes on the subject and they're both equally wrong. Ecclesiastes 7:18 says "The man who fears God will avoid all extremes."

Concerning the idea that wealth and possessions prove a believer's spiritual maturity, I recently ran into a couple of believers who embraced this mentality and find it hard to fathom. Hey, I'm all for God prospering the believer (Proverbs 10:22), but wealth and possessions are not the ultimate sign of God's blessing. If they were, then Hugh Hefner was a sterling example of godliness! Christ said we can determine the true from the false *by their fruit*, referring to the fruit of the spirit or lack thereof (Matthew 7:15-23). He also said:

> **"Watch out! Be on your guard against all kinds of greed; a man's life does not consist in the abundance of his possessions."**
>
> **Luke 12:15**

Wow, that just blows the whole theory that wealth and possessions signify spirituality, doesn't it? Please be careful not to fall into this mentality; it's not only a manifestation of greed, it's just plain arrogant. People who develop this mindset naturally start to look down on believers who lack money and expensive possessions. This is why Paul instructed a young minister like so:

> **Command those who are rich in this present world <u>not to be arrogant</u> nor to put their hope in wealth, which is so uncertain, but to put their hope in God, who richly provides us with everything for our enjoyment. [18]Command them to <u>do good</u>, to <u>be rich in good deeds</u>, and to <u>be generous</u> and <u>willing to share</u>.**
>
> **1 Timothy 6:17-18**

This was how Timothy was to urge wealthy believers in his congregation. Notice that Paul didn't say there was anything wrong with believers being wealthy, but he did warn against arrogance because it's easy for wealth to create an attitude of superiority. His instructions were that wealthy Christians are to be rich in good deeds and generous with their wealth. Nowhere does he say that riches are a sign of spiritual maturity or that wealthy believers should display their money and possessions to impress other believers; that is, put on airs of wealth. The very idea is absurd.

Unbelievably, I ran into a believer not long ago who said he judged men by their shoes. This was how he sized-up other men and I find it almost incredulous. What a shallow measure of worth! I realize that people in general ordinarily judge others by external things, like clothes, possessions, education and occupation, but this isn't the way it's supposed to be with believers:

> **<u>So from now on we regard no one from a worldly point of view</u>. Though <u>we once regarded Christ in this way, we do so no longer</u>. [17] Therefore, if anyone is in Christ, he is a new creation; the old has gone, the new has come!**
>
> **2 Corinthians 5:16-17**

What did Paul mean by "a worldly point of view"? He meant judging people by *outward appearances* alone. Paul used to view Christ in this manner back when he was a highfalutin Pharisee. As an arrogant legalist, Paul looked down on the Messiah despite his incredible ministry, likely because Jesus chose to operate outside of the religious establishment and enlisted common, uneducated individuals for his ministry, like fishermen.

God, by contrast, determines a person's worth by what's in the heart:

> **But the LORD said to Samuel, "Do not consider his appearance or his height, for I have rejected him. The LORD does not look at the things man looks at. <u>Man looks at the outward appearance, but the LORD looks at the heart</u>."**
>
> **1 Samuel 16:7**

People tend to base their judgment of others on appearances, while the LORD evaluates based on what's in the heart. Isn't that what's really important? What good is it for a man to pursue a woman who looks and dresses like a Hollywood starlet, but has a roaming eye and disloyal heart? She may *look* stunning, but a marriage to her would be doomed to misery and divorce. How much better to find a more down-to-earth woman who has a heart of love and loyalty? Proverbs 27:19 says, "As water reflects a face, so a man's heart reflects the man."

Several years ago I was a supervisor at a company and would occasionally interview applicants. I hired a young man who looked like a tall Tom Cruise and dressed immaculately. Unfortunately, he proved to be a poor employee. He was lazy, troublesome and snuck smoke breaks every hour. After nine months I had no recourse but to fire him and interviewed two new applicants for the position. One looked great and carried himself with confidence, but he smoked and was overqualified. The other applicant looked and dressed poorly, but something about his demeanor was attractive. I sensed humility. Since I didn't want to deal with another smoker and was looking for someone who would stay a long period of time, I chose the second man. He stayed with me until I decided to change occupations, which was almost five years later, and he turned out to be one of my favorite workers. Although not without shortcomings, he was a solid worker, dependable and utterly loyal. In fact, he's one of the most loyal people I've ever met. (Loyalty is so underrated). I developed the highest respect for him and maintain contact with him to this day. Why? He may look and dress shoddily, but he has a heart of gold. When all is said and done, that's what really counts.

I should add that I'm just making a point here and not encouraging people to dress shabbily, especially if you go to a job interview. Every situation and environment calls for wisdom to act and dress appropriately. You don't wear a bathing suit to a funeral. When Pharaoh sent for Joseph from the dungeon, Joseph shaved and dressed appropriately before going to see the king (Genesis 41:14). Such things are a matter of protocol and common sense.

3. Legalists Put on a Show

Putting on a show is along the same lines as putting on airs. The legalists in 1st century Israel claimed that God was their father, but Jesus plainly told them that the devil was, in fact, their father (John 8:39-47). They were putting on a show and fooled the Israelites.

Similarly, just because people *say* they're a pastor, prophet or apostle doesn't mean it's true. Jesus commended the Ephesians for testing some people who claimed to be apostles but proved false (Revelation 2:2). There are people in every Christian sect today who claim to be this or that, but they're not. They're essentially putting on a show.

For instance, one woman I knew for a handful of years insisted on being addressed as "Apostle Harris" at all times, even though she wasn't an apostle in the remotest sense. She had to be one of the most arrogant, joyless persons I've ever met, yet she claimed to be a high-ranking Christian leader when nothing could be further from the truth. She once rebuked me because I didn't pray over a cupcake, if you can believe it (!).

Years ago I sat across the desk from a pastor of a small church once a week for four months. I had to do this for an internship class. He was a gentle and likable man but every time I was around him I kept sensing that he wasn't really a pastor, that he was just playing the part. Don't take that the wrong way because I'm not one to jump to conclusions; I'm just sharing what I *sensed* every time I was around him.

If his fruit proved my impression wrong then I would have immediately dismissed it, but his fruit verified what I sensed. Maybe when he started in ministry 25 years earlier he was really a pastor, I don't know, but when I spent time with him he was clearly just going through the motions. He was putting on the airs of being the pastor while everything else proved him to be false. I felt sad for him, but when I left his assembly I had to tell him the truth. I respectfully encouraged him to step down for a season in order to draw close to God, the Fountain of Life, because he clearly needed to let go of the grind of "the ministry" for a season and get his inspiration back.

Although he was putting on a show, he wasn't malevolent in the least. His abuse of the Church was passive in nature, not aggressive. He was hurting believers simply by setting a lifeless example and not being inspiring, but he didn't intentionally seek to hurt others. Regardless, it's still an example of putting on a show, and those who put on a show aren't really what they propose to be. As such, it's impossible for them to fulfill the mandate of the position they claim.

Needless to say, be wary of those in the Church who give the impression of putting on a show. Putting on an act is the very definition of hypocrisy and the Bible blatantly teaches that believers must rid themselves of hypocrisy (1 Peter 2:1).

The above examples show that just because people say they're a pastor, prophet or apostle, it doesn't mean it's so. This includes people who are in ministerial positions at churches and insist on a title. Think about it like this: If I said I was a car, hanged out in a garage and insisted on being called a car, would that make me a car? Of course not. The same can be applied to the Church. Don't assume that just because people say they're fivefold ministers[7] (or whatever the case may be) that they are, even if they hang their credentials on the wall and their names are in lights on the church billboard accompanied by titles like "Rev." or "Pastor". Remember Jesus' words: "By their fruit you will recognize them."

"Putting on a show" is not limited to people pretending to be fivefold ministers, any Christian can succumb to this hypocritical spirit.

---

[7] "Fivefold ministers" refer to believers functioning in the office of **apostle, prophet, evangelist, pastor** or **teacher**, as detailed in Ephesians 4:11-13.

Take praise & worship, for example. Some churches encourage celebratory praise and reverent worship, and that's awesome, but this can devolve into putting on an act where the individual just goes through the motions at church services while it's not a reality in his/her everyday life. The temptation to do this isn't just an issue for regular churchgoers; it can happen to Christian leaders as well. Even worship leaders and their musicians can succumb.

I have to be careful how I word this because I don't want to be taken the wrong way, so please read with discernment. Of course it's better to enter into praise & worship once or twice a week in the assembly of the saints than not at all, that's a given. But celebration and adoration of God should become more of an everyday thing as the believer grows. Praise & worship should flow out of us as naturally as water from a spring (Hebrews 13:15). This is the way it should be for growing believers and more seasoned ones alike. But something's seriously wrong if praising and worshipping God becomes mere outward antics at church services. When this happens, the believer is essentially just putting on an act because he or she is around other believers, but it's not a reality in his/her personal life. Beware of falling into this mode because it's a form of legalism that Jesus denounced when he quoted Isaiah:

> **"These people honor me with their lips, but their hearts are far from me."**
>
> **Mark 7:6**

It's possible to praise & worship God with our mouths and yet not really mean it with our hearts. Please be careful to never slip into this legalistic mode!

Believe it or not, churches sometimes unknowingly facilitate this problem. They put so much stress on coming to every church service and being involved in the church that believers end up running around like headless chickens doing this or that for the ministry, which leaves very little time for the most important thing, their *relationship* with God. This is especially so when you factor in other life essentials like work, kids, education, shopping, cooking, physical fitness, rest and recreation.[8] In other words, believers are so pressured to run around doing this or that so their pastors will deem them faithful and godly that they don't have time and energy for the very things that create true godliness—personal time spent with the LORD and his Word.

Like I said, this could just as easily happen to pastors and worship leaders or musicians. Such people become so involved in the work of the ministry that they forsake the core of all Christian service, the Lord himself. The story of Mary and Martha applies here:

> **As Jesus and the disciples were on their way, he came to a village where a woman named Martha opened her home to him. [39] She had a sister called <u>Mary, who sat at the Lord's feet listening to what he said.</u> [40] But <u>Martha was distracted by all the preparations</u> that had to be made. She came to him and asked, "Lord, don't you care that my sister has left me to do <u>the work</u> by myself? <u>Tell her to help me!</u>"**
>
> **[41] "Martha, Martha," the Lord answered, "you are worried and upset about many things, [42] but <u>only one thing is needed</u>, Mary has chosen <u>what is better</u> and it will not be taken away from her."**
>
> **Luke 10:38-42**

Martha was so focused on the busy-ness of *working* for the Lord that she unintentionally forsook what was most important, spending time with him and "listening to what he said," an obvious reference to spending quality time with God's Word. In fact, Martha was so involved with the work of her service—i.e. her ministry—that she got mad at someone else who was free of such concerns and spending quality time with the Lord. So mad, in fact, that she started demanding things from the very One she was supposed to be serving! She TOLD the Lord, "Tell her to help me!" This is what legalism does to people; it corrupts them to

---

[8] Yes, *some* measure of recreation is essential: "There's a time to weep and a time to **laugh**, a time to mourn and a time to **dance**" (Ecclesiastes 3:4).

the point that they end up having the very *opposite* attitude they should have.

Serving God is a wonderful thing, but don't be foolish like Martha and get your priorities out of whack. Think about it, the Living Lord was AT HER HOUSE—the amazing miracle-worker—and all she does is run around in a whirlwind of activity? Mary chose what was more important on this occasion. There's a time for work, of course, but there's also a time for your relationship with your Creator. The latter's more important because our service for the Lord must spring from our love for the Lord. Otherwise it's just religious works or, worse, putting on a show.

4. Legalists Focus on the Minor Rather than the Major

Notice these two denouncements of legalism by Jesus:

"Woe to you Pharisees, because you give God a tenth of your mint, rue and all other kinds of garden herbs, <u>but you neglect justice and the love of God</u>. You should have practiced the latter without leaving the former undone."

Luke 11:42

"You blind guides! You strain out a gnat but swallow a camel."

Matthew 23:24

The first passage shows that the Pharisees were steadfast in giving their herbal tithes at the expense of godly traits like justice and love.

The second passage is figurative. Both the gnat and the camel were non-kosher to the Israelites, meaning they weren't allowed to consume these foods in accordance with Mosaic Law. Jesus' point was that these legalists concentrated so much on minor issues at the expense of more important ones that it was like straining out a gnat and then consuming a camel. In other words, it was absurd. If anything is strained out it should be the camel!

You'll observe this in people or churches infected by legalism, just open your eyes. For instance, if someone slips a cuss word it's frowned upon as the ultimate evil, but a blind eye is turned to those who run around the church lying, gossiping, slandering and provoking needless strife! I'm not saying cussing is good, but—depending on the words—it's a relatively minor issue in comparison to the others, which are way more destructive. Let's say a believer slips the "f" word or the "s" word, who does it *really* hurt? I've heard these words and worse standing in line at Dairy Queen. Gossip and slander, on the other hand, have the power to ruin lives, reputations and relationships. Many cuss words are about as shocking and harmful as saying "darn," but gossip and slander truly hurt people by causing division and strife. Which is the minor issue and which is the major?

Unfortunately, legalistic Christians focus on the minor issue at the expense of the major and we consequently have churches full of liars, gossips, slanderers and strife-makers, but—Praise God—they don't cuss! (That's sarcasm, in case you're not sure).

5. Legalists Focus on Rules above Relationship

The gospel is referred to as the "message of reconciliation" in Scripture (2 Corinthians 5:17-21). Why? Because it is through the good news of the gospel that people are *reconciled* with their Creator. 'Reconciliation' means "to turn from enmity to friendship" and this is the core of the Christian message: We can have an actual *relationship* with God through spiritual regeneration via the imperishable seed of the enduring Word of God, Jesus Christ (1 Peter 1:23). I should add that 'seed' in the Greek is "sperm"—we've been born-again of the imperishable *sperm* of Christ, the Living Word of God (see 1 John 3:9).

Since legalism is the definition of hypocrisy—putting on an act—legalists *can't* stress relationship; consequently, they divert to religious rules, including the many they make up. Why do they dream up new rules or laws? Because they're obsessed with them, that's **legal**-ism.

Notice what Jesus said about the legalists of the 1st century:

> " 'These people honor me with their lips, but
> their hearts are far from me. [7] They worship me in
> vain; <u>their teachings are but rules taught by men.</u>'
> [8]You have let go of the command of God and are
> holding on to the traditions of men..."
> [13] "Thus you <u>nullify the word of God</u> by your
> tradition that you have handed down."
>
> **Mark 7:6-8,13**

What we see here is a tendency of legalists to conjure-up rules
that go beyond Scripture. The Bible is full of moral commands, which
can be condensed into the two greatest commands, loving God and
loving people as you love yourself (Matthew 22:34-40). But this isn't
good enough for legalists; they have to add *more* rules. Paul commented
on this fleshly practice when he wrote to the Colossians:

> Since you died with Christ to the basic
> principles of this world, why, as though you still
> belonged to it, do you submit to <u>its rules</u>: [21] "Do not
> handle! Do not taste! Do not touch!"? [22] These are
> destined to perish with use, because <u>they are based on
> human commands and teachings.</u> [23] Such regulations
> indeed have <u>an appearance</u> of wisdom with their self-
> imposed worship, their false humility and their harsh
> treatment of the body, but they lack any value in
> restraining sensual indulgence.
>
> **Colossians 2:20-23**

Notice Paul is denouncing *human* commands and teachings, not
biblical ones. Such rules only have an appearance of wisdom and have
no real power to restrain carnality (verse 23). Only spiritual rebirth,
putting off the old self and putting on the new self with the help of the
Holy Spirit provides the power to walk in *true* righteousness and holiness
(Ephesians 4:22-24) .

Also observe in verse 21 how Paul literally *mocks* the goofy rules that legalists dream up: "Do not handle! Do not Taste! Do not touch!" *He's making fun of their stupid rules!*

Legalists do the same thing today as they did in the 1st century. Here are ten modern examples with my observations about each in parentheses:

- **"Don't drink caffeinated beverages"** (Why not if it's done in moderation? In fact, a recent 15-year study revealed that people who regularly consume caffeinated beverages in moderation actually live longer).

- **"Don't drink alcoholic beverages"** (But wasn't Jesus' first miracle to turn water into wine at a wedding party? Didn't Christ and the disciples drink wine at the Lord's Supper? What about Deuteronomy 14:26 and numerous other passages? Not that I'm advocating being a drunkard, of course, which is carnal according to Galatians 5:19-21, but there's a difference between being a drunkard and drinking a sip of alcohol. At the same time, those who partake of this freedom shouldn't look down on those who choose not to and vice versa; read Romans 14 for details).

- **"Don't eat meat or pork"** (Why not? Didn't Jesus and Paul declare all foods clean in the New Testament, as shown in Mark 7:18-19 and 1 Timothy 4:2-5? Didn't Paul stress that every neutral thing is permissible *if we're not mastered by it*, according to 1 Corinthians 6:12 and 10:23? I'm not saying there's anything wrong with a vegetarian lifestyle; in fact, I'm not a big meat-eater, but to make vegetarianism a rule that all believers *must* follow is a different story and wholly wrong).

- **"King James only!"** (Not that there's anything wrong with the KJV Bible, of course—except that it's written in an archaic style of English that modern readers can barely understand—but this rule is so absurd it requires no further comment).

- **"You're only welcome at our church services if adorned in dress clothes"** otherwise known as **"Suit and tie only!"** (This is more of an unwritten rule where you'll get dirty looks if you dare to come to church in anything other than the so-called appropriate apparel. There's nothing wrong with wearing dress clothes to church gatherings, but to make it a rule and look down upon those who don't is grossly wrong. See James 2:2-4).

- **"You can celebrate this and that holiday but not this or that holiday"** (Although some religious holidays have somewhat dubious origins, observing them or not is a matter that comes down to a person's heart. For example, Christmas may be about materialism to one person and it may be about a celebration of Christ and the gift of giving to another; Easter may be about colored eggs and spring vacation to one person and about the resurrection of Christ and spiritual regeneration to another. This is why Paul encouraged Christians to resist making judgments about fellow believers and the days they choose to celebrate as holidays. See Romans 14:5-8 & Colossians 2:16).

- **"You must not view an R-rated movie"** (Unless, of course, it's *The Passion of the Christ*, which proves that not all R-rated films are moral filth, even if they have scenes depicting various fleshly behaviors and extreme violence. Want proof? Are there any stories in the Bible that are heavily R-rated? Obviously: David's lust for the bathing Bathsheba and his subsequent adultery and murder of Uriah; David chopping off Goliath's head and parading it around; Lot's daughters' incestuous actions with their drunken father; the mass slaughter of infants; whole cities put to the sword, including women and children; the global bloodshed in Revelation; the naked demoniac; the witch of Endor; Judah having sex with his daughter-in-law who was posing as a prostitute; God threatening to kill Moses until his wife circumcises their son and throws the bloody foreskin at Moses' feet; wicked Jezebel being thrown alive from an upper window, splattering on the pavement, her corpse trampled by a chariot and torn to pieces by dogs; all the pregnant women of a city ripped open; lions mauling to death Gentile settlers in Israel; ten thousand captured soldiers thrown off a cliff to their deaths; etcetera. What about the Song of Songs? It's a beautifully poetic book about romantic love and sexual union with a deeper subtext, but what's it rated? Read it and be honest. God's Word obviously doesn't whitewash human nature but honestly bares it with all its potential glory or shame. The Bible isn't the "Good Book" because it Disney-fies the human experience, but because it's brutally honest about it and provides the God-given answers. Of course, someone could argue that these hardcore Bible stories include moral themes or lessons, but so does the R-rated *3:10 to Yuma* remake, which is a story of redemption with a Christ-figure. Needless to say, not all films are moral trash and believers should have the freedom to seek out the worthy ones while adhering to the principle "Above all else, guard your heart for it is the wellspring of life" from Proverbs 4:23).

- **"You can't play competitive games, like football, including board games, like chess"** (You might think I'm kidding, but I actually read this absurd rule on a Christian website. It's hard to believe, but this ministry was actually making the argument that truly holy Christians shouldn't engage in any type of competitive games whatsoever because it's inherently carnal. Incredible[9]).

- **"Marital couples can only have sex in the missionary position; all other sexual expressions are forbidden"** (As unbelievable as this one sounds, multiple believers who left a rigid sect testified that this was actually one of the groups' numerous, eye-rolling rules. I'm guessing these prudish rule-makers never read the Song of Songs).

- **"You must witness door-to-door or you're not a true believer"** (I came across a couple of believers about a year ago who regularly went door-to-door sharing the gospel. One of them was an elder and it became clear that he looked down on Christians who failed to go door-to-door as they did. I asked, "Did Jesus go door-to-door?" They quickly answered, "Of course," but failed to cite any Scripture (because they couldn't). I then asked, "How come there's not one instruction in the epistles for believers to 'witness' door-to-door?" They had no answer, except to inquire, "How else will people hear the good news?" I then listed a number of ways off the top of my head: "Natural

---

[9] This is a different issue than those who watch (or play) sports, like football, to the point that it's akin to idolatry. *Anything* can become an idol if it becomes our primary focus at the expense of God and health.

contact, revivals, internet, tracts, books, radio, TV, inviting people to church, etc." I'm not at all saying that believers shouldn't go door-to-door, as Jesus sent his disciples to do this on a couple occasions, but there's no rule in the New Testament that believers *must* go door-to-door. Why? Because not all cultures or generations are conducive to the door-to-door approach, as 1st century Israel was, and believers need to adjust their evangelistic methods accordingly. What God's Word does say is that believers should "Always be prepared to give an answer to everyone who asks" us to give the reason for the hope that we have "But do this with gentleness and respect" (1 Peter 3:15); and that we should "shine out like stars in the universe" as we "hold out the word of life" (Philippians 2:15-16). You see? There's no ironclad *law* that believers must go door-to-door, but rather general instructions to hold out the word of life in a respectful fashion as led of the Holy Spirit. Speaking of which, if the Holy Spirit guides you to go door-to-door in certain neighborhoods, by all means do so).

Eye-rolling rules like these bring to mind Jesus' potent observation about legalists: "They worship me in vain; their teachings are but rules taught by men" (Mark 7:7).

6. Legalists are Works-Oriented Rather than Relationship-Oriented

Just as legalists are rule-oriented rather than relationship-oriented, so they're also works-oriented. We see this in Jesus' confrontation with legalists in this passage:

> "Watch out for <u>false prophets</u>. They come to you in sheep's clothing, but inwardly they are ferocious wolves. [16] <u>By their fruit you will recognize them</u>. Do people pick up grapes from thornbushes, or figs from thistles? [17] Likewise every good tree bears good fruit but a bad tree bears bad fruit. [18] A good tree cannot bear bad fruit, and a bad tree cannot

bear good fruit. [19] Every tree that does not bear good
fruit is cut down and thrown into the fire. [20] Thus, <u>by
their fruit you will recognize them</u>."
[21] "Not everyone who says to me, 'Lord,
Lord,' will enter the kingdom of heaven, but only he
who does the will of my Father who is in heaven.
[22]Many will say to me on that day, 'Lord, Lord, did
we not prophesy in your name, and in your name
drive out demons and perform many miracles?'
[23]Then I will tell them plainly, '<u>I never knew you</u>.
Away from me, <u>you evildoers</u>!' "

Matthew 7:15-23

Jesus was speaking of the future occasion when those who
falsely speak for God stand before him to be judged.[10] Notice what these
people say to Jesus upon meeting him in verse 22. Unbelievably, they
immediately start *boasting* of their great works! They brag about their
prophesying, exorcisms and miracles! Interestingly, Jesus doesn't contest
that they did these works, so they're likely telling the truth. He merely
responds, "*I never knew you*. Away from me you evildoers!"

This shows two things: Firstly, legalists trust in their religious
works to obtain God's favor and salvation, which explains why these
false prophets immediately boast of their great works when appearing
before the Lord.

Secondly, Christianity's all about reconciling with God and
literally *knowing* him. This is why the gospel is called the "message of
reconciliation" (2 Corinthians 5:18-20). Christianity is a *relationship*
with the awesome Creator of the universe and our works are merely an
overflow of this relationship. But legalists reject this simple truth
because having an actual relationship with the LORD is something that's
largely done in private and legalists are all about putting on airs of
religiosity to impress others. Consequently, they divert to rule-ism and
works-oriented religion. This is why these false ministers immediately

---

[10] 'False prophets' in the Greek is one compound word *pseudoprohetes (soo-
doh-prah-FAY-tus)*; *pseudo* of course means false and *prophetes* refers to
inspired speakers or those who propose to speak for God. Hence,
pseudoprophetes or "false prophets" refers to people who falsely speak for the
LORD.

start boasting of their works when they come face-to-face with the Lord. As is typical with legalists, they thought their great works would secure them God's favor and eternal salvation, but they were wrong.

Christ's response to these legalists, "I never knew you," is a key insight about legalists—*they don't have a relationship with the Lord* and therefore don't really know him despite claims to the contrary. Take the Pharisees, for example. They claimed that God was their father, which implies close kinship, but Jesus frankly told them they were children of the devil (John 8:41-44)! Another good example is the priests of Judah just before their forced exile. The LORD spoke of them like so:

> **"The priests did not ask,**
> **'Where is the LORD?'**
> **Those who deal with the law <u>did not know me</u>;**
> **the leaders rebelled against me.' "**
>
> **Jeremiah 2:8**

He goes on to point out that they had no awe of God (verse 19). People who really know the LORD develop an overwhelming awe. Legalists lack such awe because they don't know him, even though they put on airs of veneration to impress others.

I should stress that works have their place. After all, James made it clear that "faith by itself, if it is not accompanied by action, is dead" (James 2:14-24). But, again, works are a *result of* having a relationship with God and not a *means to* the relationship. This is why Paul said it is by God's favor we are saved, through faith, and not by works so that no one can boast (Ephesians 2:8-9). Unfortunately, legalists choose to concentrate on their works so that they can boast. It's all about ego and arrogance. We see this in the passage from Matthew above.

Scholar E.W. Bullinger points out the differences between godliness and religion in his lexicon (335). The Greek word for godliness in the Bible relates to a real and vital relationship with the Almighty whereas the Greek word for religion refers to the outward acts of religious works and ceremonies. The latter can be performed by the flesh without knowing God at all, which is why legalists make it their focus, but the former—having a relationship with God—requires the human spirit. Jesus said, "God is spirit, and his worshippers must worship **in**

spirit and truth" (John 4:24) 'Spirit' here refers to the human spirit. The point being that true worship is not merely a matter of outward conformity to religious rules, ceremonies, works and places. Authentic worship springs from a regenerated spirit that's connected with the LORD and involves communion between the individual and the indwelling Holy Spirit, who guides/helps us. This is relationship. 'Godliness' means to be *like* God and stems from this relationship since we become like those we spend time with the most. In other words, **a relationship with God produces godliness**. 'Religion' by contrast doesn't refer to godliness, but to outward forms of devotion.

Let me give an example of works being a natural outflow of having a relationship with God. I always strive for a relationship with the Lord and therefore talk to him throughout the day, give thanks, etc. As a result of this relationship he has given me a general commission as well as specific tasks. For instance, teaching God's Word is my general assignment whereas writing this book is a specific task. When you focus on the LORD and genuinely seek his will he'll tell you precisely what to do in each season of your life. Whatever general assignment or specific work he gives you, you'll have a joyful enthusiasm about it. For example, it takes a lot of time and work to write books like this but it's a joy for me. I literally *love* doing it and I struggle with a sense of meaninglessness whenever I stray from my calling. Teaching God's Word is a joy because it's a natural outflow of my relationship with him. Just the same, you'll have an elated drive for whatever the LORD calls you to do. In some cases it may be something very difficult, like the last twelve hours of Jesus' life on Earth, but your Father will give you the grace, peace and power you'll need to accomplish it, just as he did for Yeshua. On a much less traumatic scale, I've taught sermons at churches where the experience wasn't very fun, but God faithfully gave me the grace, peace and power to accomplish it.

7. Legalists Love to Boast of their Works

In the above passage—Matthew 7:15-23—Jesus tells of legalists who appear before him at the judgment and they immediately start boasting of their works! Imagine standing before the very Creator of the universe, what would be your first reaction? I don't know about you, but I'd immediately fall on my face in reverence and humility! Then I'd proceed to thank him and praise him. But this isn't what legalists would do. Notice again the reaction of legalists when they stand before the Lord:

> **"Many will say to me on that day, 'Lord, Lord, <u>did we not prophesy in your name, and in your name drive out demons and perform many miracles?</u>'** [23] **Then I will tell them plainly, 'I never knew you. Away from me, you evildoers!' "**
>
> **Matthew 7:22-23**

How could anyone come before the Living Lord and start boasting away? Legalists can because they're arrogant. People who are arrogant have a superiority complex; that's what arrogance is. They think they're all that and a bag of chips—even when standing before the Almighty! I know it's crazy, but that's what carnal pride does to people. It corrupts.

Let's observe another scriptural example of this legalistic tendency:

> **To some who were <u>confident of their own righteousness</u> and <u>looked down on everybody else,</u> Jesus told this parable:** [10] **"Two men went up to the temple to pray, one a Pharisee and the other a tax collector.** [11] **The Pharisee stood up and <u>prayed about himself</u>: 'God, I thank you that I am not like other men—robbers, evildoers, adulterers—or even like this tax collector.** [12] **<u>I fast twice a week and give a tenth of all I get.</u>'**
>
> [13] **"But the tax collector stood at a distance. He would not even look up to heaven, but beat his breast and said, 'God, have mercy on me a sinner.'**
>
> [14] **"I tell you that this man, rather than the other went home justified before God. For <u>everyone who exalts himself will be humbled</u>, and he who humbles himself will be exalted."**
>
> **Luke 18:9-14**

Notice what this Pharisee does when he goes to the Temple—*he prays about himself.* Can you believe it? His "prayer" consists of boasting of how supposedly righteous he is, then putting down another man who also came to the Temple to pray and, lastly, boasting of his religious works. The tax collector, by contrast, doesn't even look up to Heaven; he looks down, confesses himself a sinner, and asks for God's mercy.

Is it any wonder that Jesus said the tax collector would go home justified in God's eyes and not the Pharisee? Keep in mind that tax collectors were viewed with disdain while Pharisees were respected religious leaders of Israel. Jesus' story shows that appearances aren't always what they seem.

Do you know people in the Church who have a tendency to boast of their great religious works? It may even be a respected pastor, prophet, teacher or evangelist. Beware. It's a blatant indication of legalism.

8. Legalists have an Unbiblical Understanding of Worldliness

Believers should conduct themselves with standards of holiness, especially since pure religion in God's sight includes keeping oneself from being polluted by the world (James 1:27), but legalists have a confused and unbiblical definition of worldliness. Their idea of worldliness is not following the priority rules of their sect to the letter. But how does the Bible itself define worldliness? Take note:

> **Do not love the world or the things in the world. If anyone loves the world, the love of the Father is not in him. [16] For all that is in the world— the lust of the flesh, the lust of the eyes, and the pride of life—is not of the Father but is of the world.**
>
> **1 John 2:15-16** (NKJV)

As you can see, this passage reveals that worldliness is three things: The lust of the flesh, the lust of the eyes and the pride of life. **The lust of the flesh** refers to all sexual-oriented sins, as well as gluttony, sloth, etc.; **the lust of the eyes** refers to things like envy, malice, greed and theft; and **the pride of life** refers to everything that stems from arrogance, like hatred, abuse, authoritarianism, slander, strife and fictitious stories (otherwise known as "Barbara Streisand" or "BS"). Keep in mind that "the lust of the flesh" refers to sexual-oriented *sins* and not to sex itself. God created sex and there's nothing wrong with sexual expression between a husband and wife who are one-flesh in God's eyes. It's sexual *immorality* that's wrong, not sex itself. God created sex.

Understanding what true worldliness is can be very liberating. You realize that someone could be a full-time pastor and also be thoroughly guilty of worldliness, just like the Pharisees whom Jesus said looked good *on the outside* but were "full of greed and wickedness" within (Luke 11:39).

We'll address this subject in more detail in **Chapter 11**.

A Note on "Disputable Matters"

As pointed out above, having standards of holiness is good but, be careful, because anything good can be corrupted.

Consider what the Bible calls "disputable matters," like any of the ten extra-biblical rules addressed earlier. The Bible instructs those who walk free of the debatable rule to not look down on those who follow it and vice versa (Romans 14:1-4). Paul taught that "Each one should be fully convinced in his own mind" (Romans 14:5) and concluded that whatever believers determine about such things should be kept between themselves and God, generally speaking (Romans 14:22). Why? Because the issue itself tends to stir up unnecessary controversy which naturally leads to strife. So seek the LORD on the matter through prayer & study and draw your own conclusions; only discuss the subject with other believers if they seem open to discussing it. Other than that, keep it between yourself and the LORD.

Usually people embrace rules in "disputable matters" because they have a problem in the area in question. Again, there's nothing wrong with this; the problem enters the picture when they impose *their personal rule* on everyone else, which isn't necessary because not everyone has a problem in the same area. Let me give a couple examples.

Not long ago I was part of a men's group that would read Christian books on male-oriented issues and regularly meet for discussion and fellowship. In one of the books the author went to extreme lengths to protect himself from his lust problem. For instance, before reading a newspaper or magazine he'd cut out any ads or pictures that featured a fetching female, especially scantily-clad ones like underwear or bathing suit ads. In addition, if he were out in public he'd never look at a comely female for more than a passing glance (approximately 0.187 seconds) and would refuse to view TV shows or movies that showed women in alluring apparel. Etcetera. These were rules that this man came up with in order to walk free of lust and serve the Lord with a clear conscience. There's nothing wrong with these rules if a man has a severe lust problem. Such a man observes the rules for the sake of personal holiness, which is pure religion in God's eyes (James 1:27). These rules are akin to the alcoholic who must stay away from any environment that includes alcoholic beverages in order to walk in victory. But not all men have such a lust problem, nor do all people struggle with alcohol like the severe alcoholic.

To be expected, this subject provoked a lively discussion at the men's group. A couple of the men admitted they needed to go to such extremes to walk free of lust, while most others felt the rules were so radical that it was the next thing to requiring women to wear robes and veils in public, like in some Islamic countries.

This was the perfect occasion for us to practice Paul's instructions in Romans 14: The men who felt it necessary to adhere to these rigid rules should not look down on those who didn't and vice versa. As Paul instructed, "Who are you to judge someone else's servant? To his own master he stands or falls. And he will stand, for the Lord is able to make him stand… Each one should be fully convinced in his own mind" (Romans 14:4-5).

Such rules are fine if you require them to keep a clean conscience before God, but be careful that religious pride doesn't seep-in and you start judging and condemning other genuine believers who don't require these rules. Otherwise you'll be infected by legalism, which is a path of spiritual darkness and death.

Carol & I went to one church where the pastor had a history of alcohol-related problems before he came to the Lord and, consequently, was hell-bent against anything having to do with alcohol. Not only was drinking a sip of alcohol a sin, it was also a sin to dine at an establishment that served alcohol, like Red Lobster. In fact, it was wrong to shop at a store that sold alcohol, like Walmart! Do you see the problem here? Because *he* had a weakness toward alcohol he developed an extreme view on the subject and tried to impose *his* personal rules of holiness on everyone else, including the vast majority who had no need of such rules.

IMPORTANT: Being Anti-Legalism is not the same as being Pro-Lawless!

Before moving on, let me stress that I'm in no way advocating lawlessness. The words 'lawless' and 'sinful' are essentially one-and-the-same because sin is the disregard of divine law. In fact, John plainly pointed out that "sin is lawlessness" in 1 John 3:4. But what is the divine law of the new covenant that believers have with the Almighty? Faith, hope and love; and the greatest of these is love—love for God and love for people (1 Corinthians 13:13 & Mark 12:28-31). How does faith work? Faith works by love (Galatians 5:6). Let me explain.

Jesus plainly stated that if we fulfill these two laws of love we'll automatically fulfill all the moral laws contained in the Old Testament (Matthew 7:12 & 22:40). How so? Through the *motivation* of love— God's love that's inside of us through spiritual regeneration, putting off the flesh and putting on the new self. This is living out of our spirit with the help of the Holy Spirit:

> **You were taught with regard to your former way of life, to <u>put off your old self</u>, which is being corrupted by its deceitful desires; [23] to be made new in the attitude of your minds; [24] and to <u>put on the new self</u>, created to be <u>like God</u> in <u>true righteousness</u> and <u>holiness</u>.**
>
> **Ephesians 4:22-24**

This is the new covenant of the spirit, which is the sound "middle ground" between legalism and lawlessness. The "old man" refers to the flesh or sinful nature. It's corrupted by "deceitful desires" and therefore must be "put off." This means that we have to learn to recognize the wrong desires of the flesh and not embrace them. Rather we put them off by counting ourselves *dead* to the flesh's deceitful desires and *alive* to God and his nature. (Romans 6:11). What's God's nature? The fruits of the Spirit *are* his nature and are opposed to the works of the flesh (Galatians 5:19-23). When we put off the old man and put on the new man in this manner we'll be spirit-controlled rather than flesh-controlled. We'll live out of our "new self" and will therefore produce fruits of righteousness and holiness "like God." This is the biblical way to be godly. It's putting the flesh on the level of a slave and dominating it by walking in the spirit.

It's actually a very simple thing, but it must be learned and become habitual, which is a process and matter of growth. We'll miss it now and then, but that's what 1 John 1:8-9 is for. You don't drown by falling in the water; you drown by staying there and eventually sinking.

Legalists, unfortunately, reject this new way of the spirit. It's too easy and they don't get the sole credit they crave. They prefer instead to subject themselves to hard labor in order to achieve their own fleshly salvation and godliness, but this type of godliness is false and is actually *self*-righteousness.

We'll address lawlessness, or libertinism, in detail in **Chapter 10** and walking in the spirit in **Chapter 11**.

Isn't Christianity a Bunch of Rules Like Legalism?

We've seen how legalism is a mentality of rule-ism where people are obsessed with outward compliance to the dos & don'ts of their belief system above all else. Someone might understandably argue that Christianity has its own endless list of rules and regulations. In other words, how does genuine Christianity differ from legalism? What makes Christianity superior?

As noted in the previous section, there are only two laws in Christianity with three applications: **love God** and **love people** as you **love yourself**:

> **Jesus replied, " 'Love the Lord your God with all your heart and with all your soul and with all your mind.' [38] This is the first and greatest commandment. [39] And the second is like it: 'Love your neighbor <u>as yourself.</u>' [40] <u>All the Law and the Prophets hang on these two commandments.</u>"**
>
> **Matthew 22:37-40**

> **Let no debt remain outstanding, except the continuing debt to love one another, for <u>he who loves his fellowman has fulfilled the law.</u> [9] The commandments, "Do not commit adultery," "Do not murder," "Do not steal," "Do not covet," and whatever other commandment there may be are summed up in this <u>one rule</u>: "Love your neighbor as yourself." [10] Love does no harm to its neighbor. Therefore <u>it is the fulfillment of the law.</u>**
>
> **Romans 13:8-10**

Love does no harm to God, it does no harm to others and it does no harm to self, so it's the fulfillment of the Law. Walking in love doesn't just refer to gentle love; sometimes tough love is necessary, like when Jesus sternly rebuked the Pharisees and boldly cleared the temple.[11]

So love is the *sole rule* of Christianity, that's it.

How is the believer able to successfully walk according to this rule? It starts with spiritual rebirth:

> **He saved us, not because of righteous things we had done, but because of his mercy. He saved us through the <u>washing of rebirth and renewal by the Holy Spirit,</u>   Titus 3:5**

---

[11] See the teaching *Gentle Love and Tough Love* at the FOL website for details.

As Jesus said, "I tell you the truth, no one can see the kingdom of God unless he is born again... Flesh gives birth to flesh, but Spirit gives birth to spirit" (John 3:3,6). When believers are spiritually regenerated God gives them new "God-ware":

> **"This is the <u>covenant</u> I will make with the house of**
> **Israel**
> **after that time," declares the LORD.**
> **"I will put my law in their minds**
> **and write it on their hearts.**
> **I will be their God**
> **and they will be my people."**
>
> **Jeremiah 31:33**

The passage speaks of the time of the new covenant, which is the Church Age, meaning NOW. In the new covenant all believers are of the house of Israel in a spiritual sense:

> **A man is not a Jew if he is only one**
> **outwardly, nor is circumcision merely outward and**
> **physical. [29] No, <u>a man is a Jew if he is one inwardly</u>;**
> **and circumcision is <u>circumcision of the heart</u>, <u>by the</u>**
> **<u>Spirit</u>, <u>not by the written code</u>.**
>
> **Romans 2:28-29**

The passage is talking about spiritual rebirth. This is how the LORD puts his moral law in the minds and hearts of his people. This is the first essential step for people to fulfill God's law. The second step is noted in the previous section: Learn to distinguish the desires of the flesh—your old nature—from the desires of the spirit—your new nature. Put off the old and put on the new. When you do this you will naturally produce the fruit of the spirit, which are the very character traits of God. Consequently, you'll be spirit-controlled rather than flesh-ruled, you'll be an "imitator of God," you'll be godly or like-God (Ephesians 5:1).

Since love is the primary fruit of the spirit and love is the fulfillment of the law, believers fulfill this single law of Christianity when they walk in the spirit. It's actually very simple, but religion unnecessarily complicates everything.

So Christianity is vastly superior to legalism because believers fulfill the Law by living according to the law of love that is *within* them and not by futilely disciplining their flesh to conform to an endless list of *external* rules.

Someone might respond, "If believers have the law of love written in their hearts why do they need the Bible and all its instructions?" Several reasons, starting with the fact that the Bible shares a lot of information that isn't moral law. For instance, it includes historical, prophetic and psychological truths, as well as passages of encouragement and comfort. It shows believers who they *are*, spiritually speaking, and therefore how God sees them (Colossians 1:22 is a good example). There are also instructions that are not of a moral nature, such as information on church order, church government, spiritual gifts, prayer, spiritual warfare, faith and healing. As far as the actual moral law is concerned, it's important to have it documented for reasons that will be explained next chapter. Furthermore, the Bible instructs us to "not go beyond what is written" (1 Corinthians 4:6). In other words, the Scriptures set the boundary lines for believers and the Church in general. For instance, when someone strays into false doctrine God's Word can be used as a corrective.

But, as far as the moral law goes, it's written in the believer's spirit. All the believer has to do is learn how to live by their spirit led of the Holy Spirit and he or she will fulfill all the moral law through the love of God that's been poured out into our hearts by the Holy Spirit (Romans 5:5).

All Moral Truth is Obvious

One last thing in this vein: All moral truth is obvious the more a person develops discernment or wisdom. For example, I wrote a book about forgiveness, released in 2012, and it goes into a lot of detail in its 256 pages[12] but, generally speaking, all the truths conveyed in it are obvious if one simply reflects on any of the many issues. It's really all

---

[12] *The Believer's Guide to FORGIVENESS & WARFARE.*

just common sense. Truth is simple, but religion unnecessarily complicates it.

For instance, say a married man meets a comely woman on the job who conveys interest. Should he commit adultery with her or not? You don't have to be a Christian or know any passage in the Bible to know that it's wrong. Why? Because it's wrong to be unfaithful to one's spouse. Or take homosexuality, a hot topic today. Is it right or wrong? It's a matter of being honest about the obvious facts of reality. It's common sense and you don't need the Bible to tell you one way or another.

Moral truth is obvious because we all instinctively know the difference between good and evil due to conscience (Romans 2:15). So why do people rebel against this inherent moral code? Paul explained it this way: "They are darkened in their understanding and separated from the life of God because of the ignorance that is in them due to the hardening of their hearts" (Ephesians 4:18). You see? They harden themselves to the voice of their conscience to the point that they no longer even realize moral common sense.

Consider belief in God. Why are atheists so mad about someone they don't even believe exists? Why don't they get all irate in denouncing, say, Bigfoot or leprechauns? Because they know Bigfoot and leprechauns don't exist. But they *know* deep down inside that God exists and they *have* to get all worked up to deny it.

What's my point? If moral truth is obvious to unbelievers, as long as they don't harden their hearts, how much more so the born-again believer who's in spiritual union with their Creator? We just have to open our eyes and look beyond the false indoctrination of secular and religious culture, which is what being transformed by the renewing of the mind is all about (Romans 12:2).

All moral truth is obvious. Think about it.

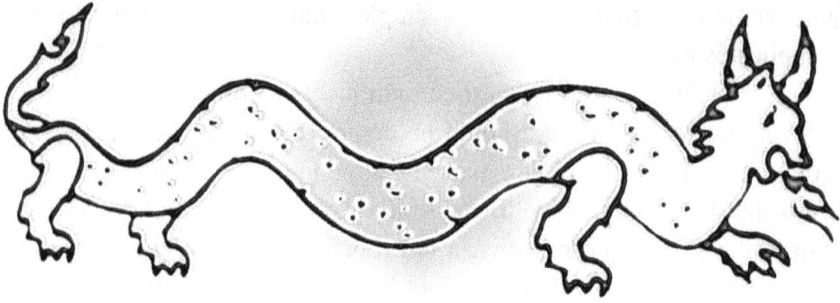

Chapter 3

General Legalism Continued

Continuing with our list of 16 legalistic traits:

9. Legalists are Obsessed with the LETTER of the Law

Legalists by definition are obsessed with strict adherence to the letter of the law, whether the rule in question is biblical or extra-biblical. This would include things they feel the Lord instructed them to do or not do.

A good example from the New Testament is when the Pharisees objected to Jesus' mere intention of healing a man's deformed hand on the Sabbath (Mark 3:1-6). The Pharisees were so ridiculously detailed and rigid with their rules concerning "working" on the Sabbath that they objected to Christ doing any type of healing "work" on that day. The Lord was so disgusted by their stubbornness that he shot them all a glance of *anger*. This was righteous anger, of course, but anger nevertheless. He then proceeded to heal the man despite their legalistic objections. This was a wordless reprimand and the Pharisees were so offended they decided to murder him!

Can you imagine people being so blinded by legalistic zeal that they object to an incredible healing?! Make no mistake, this is what the poison of legalism does when people are seriously infected. Those who are not contaminated, by contrast, are ever-ready to praise God when people are miraculously healed and set free. Take, for instance, the occasion where blind Bartimaeus received his sight through faith and immediately glorified God. The passage goes on to say, "And all the people, when they saw it, gave praise to God" (Luke 18:43 NKJV). This is how *normal* people react to incredible healings and life-changing miracles. Not so with legalists. They're so corrupted by rule-ism they can't see the forest for the trees!

Here's a more mundane example: Say you feel inspired to declare a two-day fast and at around 46.5 hours you have a peace after accomplishing everything you intended, but you sit there for 90 minutes watching the clock in misery until exactly the 48-hour mark to break the fast. This is letter-of-the-law-ism, which is a form of legalism. It's stupid and unnecessary. If the Spirit inspires you to take a two-day fast and you feel peace and release to break it at 46.5 hours, please do so. You're not committing a grievous sin by not waiting till *precisely* the 48-hour mark.

To have this attitude with scriptural laws is bad enough, but legalists obsess over the many nitpicky, joy-sapping rules they continually dream-up. For instance, Jesus and his disciples were walking through the fields one Sabbath and picked some heads of grain to quell their hunger. Since it was the Sabbath the Pharisees argued that the disciples were guilty of working because they plucked the grain and rubbed it in their hands before eating. To their legalistic way of thinking this was equal to reaping and threshing. The Law did forbid working on the Sabbath but it was intended to be a blessing not a burden. The Sabbath was supposed to be a welcomed rest and celebration of God after a 6-day work week, not a joyless ritual observing man-made technicalities. Christ's simple-yet-brilliant response says it all: "The Sabbath was made for man, not man for the Sabbath" (Mark 2:27).[13]

God is always interested in blessing people by setting them free while religionists are intent on burdening others and putting them into spiritual bondage. Concerning the Teachers of the Law and the Pharisees, Christ said: "They tie up heavy loads and put them on men's shoulders, but they themselves are not willing to lift a finger to move them" (Matthew 23:4). By contrast, the Bible says:

> **This is love for God: to obey his commands. <u>And his commands are not burdensome</u>, [4] for everyone <u>born of God</u> <u>overcomes the world</u>. This is the victory that has overcome the world, even our <u>faith</u>.**
>
> **1 John 5:3-4**

As we saw at the end of the last chapter, all of God's moral laws in the Old Testament can be condensed into two basic commands with three applications: **Love God** and **love people** as you **love yourself**. That's it. And these commands are not burdensome because believers are born of God and have the spiritual nature to fulfill them with joy. The only believers who can't do this are those who fail to put off the flesh and are therefore flesh-ruled. As such, the "law of sin and death" is at work in their lives and this is no fun because sin's reward is death. But those who walk in the spirit are spirit-controlled and therefore the "law of the Spirit of life" is in motion, which is a higher law than the law of sin and death (Romans 8:2).

Did you ever marvel at how huge aircrafts are able to defy the law of gravity and soar above the landscape? How do they do this? It's simple: They activate a higher law, the law of lift and propulsion, which neutralizes the law of gravity. As long as the higher law is in motion the lower law is rendered powerless. Just as the physical law of lift and propulsion enables people to conquer gravity and fly, so the law of the Spirit of life deactivates the law of sin and death when it is in motion.

---

[13] You can compare the three accounts of this occasion as shown in Matthew 12:1-8, Mark 2:23-28 and Luke 6:1-5.

This is "walking in the spirit" or "participating in the divine nature." This law is not burdensome, but human religion is.

Notice what Christ said on this matter:

> **"Come to me, all you who are weary and burdened, and <u>I will give you rest</u>. [29] Take my yoke upon you and learn from me, for <u>I am gentle and humble in heart and you will find rest for your souls</u>. [30] For <u>my yoke is easy and my burden is light</u>."**
>
> **Matthew 11:28-30**

Yes, there is a yoke and burden to serving the Lord, but unlike the yoke of the flesh or the burden of religion Jesus' yoke is *easy* and his burden is *light*. How so? Because that's the nature of the law of love and love is the fulfillment of the Law (Romans 13:8-10).

Speaking of joy-sapping rules…

10. Legalism Saps Life, Freedom and Joy Because "the Letter Kills"

The problem with obsession to the Law—"the letter"—is that this mentality *kills*:

> [God] **has made us competent as ministers of a new covenant, not of the letter, but of the Spirit; for <u>the letter kills</u>, but <u>the Spirit gives life</u>.**
>
> **2 Corinthians 3:6**

Focusing on rules above relationship with God, including extra-biblical rules, will naturally sap life, freedom and joy because "the letter kills." Why should believers focus on relationship with God? Because **1.** loving God is the first and greatest command, and **2.** God is the Fountain of Life and therefore only in the light of his presence are we able to see spiritual light (Psalm 36:9). Consequently, the further we get away from the Creator, the further we get away from the life and light that only He gives. Life, freedom and joy will diminish and ultimately die once on the path of spiritual darkness, which is any path that distances oneself from the presence of God. I heard a minister put it like this: "Worldliness is anything that cools your affection for God." This includes anything that comes under the brackets of "the lust of the flesh, the lust of the eyes and the pride of life" (1 John 2:15-16), touched on last chapter.

As noted above, the churches in Galatia were infiltrated by the Judaizers who were legalists that insisted on circumcision and obedience to religious laws to inherit salvation and please God. Once the Galatians were infected by legalism their joy was sapped, which is why Paul asked them, "What happened to all your joy?" (Galatians 4:15). Why was their joy sapped? Because "the letter *kills*"*!*

Simply put, legalists are joy-stealers. They're grumps. When Christ made his triumphal entry into Jerusalem the crowd of disciples began to joyfully "praise God in loud voices" whereupon the Pharisees commanded Jesus to make them stop! This can be read in Luke 19:37-39. You see, legalists are never happy in the midst of exuberant believers. Whether they know it or not they're not being godly—"like God"—because joy is actually a trait of God. It's a "fruit of the Spirit" and therefore a part of the LORD's character. As such, it comes as no surprise that God wants his people to be filled with joy. As it is written: "the joy of the LORD is your strength" and "in [God's] presence is fullness of joy" (Nehemiah 8:10 & Psalm 16:11). Needless to say, the presence or absence of joy is a good indicator of where you're at spiritually. If you have little or no joy, be sure to examine yourself to see if you're infected by legalism in some way (or in bondage to the flesh, which we'll look at in **Chapter 10**).

If not, your problem may be that you need to go deeper into praise & worship. Praise is celebration, which ushers in the presence of the LORD while worship is adoration, the natural response to being in his presence (Psalm 95:1-7 & Psalm 100). Regularly experiencing God's presence is conducive to joy because in his presence is *fullness of joy* (Psalm 16:11).[14]

---

[14] I used to struggle with depression for years and shared it with a couple Christian counselors. They told me I needed "to be on medication." Around this same time I was at my back door one day when I heard the Spirit say, "This shall be a house of praise & worship unto my Name." I reflected on it for a

To further illustrate that the letter kills, let me share a couple examples from everyday life:

Carol & I were at a NFL game years ago where a beach ball was being bounced around in the stands before the game. The people were having a blast hitting the ball high into the air, which would then land on others yards away. They would do the same, and so on. It didn't take long for a security person to come along and try to confiscate the ball. He was having a hard time because the ball kept bouncing around at giant leaps as he chased it through the stands. Of course he wasn't happy about the situation; in fact, he was totally grumpy. At one point someone in the stands held the ball and waited for him to come and confiscate it, but as soon as the sourpuss arrived the guy hit the ball into the air and everyone laughed all the louder. Mad as a hatter, the curmudgeon continued to chase the big bad beach ball until he finally apprehended it.

Yes, I understand that the stadium probably had rules about beach balls bouncing around in the stands, but the game wasn't playing and the people were having a good time, which is what these events are all about. Besides, the ball was light and harmless. The sourpuss could have eased up on the rules a bit, but like all staunch legalists he was hell-bent on enforcing the rules to the letter.

Another good example would be NFL refs who are so obsessed with the rules of the game that they throw their flags at the slightest *possibility* of an offense. It's just so frustrating to see great plays canceled out due to some overzealous ref. This slows the game down and saps the life out of the players and audience. In a recent game a defending player was flagged for supposedly roughing the passer in the middle of the 4th quarter, which cost the defending team a whopping 15-

---

moment and responded, "Okay." Although I was already a praise & worshiper I upped the ante. I started blasting praise & worship music at my house 24/7. I no longer praised & worshipped the LORD now and then; I became a praise & worship *warrior!* It became a 24-7 thing more and more (Hebrews 13:15). God inhabits the praises of his people (Psalm 22:3) and so my house naturally became a habitation for the manifest presence of God. Not just my literal house, but also the house of my body. In other words, praise & worship wasn't just reverberating through the confines of my house and property, it was playing in my heart and mind. This solved my depression problem because light naturally displaces darkness: the light of joy displaced the darkness of depression—*Praise God!*

yard penalty. When the announcers showed the replay it was clear that the man didn't do anything to warrant the penalty and they stressed this. But nothing could be done and the entire course of the game shifted because of some gung-ho ref and his little yellow flag. Just the same, legalists can derail an entire church or sect with their stubborn obsession to the letter of the law.

If you watch football you know exactly what I mean—incredible plays called back because of some trivial contact that even the announcers admit wasn't really an infraction. It happens all the time. Similarly, legalists in the church prevent spiritual growth, miracles and great moves of the Spirit with their fanatical rule-ism. They sap the life, freedom and joy from the people of God! And then we wonder why believers get disillusioned and leave the church because it's so sterile, routine and impotent.

Am I saying that game rules are wrong in football? Absolutely not. Rules are necessary for obvious reasons. What I'm objecting to is overzealous refs throwing their flags at the slightest appearance of an infraction, which unnecessarily bogs down the game. I'm also objecting to the ever-increasing rules added for the sake of safety or what have you. Dreaming up more and more life-stifling rules isn't the answer. If the players can't stand the heat they should get out of the kitchen.

The same can be applied to government. Politicians keep passing more and more laws to the point that society is stifled. How many laws do we need anyway? We're over-regulated, pure and simple, and some laws are so useless they're a joke, but we keep passing more and more. It's absurd and it's sapping the life out of the citizenry and economy.

As previously stressed, Christianity is so simple: Love God and love people as you love yourself. Obviously if a person truly loves God they'll surrender to *his* means of salvation and spirituality and not their own, which is religion. When believers fulfill these two simple laws they automatically fulfill *all* the moral law (Matthew 22:36-40). Of course, this isn't accomplished by trying to force our flesh to comply, but rather by *putting off the flesh* and its deceitful desires and *putting on the "new self"* (Colossians 3:9-10).

"Law is Made <u>Not</u> for the Righteous"

Before moving on to the next trait, something should be cleared up. Many believers may find this surprising, but the Old Testament Law—the Torah—was *not* made for the righteous. Note what the Bible says in this regard:

> **We know that the law is good <u>if one uses it</u>**
> **<u>properly</u>.** [9] **We also know that <u>law is made not for the</u>**
> **<u>righteous</u> <u>but for lawbreakers and rebels, the</u>**
> **<u>ungodly and sinful, the unholy and irreligious</u>; for**
> **those who kill their fathers or mothers, for**
> **murderers,** [10] **for adulterers and perverts, for slave**
> **traders and liars and perjurers—and for whatever**
> **else is contrary to the sound doctrine** [11] **that conforms**
> **to the glorious gospel of the blessed God,**
> **1 Timothy 1:8-11**

This passage starts off by declaring that the Law is good, but only if it's used properly. This means that the Law is inherently "holy, righteous and good," as Paul pointed out in Romans 7:12, **but** *it is only good for people if it is utilized properly*. In other words, in and of itself the law is good, but it's only good for us when used appropriately.

The remaining verses reveal what this means: The Old Testament Law is not for **the righteous**, meaning believers who are made righteous in Christ through spiritual rebirth:

> **God made him who had no sin to be sin for us, so that**
> **<u>in him we might become the righteousness of God</u>.**
> **2 Corinthians 5:21**

Jesus never sinned, but he *became* sin for us on the cross so that *in him* we might become the righteousness of God. 'Become' in the Greek is a form of *ginomai (JIN-oh-may)*, which means "to come into being, to be born" (Bullinger). Whether you know it or not, when you turned to the LORD in repentance and faith you were spiritually reborn and, consequently, your spirit was *born* the righteousness of God. This explains why we are instructed to put off the flesh and put on the "new self" in Ephesians 4:22-24. This means to live out of our reborn spirit that was "created to be like God in true righteousness and holiness." When we do this we'll be spirit-controlled rather than flesh-ruled. We'll naturally bear forth fruits of the spirit rather than works of the flesh— we'll walk in "true righteousness and holiness"! This is the key to living according to the Old Testament Law, not putting the Law in front of us and trying to force our flesh to comply, which is being "under the law." This never works. In fact, it will actually *increase* the sin problem. Why do you think Paul said, "The law was added so that the trespass might increase" (Romans 5:20)? He said it because this is the reason the Law was given to humanity—to increase the sin problem and drive us to the Savior in whom we can have spiritual regeneration. Once we're reborn in this way all we have to do is learn to put off the flesh daily (or, as Jesus put it, "deny yourself") and live out of our spirits empowered and guided by the Holy Spirit. This includes transforming our thinking so that it corresponds to who we are in our spirit, which we'll address in **Chapter 11**. 'Repentance,' by the way, means to change your mind—your thinking—for the better. As such, those who try to turn away from a sin without changing their thinking are doomed to repeat the transgression.

Putting off the old man and putting on the new is being spirit-controlled rather than flesh-ruled. It's living by the spirit with the help of the Holy Spirit as opposed to living by the flesh. This is the answer to the sin problem, not putting a list of hundreds of laws in front of us and trying to force our carnal nature to conform. Again, this doesn't work and never will because the flesh is the sinful nature. It's utterly futile to try to make it produce righteousness! The entire Old Testament is testimony to this.

The passage goes on to stress that the moral law was made "for lawbreakers and rebels, the ungodly and sinful, the unholy and irreligious" (verse 9). Paul then provides a list of various sinful lifestyles, like fornicators, sodomites and liars.[15] God's moral law was "made for" such people in that it reveals to them that they're in sin, which can lead them to the Savior, the gospel, spiritual regeneration and the attainment

---

[15] See the NKJV rendering of 1 Timothy 1:8-11.

of righteousness in Christ. At which point they won't need the Law anymore; they'll just need to learn how to put off the "old self" and put on the "new self" because—when they do this—they'll walk in "true righteousness and holiness." Obviously if someone's walking in "true righteousness" they have no need for the Law.

This, by the way, explains a mysterious statement Paul made after listing the fruits of the spirit:

> **But the fruit of the Spirit is love, joy peace, patience, kindness, goodness, faithfulness, [23]gentleness and self-control. <u>Against such things there is no law</u>.**
>
> Galatians 5:22-23

When believers learn how to live out of their new natures as led of the Holy Spirit they'll be spirit-controlled rather than flesh-ruled and naturally produce the fruit of the spirit, which are the fruits of God's very nature! Such people ***need no external law to produce these godly attitudes and behaviors!***

This is why the Bible says that the Law is *not* for the righteous, but the unrighteous. The righteous have no need of the Law. Why? Because they're *already* producing the fruits of righteousness through living out of their spirits by the Holy Spirit. They're spirit-controlled, not flesh-ruled. It's the *unrighteous* who need the Law. This would include Christians who are practicing sin with no concern to repent. Say, for example, if believers are living in adultery, fornication, homosexuality, lying, slander or strife. We can show them through God's moral law that they are in sin and need to repent. This is using the Law lawfully or properly. Once they humbly repent God forgives them and they are cleansed from "ALL UNRIGHTEOUSNESS." At which point they'll no longer need the Law because they're righteous, as this passage clearly shows:

> **If we claim to be without sin, we deceive ourselves and the truth is not in us. [9] <u>If we confess our sins</u> he is faithful and just and will <u>forgive us our sins and purify us from all unrighteousness</u>.**
>
> 1 John 1:8-9

As long as believers "keep with repentance" in this manner they walk in the grace of God's forgiveness and **are** righteous in Christ because God purifies them "from all unrighteousness" when they confess. If the LORD cleanses repentant believers of *all* unrighteousness, what's that make them? Completely righteous. As such, they have no need of the Law because the Law was made for the unrighteous, not the righteous.

Genuinely "Loving Yourself" includes "Denying Yourself" (Your Flesh)

Earlier it was established that there are only two laws in Christianity with three applications: **Love God** and **love others** as you **love yourself**. Christ Himself taught this by quoting the Old Testament. Yet Jesus also instructed that we are to **deny ourselves** (Matthew 16:24). While this might seem like a contradiction, it's not.

The former obviously refers to **loving oneself in a whole, eternal sense** whereas the latter refers to **denying the flesh**, the sinful nature. For instance, the married believer who genuinely loves himself (and the Lord, his wife and family) won't entertain the adulterous attentions of a flirtatious "hottie" whereas the fool who doesn't truly love himself will. Why? Because the fool stupidly favors indulging the deceitful desires of his flesh above his own welfare.

It's for this reason that a wise woman won't consume a strawberry shortcake every day even while her flesh might crave it. She loves herself too much. Loving oneself in this manner is healthy and is not narcissistic whereas indulging the corrupt desires of the flesh is folly.

Why Do Legalists Prefer the Law?

We've talked a lot about how legalists prefer to focus on religious laws at the expense of living by the spirit. This was the problem Paul was having with the Galatian churches. Jewish legalists infiltrated these Gentile fellowships and put them into bondage to various religious laws, like circumcision, strict Sabbath observation, special fasts that were initiated by the Jews during the Babylonian captivity, the seven Jewish feasts[16] and the seven 7-year periods that culminated with the fiftieth year, the year of Jubilee (Galatians 4:10).

This understandably upset Paul, especially since he founded all or most of the churches to whom he was writing. Notice what he asks the Galatian believers in exasperation:

> **You foolish Galatians! Who has bewitched you? Before your very eyes Jesus Christ was clearly portrayed as crucified. [2] I would like to learn just one thing from you: Did you receive the Spirit by observing the law, or by what you heard? [3] Are you so foolish? After beginning with the Spirit, are you now trying to attain your goal by human effort?**
>
> **Galatians 3:1-3**

This perplexed and grieved Paul, so he felt it necessary to explain to the Galatians the actual purpose of the Law, concluding with this thought:

> **So the law was put in charge to lead us to Christ that we might be justified by faith. [25] Now that faith has come, <u>we are no longer under the supervision of the law</u>.**
>
> **Galatians 3:24-25**

Since believers are justified in God's sight by faith we are no longer under the supervision of the Law. 'Supervision' is translated as "schoolmaster" in the King James Version. The original Greek word refers to a household servant or slave whose job was to tutor and oversee male children until they came of age whereupon the sons took on the responsibilities and freedoms of adulthood. Are you getting this? Believers are no longer under the supervision of religious law. Since we are spiritually regenerated and have the Holy Spirit we are liberated to function in the responsibilities and freedoms of spiritual adulthood.

---

[16] The seven feasts are: Passover, Unleavened Bread, Firstfruits, Pentecost, Trumpets, Atonements, and Tabernacles.

If this is so, why on Earth would a believer go back to a system of dos and don'ts, like the Galatians did? Why would spiritually regenerated believers submit themselves to a former slave (the supervision of the Law) and have "him" oversee them? It's both foolish and absurd, not to mention a denial of the believer's rights as sons and daughters of the Most High!

So why do some people do it? Why revert to a system of rules and regulations that can only give the outward appearance of godliness and not the real deal? One obvious reason is laziness. In some perverted sense it's easier to submit to a system of laws than to think for oneself. You'll see this mentality in Christians who wholly submit their lives to authoritarian churches that tell them precisely what to do and believe. As such, they don't have to think for themselves; they just follow the authoritarians and their commands or rules.

Other reasons are insecurity and fear. Some believers are so insecure that they need someone to tell them what to do and believe. They're simply not secure in who they are in Christ and, consequently, they're weak. They're afraid of the responsibilities and freedoms that come with spiritual adulthood and therefore never really grow up. It's akin to the security of working for a company all your life rather than deal with the uncertainties of striking out on your own. Although the latter would provide a sense of adventure, freedom and change, the former provides security and comfort. Why risk the unknown? For this same reason millions of believers languish in dead fellowships.

Preferring the security of being an employee rather than being your own master is fine for the labor market, if that's what a person prefers, but it's unhealthy in the realm of the spirit. There are plenty of legalists and authoritarians out there who are more than willing to take advantage of believers who refuse to take the reins of spiritual maturity, libertines as well.

We looked at another reason why people prefer the law in the last chapter: Since legalists don't have an actual relationship with the LORD they have no choice but to divert to rules and regulations. This isn't to say that they won't go through the motions of having a relationship, but this is chiefly for appearances sake. In some cases they may actually pray in their private time, but it's very rehearsed, one-sided and lifeless, like talking to a wall. They likely do this to convince themselves that they actually have a relationship with God. If your prayer time is dry, one-dimensional and boring, take note. Legalism is creeping in.

Lastly, in addition to lacking an actual relationship with the Lord, legalistic leaders prefer religious rules so they can dominate others and foster a *dependent* following of sheeple. Such dependency naturally feeds the leader's ego.

Speaking of sheeple...

11. Legalism Creates Sheeple whereas True Christianity Creates Unique People

Because legalism is obsessed with outward adherence to the letter of the law and "the letter kills," it typically creates either automaton-like sheeple or prune-faced authoritarians; it can't produce unique people who are freed-up and full of the life and love of the LORD.

Consider some of the mighty men and women of God in our modern era. Are they boring and drone-like? No, they're exciting, passionate and very unique individuals. That's because they've consecrated themselves to the Almighty, who is the Fountain of Life (Psalm 36:9), and the life of God naturally brings to the fore all the magnificent aspects of their unique personalities. As such, people who are truly close to God aren't boring sheeple, but rather exciting *individuals* who stand out from the crowd, albeit in a godly way, not worldly. Do you think for a second that if Jesus Christ was some dull, lifeless milksop—as religion and the world depict him—he'd have turned the world upside down as he did? Would such an impotent person inspire large numbers of people to want to murder him and others to be willing to die for his cause, even up to the present day, two thousand years later?!

Unfortunately, the typical image of a Christian in the eyes of the world is either some dull, feeble "goody-goody" or a sourpuss bigot. The reason they have these images is because legalism has so thoroughly infected the Church, but nothing could be further from the truth. Anyone who simply reads the Bible without blinders on will see that both images are profoundly false.

Make no mistake, true Christianity sets free, gives life and empowers. These are the hallmarks of genuine Christianity, not being some lifeless, drone-like, powerless sheeple.

12. Legalists are Unreasonably Judgmental and Increasingly Hypocritical about It

In other words, they're hell-bent on picking out people's flaws and criticizing. They're faultfinders, pure and simple, which is a severely fleshly characteristic according to the Scriptures (Jude 1:16). Even worse, they're often guilty of the very things they criticize in others. This isn't *righteous* judging, like Paul's judgment and public rebuke of Peter's legalism in Galatians 2:11-14, but *hypocritical* judging. Notice what Jesus said about this type of judging:

> **Do not judge, or you too will be judged. [2] For in the same way you judge others, you will be judged, and with the measure you use, it will be measured to you. [3] Why do you look at the speck of sawdust in your brother's eye and pay no attention to the plank in your own eye? [4] How can you say to your brother, 'Let me take the speck out of your eye,' when all the time there is a plank in your own eye? [5] You hypocrite, first take the plank out of your own eye, and then you will see clearly to remove the speck from your brother's eye."**
>
> **Matthew 7:1-5**

As you can see, Jesus wasn't denouncing *righteous* judging, like judging a fellow believer's bad fruit and offering a corrective word, as when Paul reprimanded Peter. Jesus was condemning *hypocritical* judging, which is criticizing others for things that the criticizer himself (or herself) practices.

It goes without saying that being a grumpy faultfinder is a big red flag. Beware the Pharisee!

Along the same lines is the tendency to criticize and condemn anything that exists outside the scope of one's experience. For instance, a pastor might get on a high horse and condemn things that are actually neutral and may be used in God's service to spread the gospel, encourage believers or educate the public in general. I recently read an article in a Christian magazine by a well-known pastor who went on a tangent, condemning styles of music he obviously wasn't familiar with, like various forms of metal. What he didn't realize is that each form he mentioned has been used to share the truths of God's Word by various bands. Sure, Christ-hating groups use these styles to spread their anti-Christian garbage, but that doesn't make the style itself evil. My point is that it's wrong to make blanket-denouncements of things simply because they're beyond the scope of our experience. All forms of art, music, film and storytelling can be used by believers in the Lord's service. Making blanket vilifications of these types of things is arrogant and legalistic, although denouncing a *specific* band, film or book may sometimes be in order.

This is also true regarding judging cultures or sub-cultures that are alien to us. For example, I was reading an article by a minister whom I respect where he mentioned a run-in with a group of people he described as "hippies." We're talking long-hair, beards, tie-dyed shirts, tattoos, headbands and the like. He said they drove into town from the desert to do some shopping. That's it. They didn't do anything bad, yet he criticized them. He denounced them by appearances alone. The minister was elderly and missed the whole counterculture movement of the late 60s and early 70s. As such, people who looked like "hippies" were largely beyond the scope of his experience. He consequently made a blanket judgment of anyone who looked like a hippie, likely because they're known for drugs and casual sex. This is wrong—it's arrogant, ungodly and thoroughly legalistic! God looks at the heart of the individual regardless of appearances (1 Samuel 16:7). Anyone who wants to be godly will do the same (2 Corinthians 5:16).

Nosiness fits into this category as well. Legalists have a tendency to pry into other people's business. We see this after Jesus prophesied how Peter would eventually die over three decades later. This prompted Peter to inquire about how John would die, whereupon Jesus responded, "If I want him to remain alive until I return, **what is that to you?** You must follow me" (John 21:18-23). In other words, "Don't concern yourself with John; *your business* is to focus on what I've called YOU to do." This was a soft correction, but a correction nevertheless. Needless to say, if you sense someone is snooping into your personal business put an immediate stop to it, even if it's a pastor or pastor's wife, but please don't overreact. This will erect a protective boundary in your relationships, which is important because people who are nosey also tend to be gossips, even some pastors and their spouses. In short, if you don't want private matters spread to the community, don't give-in to inquisitive minds.

There's a freeing revelation here: Don't concern yourself with other people's business; it's not your job. If you sense something is wrong with a certain person or group, pray for them; if they ask for counsel, give it. But don't nose into other people's lives, unless a crime is being committed. And, even then, you have to use wisdom to tackle the situation effectively. How God works in other believer's lives is none of our concern. Our concern is to follow the Lord and the responsibilities thereof. Paul expressed it perfectly when he asked, "Who are you to judge someone else's servant?" (Romans 14:4). He was referring to judging other believers on disputable matters, as addressed in the last chapter. By "someone else's servant," Paul meant *God's* servant, that is, other believers.

This is a very liberating! Being a legalist is an exhausting and unhappy life—constantly nosing into other people's affairs, negatively judging them, enforcing the rules to the letter, stalking "heretics" and "heresies," keeping up appearances, putting on airs, etc. What a burden! No wonder the Pharisees were so joyless and mean. By contrast, Jesus' yoke is easy and his burden light (Matthew 11:30). We're *free* of all these legalistic encumbrances. Praise God!

13. Legalism Offers an Unbalanced View of God that Stresses Judgment and Wrath above Love and Compassion

Some Christians emphasize God's love and mercy to the point that the Almighty is reduced to a cuddly teddy bear in the sky, while others emphasize his judgment and wrath to the extent that He's some merciless ogre who can't wait to obliterate humanity. To lean toward one extreme or the other is wrong because God isn't one or the other. Notice how a *balanced* believer acknowledges BOTH sides of God:

> **Consider therefore <u>the kindness and sternness of God</u>: sternness to those who fell, but kindness to you, provided you continue in his kindness. Otherwise you will be cut off.**
> **Romans 11:22**

The LORD was able to use Paul so mightily because he was always *balanced* with what he taught and preached about God. He never swung to one loony extreme or the other. As you can see in this passage, he stressed BOTH God's kindness and sternness: sternness to those who forsook Him by walking in the flesh with no concern of repenting, and kindness toward those who respected Him and kept in repentance. Paul elsewhere stated:

> **Do not be deceived: God cannot be mocked. A man reaps what he sows. [8] The one who sows to please his sinful nature, from that nature will reap destruction; the one who sows to please the spirit, from the spirit will reap eternal life**
> **Galatians 6:7-8**

We see both God's kindness and sternness in this passage. The spiritual law of sowing & reaping is equally kind and stern: The one who sows to please the flesh will reap destruction from that nature while the one who sows to please the spirit will reap life from that nature. One will experience destruction and the other life. It's a spiritual law set in motion by God Himself and cannot be altered, unless of course the person *chooses* to switch from one to the other. In other words, if a spiritual man decides to stop sowing to please the spirit in preference to pleasing the flesh without care of repentance, he'll reap destruction; just the same, if a carnal woman chooses to stop sowing to please the flesh and starts sowing to please the spirit—that is, she repents—she'll reap life. These common-sense principles are detailed in Ezekiel 18:21-24 by YaHWeH Himself.[17]

14. Legalistic Leaders Relish Power, Praise & Prestige Rather than Humble Service

Let's look at a few passages that reveal this legalistic tendency:

> "**Everything they do is done for men to see:** **They make their phylacteries wide and the tassels on their garments long;** [6] **they love the place of honor** at the banquets **and the most important seats** in the synagogues; [7] **they love** to be greeted in the marketplaces and **to have men call them 'Rabbi.'** "
>
> **Matthew 23:5-7**

---

[17] YHWH is the Tetragrammaton *(teh-truh-GRAM-uh-tawn)*, which is the actual name of God in the Bible, typically rendered "LORD" in English versions (all capitals). From the 2nd or 3rd century BC The Name was considered too holy to speak and therefore substitute words for YHWH were used, like *Adonai (ah-doh-NAHY)* and *Elohim (eh-LOH-him)*. *Adonai* is a title of reverence for God and *Elohim* simply means "God." Since YHWH became ineffable, the actual pronunciation was lost over time, although *YAH-way* is the likely pronunciation (or *YAH-hoo-way* to devout Jews). 'Jehovah' is merely the English form of the Tetragrammaton (JHVH) with the vowels of *Adonai* inserted. Basically, when God said, "I AM WHO I AM," he was giving the translation of what Yahweh means (Exodus 3:13-14). "I AM WHO I AM" is *Ehyeh Asher Ehyeh* in Hebrew. He was saying in effect, "My name is the fact that I exist." Etymologically, 'Yahweh' is related to words that mean "to be" or "to create".

Who was Jesus talking about in this passage? Verse 1 shows that he was referring to the Pharisees and Teachers of the Law, the quintessential examples of legalism in the Bible. Notice Jesus' telltale description of these legalists in the opening verse: "Everything they do is done for men to see". This is one of the major driving forces for everything legalists do—dressing and putting on airs for appearance's sake. They want others to perceive them as godly when, in reality, they're not.

In verse 6 Jesus goes on to say that legalists love the places of honor at festivities and the most important seats at religious gatherings. When people are always gravitating toward the most honored seats at such events it's a big red flag. It reveals a carnal obsession. They covet the superior position because of arrogance. Arrogance is a superiority complex. Beware!

Verse 7 shows that legalists love to be greeted with a title, in this case "Rabbi," which means "teacher" (John 20:16). 'Rabbi' isn't used in Christendom but modern legalistic leaders obsess over numerous other titles: Pastor, Reverend, Apostle, Master Prophet, Doctor, Bishop, etc. Of course, Jesus wasn't saying there's anything wrong with legitimate church *positions* or *offices*, since the New Testament indicates some of these; he was simply sharing a telltale trait of legalists—they're *obsessed* with people referring to them with a title. Look what Jesus went on to say to his disciples:

> **"But you are not to be called 'Rabbi,' for you have only one Master and <u>you are all brothers</u>. [9] And do not call anyone on earth 'father,' for you have one Father, and he is in heaven. [10] Nor are you to be called 'teacher,' for you have one Teacher, the Christ. [11] <u>The greatest among you will be your servant</u>. [12] For whoever exalts himself will be humbled, and whoever humbles himself will be exalted."**
>
> **Matthew 23:8-12**

Jesus is contrasting the way believers should be with the way legalists are. Legalists, like the Pharisees, relish titles whereas believers shouldn't. No matter who's in the leadership position Jesus stressed that *we are all brothers* (verse 8) and that the truly great amongst us will have a servant's heart, not be on some ego-trip obsessed with a title.

Again, leadership positions in the Church are scriptural (Ephesians 4:11-13) and hard-working servant-leaders are to be respected (1 Thessalonians 5:12). The problem enters the picture when leaders insist that their positions become titles. Keep in mind that *there are no examples in the New Testament of Church leaders being addressed with titles.* None. Paul was the greatest apostle—certainly greater than anyone today—and he was simply referred to as "Paul" or "our dear brother Paul" (2 Peter 3:15). It's the same thing with Peter, Timothy, Apollos and Barnabas. This is the example set in God's Word, which is the blueprint for authentic Christianity. It's the example set by the Holy Spirit, the writer of the Word. I'm not saying you can never refer to a Church leader with a title, but rather that it's wrong for leaders to be caught up in the "title syndrome" because Jesus said this was a trait of the Pharisees and Teachers of the Law, the ultimate scriptural example of legalists.

Of course, most churches and ministries have a rule about addressing leaders with titles, written or unwritten, and so congregants pretty much have to follow suit if they want the favor of the leadership and be a functioning member. If you feel led to be a part of such a group you'll have no choice but to make a concession in this area. It's simply an eye-rolling religious rule that you'll have to abide by in order to fulfill your call within the group. But this doesn't make the practice biblical. Not all leaders within these groups are hardcore legalists, of course; most aren't. They're sincere men and women of God following in the footsteps of tradition. It's what they're familiar with, but—again—this doesn't make the practice biblical.

If you find yourself in this situation do your part to enlighten others to the scriptural truth since only the truth will set people free from false doctrine and practices, but don't harp on it to the point of being one-dimensional and annoying. Be wise, subtle and led of the Holy Spirit. Also, as you move up in the ranks, so to speak, set the example by playing down the title syndrome. For instance, if someone calls you "Pastor" respond with, "Please call me Joe or brother Joe." This speaks volumes and testifies to your security and humility.

This is fitting because those who propose to be leaders in the Church should strive for humility and a servant's mentality. Notice what Jesus said on this:

> **"You know that those who are regarded as rulers of the Gentiles <u>lord it over them</u>, and their high officials <u>exercise authority</u> over them. [43] Not so with you. Instead, whoever wants to become great among you must be your servant, [44] and whoever wants to be first must be slave of all. [45] For even the Son of Man did not come to be served, but to serve, and to give his life as a ransom for many."**
>
> **Mark 10:42-45**

Jesus wasn't at all saying that Christian leaders should be pathetic milksops or "doormats." After all, there are numerous biblical examples of Jesus being courageous, astonishing, amazing, authoritative and even frightening. If you don't think these are accurate descriptions of Jesus Christ simply read the four Gospels for verification.[18]

What Jesus was condemning in this passage was an arrogant and abusive "lord it over" spirit. This is a dictatorial air where the person in question is constantly barking orders, throwing his/her weight around and generally making those around him/her feel like inferiors. A godly woman once told me about the previous pastor of her church. She didn't badmouth him or anything, she simply pointed out that she felt intimidated when she was around him. Just the same, I was once at a church for a couple of months where I felt like a little boy every time I tried to talk to the pastor. Whether this pastor knew it or not, she was projecting a sense of inferiority on me; of course, I refused to accept it. Genuine Church leaders are not to be like this; they're called to prepare believers for works of service by **building them up**, not lording it over them, tearing them down and making them feel like insignificant worms (Ephesians 4:11-13, 2 Corinthians 10:8 & 13:10). We'll address this in more detail in **Chapter 7**.

---

[18] See, for example, Matthew 7:28-29, 14:26, Mark 1:27, 2:10-12, 4:37-41, 7:37, Luke 5:8-11, 7:14-16, 20:20-26, 20:40 and John 2:13-17.

As Jesus said in verse 44, anyone who wants to be first in the body of Christ must be willing to be "slave to all."

Needless to say, if you ever come across such a spirit of carnal authoritarianism, head for the hills. It's a trait of legalism.

15. Legalists Relish Burdening People Rather than Setting them Free

We see this trait in these two statements by Jesus:

> **"And you experts in the law, woe to you because <u>you load people down with burdens they can hardly carry</u>, and <u>you yourselves will not lift one finger to help them</u>...**
> **⁵² Woe to you experts in the law because <u>you have taken away the key to knowledge</u>. You yourselves have not entered, and <u>you have hindered those who were entering</u>."**

> **Luke 11:46,52**

As you can see in verse 46, legalists lack the capacity or desire to set people free. On the contrary, they do the very opposite—they load people down with heavy and unnecessary burdens that they're unwilling to help carry. This is what legalists do.

Verse 52 goes on to show that legalists aren't interested in giving anyone the "key of knowledge." What is the "key of knowledge"? It refers to understanding what the Law is all about—it's simply *correct* interpretation of the Scriptures. In short, it's **truth**, which is the only thing that can set people free (John 8:31-32), the primary truth being **Jesus Christ is Lord and Savior**. After all, the Messiah is the main theme of Scripture (John 1:45 & 5:39-40). And the Living Word and the written Word are both **truth** (John 14:6 & 17:17). But legalists aren't interested in giving people this key because **1.** they don't really know the LORD and **2.** they don't really want people set free. In fact, they actually *hinder* others from discovering the truth and walking in freedom. They ironically offer the precise opposite to the services they're *supposed* to offer. Is it any wonder that Christ called their converts "twice the sons of hell" as they were?

But why? Why don't legalists want people set free? Why do they actually hinder others from finding the truth? Because of pride. It makes them feel needed and superior if people are weak, dependent and needy. If people are set free they'll no longer have control over them. In fact, they're intimidated by strong individuals who are free, which is why they wanted to kill Jesus Christ (Matthew 12:13-14 & John 8:40). As a matter of fact, legalists *can't* set people free since they're not free themselves and people can only give what they've got. If they don't *have* freedom they can't *give* freedom.

You'll see this spirit seep into some churches or ministries. The pastor and staff will only go so far in helping others because they want to keep congregants weak and needy. It's an issue of pride and even job security; it's also totally absurd. It's like a guitar teacher holding back important theory and techniques because he doesn't want the student to surpass him one day and steal his thunder. Ridiculous!

The true Christian spirit, by contrast, is intent on setting people free above all else. As a minister friend told me, "My job is to become unnecessary in the life of the believer." As disciples get to know the LORD they'll naturally become stronger and freer. In time, the minister's services will no longer be needed.

We'll look at this topic further in **Chapter 6** and **7**.

16. Legalists Cease to be Learners (Disciples)

Lastly, legalists tend to cop a "know it all" spirit and cease to be learners. This is not good because the Greek word translated as 'disciple' means "learner." As such, anyone who's a disciple of Christ must also be a learner or pupil of Christ. Even those who are apostles, prophets, evangelists, pastors and teachers in the Church are *still* disciples of Christ so they must still be learners, not only learners of the living Word but also of the written Word. In other words, being a disciple of Christ – a learner of God—is a **foundational** calling that believers will *always* have, regardless of how far they go in the Lord and how great they are in the kingdom of God.

There's a saying: The more you know, the more you know you don't know. The more you acquire knowledge the more you realize the many things that you don't know and the innumerable things that remain mysterious and wondrous. This has to do with humility because it takes humility to admit you don't know something. But legalists become proud of their "great learning" and consequently become stuffy, know-it-all windbags. Even if someone comes along who shows that they know more on a particular topic or have more understanding, they won't likely admit it.

Take, for example, Jesus and the Pharisees. Jesus showed them over and over that he was more advanced than they were in knowledge, understanding and wisdom. His arguments repeatedly stunned them to silence. He performed incredible miracles again and again. Yet they were so stubborn they refused to be open to even the possibility that he was more spiritual than they were; that he was perhaps closer to God; or that he knew things they didn't. Nicodemus was the only Pharisee recorded in Scripture who was moved by Jesus' ministry and open to his instruction. He had to meet Yeshua under the cover of darkness for fear of the backlash of his fellow Pharisees (John 3:1-10). On another occasion Nicodemus openly spoke up for Jesus (John 7:45-52) and the Scriptures give evidence that he ultimately became a believer (John 19:38-42). This is great news for legalists throughout the ages—just because you're a legalist who's functioning within a highly legalistic group doesn't mean you have to stay that way!

The question needs to be asked: Why are legalists so stubborn that they can't receive from someone like Jesus or even admit that he was anointed of God? Because legalism cultivates arrogance, which is a superiority complex. It looks down on everyone else except other legalists who are higher up on the totem pole. Anyone who functions outside of their spiritual tunnel vision, like Christ did, won't be given the time of day. Why? Because they've already studied within their religious circles and think they have everything down. As far as they're concerned, they *already* know everything there is to know and you can't give something to someone who thinks they already have everything,

People like Christ are a threat to the authority and livelihood of legalists and so must be ignored, discredited or even killed. If the legalists can't kill them literally they'll cowardly kill them with words to ruin their reputations. It's what legalists do. If the Pharisees and other legalists actually dialogued with Jesus it wasn't to learn something spiritual and get closer to God, but rather to somehow trap him so they could denounce him to the people as a violator of the Law.

If you know elders or leaders in the Church who regularly speak ill of legitimate ministers who are doing wonderful things for the kingdom of God, at least as far as their assignment goes, beware! They're infected by legalism.

Legalists can get so puffed-up that they stop being learners in preference to being spurners—always quick to respond to anything outside of their legalistic prism with scorn and disdain. Paul said, "Knowledge puffs up, but love builds up. The man who thinks he knows something does not yet know as he ought to know" (1 Corinthians 8:1-2). The apostle was well-familiar with this since he used to be a Pharisee named Saul who thought he knew it all about God and Mosaic Law. He also thought Jesus Christ was a false teacher and therefore severely persecuted his followers, that is, until Christ appeared to him on the road to Damascus and humbled his arrogant behind. Saul suddenly discovered that what he believed was a lie, that his sect wasn't the one true sect and, in fact, that they were actually *enemies* of God!

Think about Paul's words in this passage and what he was saying between the lines: When we truly start knowing as we ought to know we'll become increasingly aware of our ignorance! True spiritual growth creates a spirit of humility and wonder concerning God and the many mysteries of life whereas religion creates arrogant legalists who shut themselves off to greater knowledge and the marvels of the universe. Humility maintains that childlike wonder we need in order to grow spiritually. Reflect on the passage: "God *opposes* the proud but gives his grace (favor) to the humble."

Every genuine believer is excited about the things of God when they first turn to the Lord, but this sense of awe can gradually wane as they settle down into the day-to-day activities of churchianity and everything that goes with it—the expectations, the endless rules, the grind, the constant demands on one's time, etc. Don't get me wrong here, healthy churches with godly, loving servant-leaders are always good, but experiences with believers or ministries infected by legalism will sap the life and faith right out of you, unless you're very mature and familiar with the warfare tactics detailed in **Chapter 9**.

Paul asked the Roman Christians an important question: "you, then, who teach others, do you not teach yourself?" (Romans 2:21). In other words, those who are teachers or want to become teachers must be teachable themselves. Why? Because it goes with humility. Proud people think they know it all and therefore are unteachable whereas humble people—no matter how much they know—realize they couldn't possibly know it all and, consequently, remain open to learning and, in fact, continually crave more accurate and enlightening information.

It goes without saying that we need to guard ourselves against an unteachable, know-it-all spirit as we grow in the Lord because this is a characteristic of legalists who **1.** don't really know God as they claim to, and **2.** have actually ceased from growing spiritually.

You read that right. Anyone who becomes a legalist will actually stop growing due to the infection of pride. Spiritual rigor mortis will set in. Christ said: "I tell you the truth, anyone who will not receive the kingdom of God like a little child will never enter it" and "the kingdom of God belongs to such as these [children]" (Mark 10:15 & Matthew 19:14). The Messiah wasn't encouraging childish behavior, of course, but rather childlike humility, innocence, receptivity, faith and lack of self-sufficiency in regard to God and his kingdom. This is meekness. It draws God's grace, whereas arrogance repels him.

Please be sure to maintain your child-like wonder before the LORD as you continue in the faith.

Religion Kills!

Earlier this chapter we looked at this passage:

[God] **has made us competent as ministers of a new covenant, not of the letter, but of the Spirit; for <u>the letter kills,</u> but <u>the Spirit gives life</u>.**

2 Corinthians 3:6

Paul and his team were anointed servants of the *new* covenant, not the old. The old covenant was a contract of the Law, while the new one is an agreement of the Spirit. The covenant of the Law kills because people can never fulfill the Law in their un-regenerate state. Since the disregard of divine law is the definition of sin (1 John 3:4) and the wages of sin is death, "the letter kills."

Thankfully, "the Spirit gives life." How so? Jesus plainly taught that people must be spiritually born-again to see the kingdom of God and conveyed how this is done: "Flesh gives birth to flesh, but the Spirit gives birth to spirit" (John 3:3-6). When a person accepts the gospel and turns to the Lord the Holy Spirit regenerates the human spirit so that it can connect with God and transfer eternal *life*. At this point, the believer simply needs to learn how to put off the flesh and live out of his/her spirit as led of the Holy Spirit. He/she will then be spirit-controlled rather than flesh-ruled and will consequently fulfill the righteous requirements of the Law internally. In other words, the believer lives free of outward rules and regulations because the Law is written *inside* him/her. This is how the new covenant of the Spirit gives life—life to the full.

Let's focus on the statement "the letter kills." Another way to say this is religion kills. Reflect on that. It provides a fuller meaning.

Religion kills, and in more ways than one. How so? I realize that human religion in general provides structure for people and often keeps them from lifestyles of sin, at least as far as outward appearances go, but what the individual loses is often greater than the gain. To clarify, when I say "human religion" I'm also referring to Christian religion, which is legalistic "Christianity" or counterfeit Christianity.

How exactly does religion—legalism—kill? How does it take more than it gives? By forcing people into a box of rules and regulations that never end. Many of the rules are eye-rolling and absurd, as detailed in **Chapter 2**. Legalistic systems of dos and don'ts are life-stifling and growth-stultifying. Religion *limits* people in so many ways that a book could be written on the topic. It not only kills a relationship with God, it saps joy, peace, power, creativity and adventure.

Here's one confining rule, for example: "If you're a Christian you can't perform in a pop/rock/metal band." Really? Well then explain Alice Cooper and his overtly Christian album *Brutal Planet*, amongst others, like *Dragontown*. Although Mr. Cooper confesses to being an entertainer and not a preacher, his art is able to reach people that the conventional Church wouldn't likely ever reach. Or how about the radical singer/songwriter of the infamous band W.A.S.P. who turned to the Lord in his later years and now writes Christian-themed songs, as the albums *Babylon* (2009) and *Golgotha* (2015) testify?

Here's another example: "If you're a Christian you can't be involved in comic books, particularly the more hip or edgy ones." Really? Well then explain a minister friend of mine who writes for *The Simpsons* and other comics. Besides, shouldn't we want Christians working in these environments to "salt" these works and be ambassadors of Christ?

Another one: "If you're a Christian you can't take a long break from church without being out of God's will." Really? Then explain a popular Christian writer's decision to take a year off from local church attendance to write a book he discerned God was leading him to write, which became hugely popular and launched his successful international ministry. This is akin to Jesus going out to the desert for almost six weeks to be tempted by the devil and prepare for public ministry (Matthew 4:1-2). What do you think the religionists back at the synagogue were saying about his long absence? I'm sure they gossiped about him and spoke derogatorily. They probably said things like, "And he claims to be such a devoted follower of God!" Legalists will criticize and denounce you in this manner when you are led to do something out of the ordinary. Why? Because you're breaking their legalistic rules and upsetting their religious apple cart.

These are five examples of believers who refused to allow Judeo-Christian religion to prevent them from fulfilling their God-given calls. What's your God-given assignment? Who are you called to reach? Whatever the answer, you can be sure legalists will resist you and slander you for obeying the Lord.

The religious mindset is so ridiculously confining that it restricts practically everything outside the norm of churchianity, everything that's "different." I'm not talking about morals here since immorality is always wrong, whether sexual immorality (adultery, fornication, homosexuality, incest, etc.) or otherwise.

Needless to say, be ever conscious of the tangled web of religion and refuse to allow yourself to be trapped and consumed. Religion kills!

God Wants His Church Free of Legalism!

As you can see from these last two chapters, legalism is a colossal beast. It's much more than just doing a good work to secure God's salvation or favor, which is the common definition. No, legalism is a big, ugly religious behemoth. Some find it surprising when they discover just how much the Scriptures have to say on the subject.

What can we conclude from all this material? GOD DOESN'T WANT HIS PEOPLE DEFILED BY LEGALISM. As such, it's important to be able to recognize this spiritual disease in all its various manifestations for your own spiritual health as well as the health of believers around you, including your church fellowship and especially the servant-leaders. This is why I wrote this book—to liberate believers and ministries from legalism in all its ugly forms.

Let's now move beyond general legalism and consider its four prominent "limbs," some of which we've already touched on a bit.

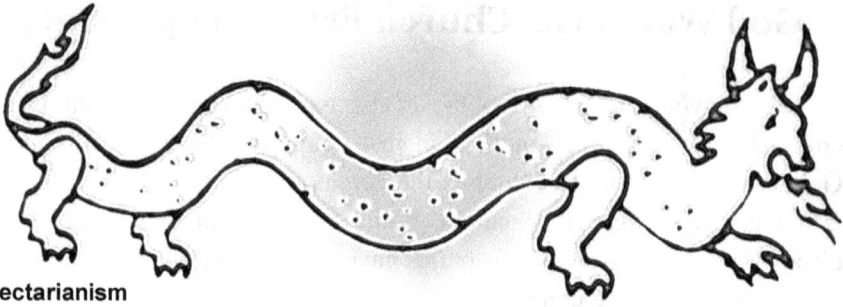

Sectarianism

Chapter 4

Limb One: Rigid SECTARIANISM

Most believers favor their church/sect. They have a history with this group and, in many cases, it's the only ministry or denomination with which they're familiar. This is understandable. *Rigid* sectarianism, on the other hand, is both unhealthy and arrogant. The more deeply believers fall into the pit of legalism the more rigid they'll be concerning their group. It's a mentality of exclusivity and superiority. Such people can become so narrowly confined and staunchly devoted to their fellowship or denomination that it smacks of cultism. They'll even preach their church or sect and its distinctive (sometimes peculiar) doctrines above the freeing power of Jesus Christ and the Word of God!

This brings to mind quasi-Christian groups, like the Jehovah's False Witnesses and Mormons, but Mainstream, Evangelical and Charismatic sects can fall prey to this same mentality. For instance, I came across a Lutheran pastor from Michigan on the internet and we corresponded for over a month. It became clear that he considered the Lutheran church to be the one true Church, pure in doctrine. All other believers were somehow misled or darkened in their understanding, if believers at all. Such idolization of one's church or sect is a form of legalism.

Jesus Condemned Sectarianism

Those who develop a spirit of rigid sectarianism increasingly view "outsiders" with an eye of suspicion. By 'outsider' I mean anyone who's not part of their church/sect or anyone who has chosen to leave. Consider this scriptural example:

> **"Master," said John, "we saw a man driving out demons in your name and we tried to stop him, <u>because he is not one of us.</u>"**
> [50] **"Do not stop him," Jesus said, "for whoever is not against you is for you."**
> **Luke 9:49-50**

As you can see, John and the other disciples were upset that someone besides them was driving out demons in Jesus' name and their knee-jerk response was to oppose him. This is the spirit of rigid sectarianism. Those who cop such an attitude view people outside their group with a suspicious, rivalrous eye. What's absurd is that this man was doing an incredibly good work—driving out demons—but it didn't matter to John and the other disciples because they were blinded by their sectarian spirit.

Christ put an immediate stop to this nonsense. His response was simple: "Do not stop him, for whoever is not against you is for you." Obviously it didn't bother the Lord that the man was operating outside their group. It didn't irk him in the least that the man didn't go to his "seminary." The man was doing a good work by faith and he was obviously on their side, so what was the problem? There wasn't one, but those infected by legalism will always create a problem where there isn't any, you can bank on it.

It should be noted that the Messiah didn't come down too hard on the disciples here. He saw that they were developing a sectarian spirit and simply nipped it in the bud. Jesus' general strategy on such occasions was to correct the negative behavior or attitude in a fairly mild manner and only take a sterner approach when the person or people failed to respond positively. This should be our approach as well.

Sectarianism is a Work of the Flesh

The reason Christ corrected them was because sectarianism is of the flesh, which is why Paul listed it as one of the works of the flesh:

> **The acts of the flesh are obvious: sexual immorality, impurity and debauchery; [20] idolatry and witchcraft; hatred, discord, jealousy, fits of rage, selfish ambition, dissensions, <u>factions</u> [21] and envy; drunkenness, orgies, and the like. I warn you, as I did before, that those who live like this will not inherit the kingdom of God.**
>
> **Galatians 5:19-21**

The word 'factions' in the Greek is *hairesis (HAH-ee-res-is)*, meaning "a religious or philosophical **sect**" and the resulting division it causes. As such, some translations render the word as "divisions," like the English Standard Version. It's a "self-chosen opinion" rooted in sectarian loyalty—i.e. one's favored sect—rather than a viewpoint rooted in the rightly-divided Word of God.

There's nothing wrong with being part of a sect, of course, as long as it's a healthy and legitimate group. In fact, to go through the foundational stage of spiritual growth it's nigh *necessary* to hook up with a specific group; and every group has its governing structure and a list of official doctrines, written or unwritten. To function in this organization believers *have* to submit to the servant-leaders thereof and assent to their major doctrines, which doesn't mean they'll agree 100% because young believers simply don't know enough to agree with absolute certainty (and by 'young' I mean young-in-the-Lord, not young-in-physical-age; someone could be 75 years-old and be young-in-the-Lord).

So there's nothing wrong with being a part of a sect in this manner. It's *sectarianism* that's of the flesh, as observed with the disciples above. Staunch sectarianism is **an arrogant and divisive attitude of superiority & condemnation toward anyone who's not part of the group in question**. This is what 'factions' refers to in the above passage.

Believers make a mistake when they join a church/camp/sect and then limit themselves to the official ministers and doctrines therein. By doing so they cut themselves off from any minister or teaching that doesn't jibe with their group. Why is it a mistake? Because it will bar them from vital biblical information that can bless them and set them free in one area or another. I could list scores of examples off the top of my head. For example, if you join a camp that supports amillennialism and strictly embrace that theology you can pretty much kiss goodbye the awesome biblical truths that reveal the nature of eternal life and everything surrounding it—literal glorified bodies, the new Jerusalem, the new Earth, the new heavens (universe), etc.[19]

When I first became a Christian I visited several local assemblies before finally settling down in a quality fellowship for a decade where I was fed the best spiritual diet you could imagine. Like most people in the beginning levels of spiritual growth (STAGE TWO[20]) I thought this church and its camp was the best on Earth and in many ways it was; it was a top-of-the-line ministry. However, I didn't make the mistake of only feeding from the teachings of this ministry/sect. At least half my spiritual diet was from my own studies in the Scriptures, which I supplemented with the teachings from quality ministers inside and outside this camp via books, tapes, radio, TV and so on.

---

[19] For insights on the nature of eternal life see the article *Eternal Life—What will it be Like?* at the FOL site, also featured in the Epilogue of *SHEOL KNOW*.

[20] For those not familiar with the Four Stages of Spiritual Growth, they are explained in the next section.

Somehow I instinctively knew that it was a mistake to limit myself to *one* general mindset in the body of Christ and I've been exponentially blessed because of it.

Sectarians would argue that doing this creates confusion in believers because they'll expose themselves to conflicting beliefs. For instance, one camp will say that Jehovah is a healing God and it's *always* His will to heal whereas another group will argue that the LORD sometimes heals, but it's not always his will and so you can never be sure. Yes, facing such contradictions can cause some immature believers to throw the baby out with the bathwater, so to speak, and use it as an excuse to backtrack to darkness (STAGE ONE). Keep in mind, however, that people like this would've likely found another excuse to revert back to STAGE ONE. Let 'em go. Christ said it's only those who "continue in his word" and don't give up who find the truth and are set free (John 8:31-32). God is a rewarder of those who diligently seek Him, not of those who throw in the towel because one ministry teaches such-and-such and another contradicts it (Hebrews 11:6).

The Four Stages of Spiritual Growth

Since the Four Stages of Spiritual Growth have come up, let me take this opportunity to briefly explain them. (Please jump to the next section if you're already familiar with them).

The apostle John referenced the Four Stages in 1 John 2:9-14, which can be summed up as follows:

1. **"In the darkness"** refers to the spiritual darkness of STAGE ONE where the unbeliever is separate from the light of God because his/her spirit is dead to their Creator.

2. **"Children"** is a reference to STAGE TWO where the individual turns from darkness (STAGE ONE) via repentance & faith and has spiritual regeneration (Acts 20:21 & Titus 3:5). This is the boot camp stage of Christian growth where the believer establishes a **foundation**. You could also call it the fundamentalist stage because it's where believers learn the fundamentals of the faith. Unfortunately, too many Christians get

stuck in this stage and never grow beyond it. They live and die in STAGE TWO as spiritual children.

3. **"Young men"** refers to the growing individualism and sense of freedom and adulthood of STAGE THREE. This is where the believer learns to think "outside the box" of his/her church & sect.

4. **"Fathers"** is a reference to the maturity and independence of STAGE FOUR wherein believers naturally propagate. This is where you *know* God in an intimate sense rather than know *about* God, which is not to say that people in this stage are perfect, of course.

While believers are in one stage they should *ideally* have a foot or finger in the next level or stage.

Here's a simple diagram of the Four Stages of human spirituality:

The arrowhead at the end of STAGE FOUR shows that spiritual maturity is an *ongoing* stage of growth as the believer knows and walks with the LORD by the Holy Spirit. Because there's no limit to knowing God there's no limit to advancing in this stage.

Since there is neither male nor female in Christ (Galatians 3:28) we can broaden John's terms for STAGE TWO, THREE and FOUR as such: children, young people and parents or, better yet, **childhood**, **youth** and **maturity**. Let's fit these into our Four Stages diagram:

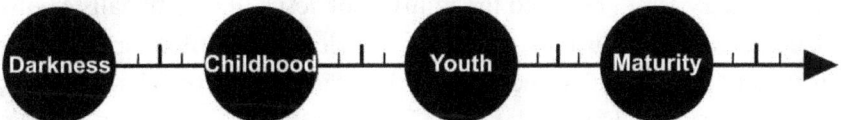

For important exposition on the Four Stages see the article *Spiritual Development—The Four Stages* at the FOL site or, better yet, pick up my book *The Four Stages of Spiritual Growth*.

Biblical Examples of Sectarianism

The aforementioned Greek word for sectarianism—*hairesis (HAH-ee-res-is)*—appears nine times in the New Testament and is used in reference to the two major **factions** of Judaism at the time of Christ, the Sadducees and Pharisees:

> **Then the high priest and all his associates, who were members of the <u>party</u> (*hairesis*) of the Sadducees, were filled with jealousy.**
>
> **Acts 5:17**

> **Then some of the believers who belonged to the <u>party</u> (*hairesis*) of the Pharisees stood up and said, "The Gentiles must be circumcised and required to keep the law of Moses."**
>
> **Acts 15:5**

The Sadducees and Pharisees were two rigid sects of Judaism, both of which Christ charged with false teaching (Matthew 16:5-12). This doesn't mean that *all* of their doctrines were false, of course, but some of them were and they were important topics. For instance, the Sadducees didn't believe in a future resurrection, angels or demons (Acts 23:8).

In John 5:39-40 Christ told the Hebrews who rejected him: "You pore over the Scriptures because you presume that by them you possess eternal life. These are the very words that testify about Me, yet you refuse to come to Me to have life" (BSB). Why did they reject the Messiah? Because of their rigid sectarianism. While the common people of 1st century Israel received the ministry of Jesus, the factionalists—the Pharisees and Sadducees—were too blinded and puffed up by their sectarian "orthodoxy" to receive and therefore considered Christ a rival; in fact, they wanted to murder him!

Interestingly, Christianity itself was referred to as a "sect" by non-Christians during the early Church. Notice what the apostle Paul said to the procurator of Judea:

"I do confess to you, however, that I worship the God of our fathers according to the Way [i.e. Christianity], **which they call a <u>sect</u>** (*hairesis*)**."**

Acts 24:14

Christianity may have been written off as just another "sect" by non-believers, but it really wasn't. It's "**the Way**" of truth (reality).

Paul Condemned Sectarianism

Like Jesus, Paul also had to correct believers who were starting to fall prey to a sectarian spirit:

My brothers, some from Chloe's household have informed me that there are quarrels among you. [12] **What I mean is this: One of you says, "I follow Paul"; another, "I follow Apollos"; another, "I follow Cephas"; still another, "I follow Christ."**
[13] **Is Christ divided? Was Paul crucified for you? Were you baptized into the name of Paul?**

1 Corinthians 1:11-13

Believers at Corinth were starting to separate and look down on other believers based on their favorite teachers. This is bullheaded sectarianism. Paul corrected the problem by asking if Christ is divided because this is what the sectarian mindset does, it *divides*. Many believers in the body of Christ today won't give heed to a word you have to say if you're not part of their sect or camp. Some will even shun you; they'll refuse to associate with you or even give you the time of day.

Paul then addressed the fact that some Corinthians insisted that they followed Paul. In other words, they were "Paulites." This didn't stroke Paul's ego, as it would many ministers today; being a spiritual man, it offended him and he rebuked it by rhetorically asking if he was crucified for anyone or if anyone was baptized into his name. No human leader should be given the accolades and loyalty that belong to the Lord, not even someone as great as the apostle Paul.

Someone might understandably ask: "What's wrong with the ones who claimed to 'follow Christ,' as shown in verse 12?" Nothing per se, as "following Christ" is the non-sectarian attitude all Christians should have, but we need to read between the lines here. The believers in Corinth who claimed to only "follow Christ" were actually saying that, since they followed Christ, they weren't going to receive from (or submit to) the other genuine ministers in their midst, whether Paul, Apollos, Peter (aka Cephas) or otherwise. This was itself a sectarian spirit, which is why Paul rebuked it.

Paul addressed this problem again a little later in his letter:

You are still worldly. For since there is jealousy and quarreling among you, are you not worldly? Are you not acting like mere men? [4] For when one says, "I follow Paul," and another, "I follow Apollos," are you not mere men?

1 Corinthians 3:3-4

Copping a rigid sectarian mentality is worldly! It provokes jealousy and strife. Those who succumb to it are not "participating in the divine nature," as all Christians are called (2 Peter 1:4); on the contrary, they're walking according to the flesh or, as Paul puts it here, behaving like "mere men." For people in the world this is understandable, but for believers who are spiritually regenerated and able to walk in the spirit with the help of the Holy Spirit it's totally unacceptable.

Sectarianism Comes to Antioch

The Bible offers an excellent example of how easy it is for sectarianism to slip into a church and infect the people; not only members of the congregation, but leaders as well:

The church at Jerusalem was established on the day of Pentecost. It was the first Christian assembly and there's evidence that it succumbed to some forms of legalism early on. Perhaps not wholly, but any amount of legalism is too much. After Stephen's martyrdom great persecution broke out against the church and the believers were scattered in every direction (Acts 7:54-8:1). Some of these Jews went to Antioch, over 300 miles north, and shared the gospel with Gentiles (non-Jews). Antioch was in the Roman province of Syria, which is now southern Turkey. The Jerusalem church decided to send a minister up there to see what was going on and chose Barnabas, likely because he was from the same general region (Tarsus). Barnabas had nothing but good things to say about the awesome move of God in Antioch and enlisted the aid of Paul in teaching the "great numbers" of believers there for a whole year. Antioch wasn't only the first non-Jewish church; it was the first one where believers were called "Christians." These facts are relayed in Acts 11:19-26.

The church in Jerusalem was basically the headquarters of Christianity and, after some time, they sent Peter up to Antioch to check on the assembly there. Why? Likely for the sake of oversight since, in a sense, the Antioch church was a satellite fellowship. Perhaps they wanted to make sure it was orthodox.[21] Keep in mind that many in Jerusalem never met Paul and were suspicious of him due to his infamous past. Another possibility is that some were jealous of the non-Jewish church's success. Regardless of the reason, Peter visited the believers in Antioch and became so involved that he stayed quite some time, evidently longer than expected.

It's at this point that "certain men came from James" to the Antioch fellowship (James was the Lord's brother, the pastor of the church at Jerusalem):

> **When Peter came to Antioch, <u>I opposed him to his face</u>, because he was clearly in the wrong. [12]Before <u>certain men came from James</u>, he used to eat with the Gentiles. But when they arrived, he began to <u>draw back and separate himself from the Gentiles because he was afraid of those who belonged to the circumcision group</u>. [13] The other Jews joined him in his <u>hypocrisy</u>, so that by their hypocrisy <u>even Barnabas was led astray.</u>   Galatians 2:11-13**

---

[21] By 'orthodox' I mean what the word literally means, "*correct* view," and not what it has been corrupted into meaning over the centuries of Church history.

There's debate as to whether these men actually came with James' blessing because the passage indicates that they were infected by legalism. What kind of legalism? The kind that insists on circumcision to be saved and refuses to eat with non-Jews in accordance with Jewish tradition. Because of this, some commentators suggest that the men lied about having the support of the Jerusalem church, but the passage doesn't state this. It literally says that they "came from James." Besides, Peter was *from* the Jerusalem church and was, in fact, the previous pastor. Surely he would know if these men were lying about coming from the very church he was a leader!

The reason some commentators suggest that this group lied about coming "from James" is because they find it hard to believe that the Jerusalem church would send a team to Antioch who were infected by legalism, but that's the insidious nature of this spiritual disease. It can infect anyone, any church, anywhere, anytime. In fact, it infected Peter in this very situation, a man who walked with the Lord for three years; a man who led the very first church on Earth; a man who wrote two books of the New Testament inspired by the Holy Spirit. If Peter can fall prey to legalism anyone can!

Peter should have known better, of course, and this is why Paul boldly corrected him in public. Years prior, God gave Peter an amazing vision to show that non-Jews were granted the message of "repentance unto life" and, therefore, Jewish believers were no longer to disassociate from Gentile believers (Acts 10:9-11:18). This is why Paul said, "There is neither Jew nor Greek, slave nor free, male nor female, for you are all one in Christ Jesus" (Galatians 3:28).

Unfortunately, Peter succumbed to fear. He was "afraid of those who belonged to the circumcision group" and therefore "separated himself" from the Gentile believers. Peter's sectarianism was so great that he stopped eating with the non-Jewish believers! How would you feel if you were one of the Gentile believers in Antioch? You'd feel like a lesser Christian than the Jewish ones; you'd feel unworthy, especially since Peter literally walked with the Lord for three years and was the former pastor of the first church on Earth! Peter had such influence that the other Jewish believers *followed his **example*** of separating from the Gentile believers, even Barnabas who was a leader at the Antioch church!

Is it any wonder that Paul couldn't keep silent, that he was so incensed he openly rebuked Peter right then and there?

Make no mistake, although there are many different "camps" of believers in the body of Christ today, there is *no place* for the rigid sectarianism with which Peter temporarily fell prey. And, please, don't think you or your church leaders are immune to this spirit of arrogance and exclusivity; if pillars like Peter and Barnabas can fall prey to it, any of us can if we're not careful. Needless to say, be on your guard and refuse to tolerate it, in yourself or others, like Paul.[22]

Rigid Sectarianism is Spiritual Immaturity

When Jesus' disciples automatically condemned someone outside their group who was simply doing a good work in Luke 9:49-50 they revealed their immaturity. They were young believers at this point (STAGE TWO) while Christ was spiritually mature (STAGE FOUR) and this is why he didn't mind one bit that this guy was driving out demons in His name. In fact, the Lord was no doubt elated that someone believed strongly enough to take the initiative and advance God's kingdom in such an authoritative manner—and the man didn't even have formal backing!

That's a great word for us today. Why do we pathetically grovel at the feet of the stuffy established religious powers seeking favor when what we really need is God's Word, God's blessing and the empowerment of the Holy Spirit to effectively advance his kingdom? Of course there's scriptural support for seeking others' favor, learning from

---

[22] It should be added that Paul had a somewhat different attitude when he was in Jerusalem at the time of Acts 21:17-26. In the center of Jewish culture Paul accommodated it. Why? Because he wanted to insure a peaceful atmosphere *in Jerusalem* since many Jewish believers were suspicious of him. This was in accordance with Paul's attitude expressed in 1 Corinthians 9:19-23 where he said, "Though I am free and belong to no man, I make myself a slave to everyone, to win as many as possible. To the Jews I became like a Jew, to win the Jews. To those under the law I became like one under the law (though I myself am not under the law), so as to win those under the law. To the weak I became weak, to win the weak. I have become all things to all men so that by all possible means I might save some. I do all this for the sake of the gospel, that I may share in its blessings."

sound mentors, and the transference of anointing via the laying on of hands, so we must be careful to *not* veer to the opposite extreme and become secluded types with a know-it-all spirit (the proverbial "lone wolf"). Yet if the powers that be are in any way arrogant, erroneous and lifeless as the Pharisees and Teachers of the Law of the 1st century it'd be better to just go out into the wilderness and get your blessing and anointing from the Almighty Himself, like Yeshua and John the Baptist did.

I see unhealthy sectarianism fairly regularly in the Church and it always repels me. Here's a good example: I worked with a guy for a number of years and, at first, he couldn't say enough praise about the church he was attending. This is good to a degree. We *should* have a positive attitude toward the fellowship God calls us to; otherwise we should go somewhere else (after all, "two visions create di-vision"). Yet this guy's attitude bordered on excessive. He kept trying to get me to come to his church for this or that function when I was perfectly happy at the fellowship I was serving. Then something went sour and he left the assembly. All his accolades suddenly vanished. Although he didn't revert to overt backbiting, he now had nothing good to say about his former church. A year or so later he found another fellowship and, once again, it was the greatest church on Earth and any person who wasn't going there was somehow a lesser Christian. He never put it this way, of course; it was just the general vibe he gave. Frankly, this is arrogance—a superiority complex—which isn't a good trait to develop because "God opposes the proud, but gives his grace (favor) to the humble" (James 4:6 & 1 Peter 5:5).

I ran into this same guy recently and happened to mention a minister who functioned outside of the normal Christian circuit. Hostility suddenly flared on his face and it was clear that he couldn't stand the man. Did this minister offend him in some personal way? Nope, never. He rejected him simply because the minister operated outside the typical church circles with which he was familiar. God forbid that the Lord would use someone outside the normal church circuit to serve people most believers would never likely reach!

Anytime you see professing Christians showing signs of staunch sectarianism like this, it signifies spiritual immaturity. It doesn't matter if they're elders, pastors, deacons, worship leaders or 80 years old. It's a one-dimensional, puerile mindset. It's spiritual tunnel vision. Yes, we all go through a period in our formative years thinking our church or camp is the best and most blessed on the planet, but then we grow up. All believers grow older, but not all believers grow up!

Sectarians argue Doctrine from a Sectarian Standpoint

You may have noticed that certain believers defend or denounce certain doctrines according to sectarian loyalties and boundaries. For instance, someone might denounce something you believe or teach because there's a group s/he objects to that also teaches it, at least in some form. Or say you teach something that doesn't gel with the religious tradition of another believer and s/he instantly writes it off as false doctrine without even studying the issue.

Let me give an example: In my book *HELL KNOW* I have a fairly long section on the Judgment Seat of Christ. A prominent international minister wrote and lambasted me for deviating from the standard position of modern American Evangelicals. As I read his email it became clear that he didn't even read the section of the book in question, at least not fully. Moreover his scriptural "evidence" was scant and he relied on quoting Evangelical slogans that aren't actually in the Bible. I replied to him the same day and explained the matter in detail. The only answer I got back was chirping crickets.

For the record, I'm an Evangelical believer, but I'm not sectarian about it, as was evidently the case with this minister who wrote me. If what Evangelicals teach is thoroughly biblical then I'll embrace it; if not, I'll reject it and expose it as unbiblical with clear scriptural support (if there wasn't strong biblical support I wouldn't reject it in the first place). The Bible teaches: "Do not go beyond what is written [in God's Word]" (1 Corinthians 4:6), not "Do not go beyond what American Evangelicals say is truth."

Here's a truth that all spiritually mature believers embrace: It doesn't matter what one group believes or another group believes on any given issue, nor does it matter what this or that pastor or minister believes; **the only thing that matters is what the truth is**. Why?

Because truth in the Greek is *alétheia (ah-LAY-thee-ah)*, which literally means "reality." In other words, 'truth' simply means the way it really is. My point is that the truth is the truth regardless of what any person or group believes. So when you're trying to discover the truth on a certain issue it's irrelevant what this or that sect believes or what this or that minister believes. All that matters is the truth and the truth is the clear revelation of the Word of God (John 17:17) as we continue in it, interpreting in context and in light of the greater context of the entire Bible (John 8:31-32). Here are the four common-sense rules of hermeneutics; that is, Bible interpretation:

1. **Context is king:** Meaning the surrounding text reveals the obvious meaning of each passage. The context also includes obvious questions like: **Who** is speaking? **Who** is being spoken to? **What** is the topic? **What** is taking place at the time? And **where**? **Whom** does it involve? And **what is their covenant** with the LORD (their agreement or contract), if indeed they even have one?

2. **Scripture interprets Scripture:** Meaning every passage must be interpreted in light of the context of the entire Bible and that the Bible itself is its best interpreter. In other words, one's interpretation of a passage must gel with what the rest of Scripture teaches on the subject, providing it's relevant; the more overt and detailed passages obviously expand our understanding of the more sketchy and ambiguous ones.

3. **Take the Bible literally unless it's clear that figurative or exaggerated language is being used:** In which case you look for the literal truth that the symbolism or hyperbole intends to convey. This rule is important because there are those who unnecessarily spiritualize God's Word based on *their* indoctrination rather than on what the Scriptures plainly teach. Without this rule people can take any passage and just spiritualize it into whatever they want it to mean based on their dubious ideology. The result is inevitably a bunch of worthless gobbledygook.

4. If the plain sense makes sense—and is in harmony with the rest of Scripture—don't look for any other sense lest you end up with nonsense: This includes the "plain sense" of the whole of Scripture on any given topic. In other words, if an individual or group comes up with an interpretation that is opposed to the plain-sense meaning that all the passages in the Bible obviously point to on that subject, then it must be rejected. This fourth rule is essentially the other three combined.

These "rules" are really just common-sense guidelines for discovering truth and being set free from religious error. By following them we allow the Scriptures to properly form our indoctrination with the clearer, more detailed and relevant passages trumping the more ambiguous, sketchy, irrelevant ones. This is common sense **exegesis** (*ek-suh-JEE-sis*)—meaning to *draw* **from** the Scriptures—as opposed to **eisegesis** (*ahy-suh-JEE-sis*)—which is *reading* **into** the Scriptures.

Although the Bible is simple enough that the simplest of persons can receive from it and be blessed, it's also deep and complex, which means that as believers grow in the Lord they naturally grow in knowledge, understanding and wisdom. As such, one believer might have a grasp on a passage or topic and another might have a fuller understanding. A good example of this can be observed in Acts 18:24-26 where Apollos, a very learned man and powerful speaker, had a limited understanding of the gospel of Jesus Christ. What he knew was good and accurate, as far as he understood it, but it wasn't a full or complete understanding. Aquila and Pricilla discerned this when they heard him speak; so they took Apollos aside, and "explained to him the way of God more adequately" (verse 26).

Staunch sectarians aren't like this, however; they argue for or against a doctrine based purely on sectarianism. If what you teach doesn't gel with their sect you're automatically wrong; if what you teach is adhered to by a group they object to, you're automatically wrong. What the Scriptures clearly and consistently teach on the topic is irrelevant to them (even though they claim otherwise). All that matters to them is strict adherence to *their* group's official doctrines. It's a spiritually immature mindset and decidedly STAGE TWO.

"You're Not One of Us"

When you get around rigid sectarians the general vibe you'll get is, *"You're* not one of us." This is precisely why the disciples tried to stop the man who was exorcizing demons in Jesus' name in Luke 9:49-50—he wasn't one of them. If you're not officially part of their group, legalists will typically perceive you as an outsider and view you with a suspicious eye. You'll even sense them looking down on you. It's arrogance.

Back in the late 80s I stopped over my boss' house for something work-related. It just so happened that his church was having a cell group meeting there. The lady who answered the door was an elder from this assembly and she gave me this overtly suspicious look, apparently because I wasn't "one of them." It was very odd. Shortly later the head elder cornered me in the kitchen and kept robotically asking with strangely dead eyes, "Why don't you come to our church sometime?" "Why don't you come to our church sometime?" I'm not making this up.

In a less extreme sense, Carol and I have experienced this "You're not one of us" mentality at a couple of churches we've visited over the years. It's a form of legalism.

Sectarians think they have a Patent on Truth

To be expected, rigid sectarians believe they have a monopoly on faith. In other words, they think *their* group is pure in doctrine and practice or, at least, vastly more accurate than other sects or ministries. For example, in 2001 Carol and I were attending a church where I taught adult Sunday school and a handful of sermons. I was considering getting credentials with this group. On one occasion the top elder and I had to travel together for over an hour by car; this gave us the opportunity to really talk. Although we were from altogether different generations and sub-cultures we were both believers and that's all that really mattered. At one point he made the statement, "Dirk, I believe *we* have the truth," referring to his denomination. You see? He was convinced that his denomination was the one true Christian sect, pure in doctrine and practice.

God bless this elderly brother. He was sincere, but sincerely wrong. Don't misunderstand me, they were a legitimate Christian denomination, but they were hardly the most accurate sect in Christendom.

I observed this same mentality in a woman I was corresponding with last year. We were discussing a theological issue. Before the discussion got going I informed her that I was open to other viewpoints but wouldn't embrace anything if it **couldn't be *clearly* proven from the Scriptures through multiple passages**. Proving something scripturally of course includes *dis*proving clear texts that counter the position.[23] She was courteous as we dialogued, but she kept insisting that her position was the right one despite clear evidence to the contrary. I cited this evidence and elaborated again and again, but it failed to persuade her. We kindly went back and forth as I gave her ample opportunity to prove her position and disprove the evidence that contradicted it, but she wasn't able to do it. The plain-as-day passages I kept citing were unable to penetrate her indoctrination. Finally, she got upset and said she wasn't going to write again. To her credit, she was willing to break away from erroneous tradition in certain areas, and I respected that, but one of the most important hermeneutical rules is "Scripture interprets Scripture" and she was unable to support her position in light of the six or so clear passages that proved it false.

During the course of our discussion I discovered, unsurprisingly, that she staunchly followed some peculiar teacher in Florida and the position she advocated was, of course, the official position of this man's small group. In fact, she often parroted his words. You see? She was believing and arguing from the basis of sectarianism and not from the basis of Scripture alone. When people are like this you can dialogue with them until you're blue in the face with as many clear Scriptures as you can muster but it's not going to change anything. Why? Because they've developed a rigid sectarian spirit and are stubbornly intent on only believing what their preferred teacher(s) or sect advocates.

The only thing you can do for rigidly sectarian believers like this is pray for them and share a scriptural truth by the Spirit now and then—

---

[23] See the article *Berean Spirit — What is it? How Do You Cultivate It?* at the FOL site for details.

if you have the opportunity. Hopefully, they'll grow up and walk free of sectarianism one day.

Rigid Sectarianism Limits
and Confines Believers

This is actually one of the worst things about sectarianism in general and especially rigid sectarianism—it can limit and confine the believer and actually prevent him/her from healthy spiritual growth. How so? Practically every church is part of a larger ministry or denomination. The pastor and associates of each assembly are generally educated and trained at the schools of these sects and understandably espouse the same doctrines and doctrinal parameters. Here's the problem: What if they're wrong in certain areas? If they're wrong that means that what they believe is false or, at best, only partially true. The problem with this, of course, is that inaccurate beliefs are false and therefore can't set the believer free since only the truth can set us free (John 8:31-32). Depending on how unbending the group is about their set of doctrines, the believers in the congregation are limited and confined by the beliefs of the group. Let me give an example.

I was communicating with a brother in the Lord from the other side of the country via email and we started to develop a good relationship over the course of a couple months. We compared insights from our studies and experiences and it was a blessing. One day he informed me that he didn't believe in the devil or evil spirits, which is nothing new since the Sadducees didn't believe in them either, as shown in the Gospels and Acts. As a non-sectarian Bible teacher, I know that no one would come to this conclusion by simply studying the Bible. In other words, I knew that this peculiar belief had to be an official doctrine of the church or sect he was hooked-up with and, sure enough, this was the case.

The fact that he didn't believe in the devil or demonic spirits didn't make him an unbeliever because it's not an essential doctrine to salvation, like the Lordship of Christ. But this belief would certainly limit his spiritual growth in some ways. For instance, it would negatively affect his understanding of spiritual warfare as well as limit his appeal in the body of Christ, confining him to his peculiar group.

Another good example would be the untold millions of believers who reject the baptism and gifts of the Holy Spirit because their church or sect is either ignorant of them or, more likely, teaches that they've been "done away with" after the 1st century. Either way, believers in these churches are restricted from these powerful truths of God's Word because of their allegiance to such groups. In other words, rigid *sectarianism* prevents them from seeing and experiencing life-changing truths.

The bottom line is this: Just because a certain pastor, church or denomination labels something a "false doctrine" doesn't necessarily mean it's really an unbiblical teaching. It may simply be a biblical teaching of which they're ignorant. If this is the case it's a truth they actually need because it would bless them.

Untold thousands of believers limit their spiritual growth because of foolish sectarianism. It's often a case of just not wanting to leave the comfort of what they know and believe. They refuse to change churches or denominations. They stay where they're comfortable while others move up the mountain of spiritual growth because they're willing to go through a little discomfort to reach new levels of glory in Christ.

Along the same lines is a group's resistance to questions by members within their group. Say a member questions some of the sect's doctrines or asks why God would do this or that and allow such and such. There's nothing wrong with this, of course, but in many sectarian groups asking questions like this would mark the individual as a doubter and that's a no-no.

Resistance to questions isn't good because it assumes that the believer has all the answers and that's just not the case. Believing in God is merely the *beginning* of the journey, not the end (Proverbs 1:7, 9:10 & Psalm 111:10). Once a person finds the LORD s/he will have more questions than ever, not the reverse. Christ said to *believers* "seek and you will find" not "if you seek answers to questions you're an evil doubter and must be excommunicated!"

Every day I have questions swirling around in my mind for which I seek answers. Questioning is good because it inspires you to find the truth and, once you discover it—even if it's in partial form—the truth will set you free (and, by "truth," I mean the way it really is).

It goes without saying, don't allow your spiritual well-being and growth to be limited or confined by the rigid sectarianism of any pastor, group, church or ministry.

We'll touch on this topic more in **Chapter 6**.

Rigid Sectarianism Needlessly Separates Believers

Another major problem with rigid sectarianism is that it unnecessarily separates Christians—genuine brothers and sisters in the Lord can't have close fellowship because of some non-essential doctrine. I see this all the time. Take, for example, a believer from an Evangelical sect who doesn't believe in faith-based healing and another from a Charismatic camp who does. The former might think the latter is loony or fanatical (even though faith and healing are huge topics of the Bible) whereas the latter might look down on the former for not adhering to what s/he considers the full gospel.

You can insert practically any non-essential doctrine into this scenario and it results in the same problem—genuine believers separated from close fellowship with other believers due to rigid sectarianism. It's both sad and unnecessary.

In the previous section I mentioned a brother who told me he didn't believe the devil was a literal spiritual being, nor did he believe in evil spirits in the commonly understood sense. Despite this, we were developing a good relationship when he just abruptly stopped communicating. I assumed it had something to do with his peculiar position. He likely investigated my teachings and saw that I overtly taught there is both a literal devil and foul spirits and he decided that it was too big of an issue to continue a relationship. Despite this difference, we were kindred spirits who could have had a rewarding friendship in the Lord. Our differences would have been addressed at some point when it came up with an open mind, an open Bible and an honest attitude. At the end of the day, people have to be free to seek things out for themselves and draw their own conclusions on their spiritual journey, but this doesn't mean the relationship has to cease if our conclusions differ. Unfortunately, it did in this case. He decided to allow our differences to put an end to our developing friendship. On the other hand, maybe he just needed some time to seek things out for himself and he'll contact me some time down the line. I hope so.

Believers cut themselves off from relationships all the time for these reasons. Take the aforementioned lady who disagreed with me on *one* very non-essential issue. When she saw that I wouldn't embrace her position because she failed to prove it, she got upset and ceased communicating.

It's for this reason that I'm extremely careful about what I reveal when meeting new believers and trying to develop relationships. I know that if I share something that they staunchly disagree with due to their spiritual upbringing—or whatever the case—our fellowship will likely end right then and there. For example, if you speak in tongues (which is synonymous with praying in the spirit[24]) be careful who you share it with and how you share it. If you come across a brother or sister who unbendingly rejects this gift they'll drop you like a hot potato.

Does the Bible teach that we should cancel relationships if we disagree on some non-essential doctrine? No. Here's what Paul taught on the matter:

> **Accept him whose faith is weak, without passing judgment on disputable matters. [2] One man's faith allows him to eat everything, but another man, whose faith is weak, eats only vegetables. [3] The man who eats everything must not look down on him who does not, and the man who does not eat everything must not condemn the man who does, for God has accepted him. [4] Who are you to judge someone else's servant? To his own master he stands or falls. And he will stand, for the Lord is able to make him stand.**

---

[24] Speaking in tongues and praying in the spirit are one-and-the-same; see 1 Corinthians 14:14-15. This is not the same as the public gift of tongues, which requires an interpreter. This will be explained in **Chapter 11**.

> **⁵ One man considers one day more sacred**
> **than another, another man considers every day alike.**
> **Each one should be fully convinced in his own mind.**
>   **Romans 14:1-5**

Paul brings up two "disputable matters" in this passage: In verse 2 he mentions the issue of eating everything or being a vegetarian; in verse 5 in mentions how some consider certain days holy—i.e. "holidays"—while others considers every day the same. The person who has the fuller knowledge and understanding on the issue is "strong" while the person with lesser revelation is "weak" (see 15:1).[25] Regardless, the one who has the fuller understanding is not to look down on the one with the lesser because it would be arrogant. Similarly, the one with the lesser revelation must not condemn the one with the fuller. You could insert any non-essential doctrine or issue into this scenario and it would apply.

Paul concluded the matter with these powerful words:

> **Accept one another, then, just as Christ**
> **accepted you, in order to bring praise to God.**
>   **Romans 15:7**

Whether someone is "strong" with fuller revelation or "weak" with lesser, we are to *accept one another **just as Christ accepted us!*** Furthermore, doing this **brings praise to God!** Do you want to bring praise to God? Then be sure to warmly accept brothers and sisters in the Lord who disagree with you on non-essential matters.

Nowhere does the Bible say we are to cancel relationships due to non-essential doctrines or issues, like the brother and sister did with me in the above examples. On the contrary, we're to *accept* one another.

---

[25] Some issues are not a matter of being "strong" or "weak" because they're issues of *preference*, like holidays. For instance, I know believers who celebrate Christmas and Easter because these days represent the birth and resurrection of Christ and I know others who refuse to celebrate them for one reason or another. It's a matter of preference or opinion, regardless of one's reasons. As Paul taught, "Each one should be fully convinced in his own mind." In cases like this it's not necessarily a matter of one being stronger and another weaker.

The only just reasons for breaking relations with other believers or so-called believers are: **1.** If the person advocates false teaching on essential matters, like the Lordship of Christ or the importance of keeping in repentance; **2.** if the individual refuses to repent of a legitimate transgression (Matthew 18:15-17); or **3.** if the person is incorrigibly contentious (Romans 16:17-18 & 2 Timothy 3:1-5). It's important to keep in mind, however, that in all these cases the offending individual should be prayed for and should receive the warm hand of fellowship if s/he makes a 180 at some point, like the fornicator who repented and was welcomed back into the Corinth church (2 Corinthians 2:6-11).

In any event, when you see brothers or sisters in the Lord who are quick to cease fellowship over non-essential issues you can be sure they're infected by rigid sectarianism. It's a form of legalism. It's sad because it needlessly separates Christians and, just as bad, limits the lives of those with lesser revelation.

What about Godly People who are Sectarian?

I said earlier that there's nothing wrong with being part of a sect, as long as it's healthy and legitimate, which means there's also nothing wrong with being a fivefold minister *within* a sect, like being a pastor. In fact, it's easier to minister and pioneer churches within an existing camp than to pioneer as a non-sectarian from scratch for obvious reasons. I knew a pastor in the mid-90s, for instance, who was pioneering a local assembly and had guaranteed financial support for five full years (!). That certainly makes it easier to start a church, to say the least.

However, the more spiritually mature a believer is the less sectarian he or she will be. Truly godly believers see the body of Christ with an increasingly universal eye rather than the limited lens of their relatively small group. You'll come across such believers and ministers in every legitimate camp. While they belong to a sect and operate within its boundaries, they're not strictly sectarian. There's nothing wrong with this and these believers are godly and mature, i.e. STAGE FOUR.

Unfortunately, there are some believers in ministry who are staunchly sectarian and they're definitely not STAGE FOUR. They're not even STAGE THREE. How do I know? Because to be STAGE THREE you have to be able to think and function independently of your sect/church and these people are unable to do this, which is why they're so staunch about their sect. Even if someone who's rigidly sectarian shows signs of genuine godliness—i.e. spiritual maturity—they're still manacled to STAGE TWO. It may be high level STAGE TWO, but it's STAGE TWO nevertheless. Such believers clearly have a hand or finger in the next two stages, but because of their blatant faction-ism they're decidedly STAGE TWO and therefore still spiritually immature to some degree. Here's how such a person would appear on the Four Stages diagram:

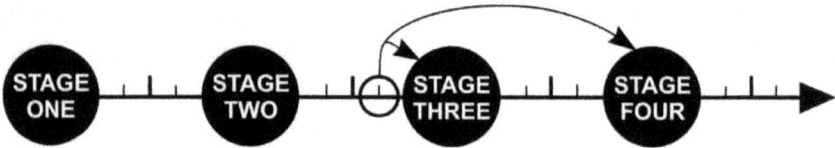

Rigid Sectarianism is a Red Flag

This particular limb of legalism can easily be observed in pseudo-Christian sects and cults, like the aforementioned Jehovah's Witnesses and Mormons. But—again—Mainstream, Evangelical and Pentecostal groups can just as easily cop the same attitude. The church that had the cell group at my boss' house was of the Evangelical-Charismatic persuasion. As emphasized before, legalism is no respecter of persons or church/denominational boundaries; it can infiltrate any individual, any assembly, any denomination.

Needless to say, if you are part of a group or trying to be a part of a group that shows signs of rigid sectarianism, it's a big red flag. Pray about it and confront it wisely. If you ultimately see no positive change I'd seriously consider heading for more spiritually healthy pastures.

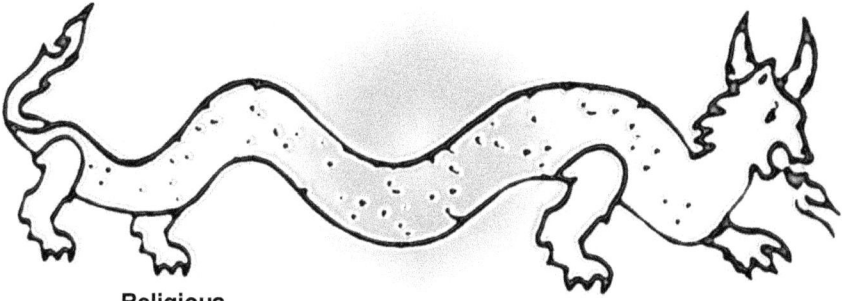

Religious
Formal
Death

Chapter 5

Limb Two:
Religious Formal
DEATH

Since legalism is a dead religious spirit that focuses on rules above relationship with God it naturally saps life, freedom, joy and spontaneity. God is the Fountain of Life from which all life flows, whether physical or spiritual, and Jesus is "the life" who came to give us "life to the full" (John 14:6 &10:10). As such, those who move away from The Life to focus on rules and ritual will move further and further away from the abundant life the Messiah came to give. If we are "made alive *with* Christ" then those who move away from him move toward death. They'll develop a sterile spirit as spiritual rigor mortis sets in. Unsurprisingly, religious gatherings of such people will have a very formal, lifeless air. Those performing the various aspects of the services—whether pastors, teachers, worship leaders, elders or deacons—will seem to be just "going through the motions." They'll function like religious zombies. It goes without saying that attending these services will be dreadfully boring. Why? There's *no life* there.

Two Biblical Examples

We see evidence of this sterile spirit in a few of the churches that Christ addressed in Revelation 2-3. The Lord gave each of these seven assemblies a report card. Why did he pick these specific fellowships? Because they characterize the seven basic types of churches that would exist throughout the Church Age. What Jesus said to these assemblies is therefore relevant in any time period.

He had nothing good to say about two of the churches, one being the church of Laodicea. Notice what Jesus said to this group of believers:

> **"I know your deeds, that <u>you are neither cold nor hot</u>. I wish you were either one or the other!** [16] **So because <u>you are lukewarm—neither hot nor cold—I am about to spit you out of my mouth</u>.** [17] **You say, 'I am rich; I have acquired wealth and do not need a thing.' But you do not realize that you are wretched, pitiful, poor, blind and naked."**
>
> **Revelation 3:15-17**

Christ rebuked these believers for being "lukewarm" and threatened to spit the whole fellowship out of his mouth if they didn't repent, meaning he would "pull the plug" on them and they'd be a church in name only.

The Lord wished that they were cold or hot rather than lukewarm. This was an allusion to nearby cold and hot springs. The cold springs were useful for refreshing and the hot springs for bathing, but lukewarm water was useless.

Notice what Jesus goes on to say:

"Those whom I love I rebuke and discipline. So be earnest, and repent. [20] Here I am! I stand at the door and knock. If anyone hears my voice and opens the door I will come in and eat with him, and he with me."

Revelation 3:19-20

Verse 20 has traditionally been used by evangelicals to witness to the lost, which would suggest that Christ was addressing unbelievers, but this wasn't the case. *Jesus was talking to believers who had pushed him out of their fellowship.* They forsook relationship with the Lord for religion and consequently became lukewarm—sterile, lifeless, useless. They were just "playing church," just going through the motions. There are assemblies like this in practically every community today, all over the world. Jesus is knocking on their doors wanting in, but they're convinced everything's fine because they have money, a nice facility, regular congregants, etc. But the Lord is ready to pull the plug on them altogether if they don't repent. Some of them he already has, like the Episcopal Church (which is *not* to say that there aren't any genuine believers still in the Episcopal Church; there's usually a "remnant" faithful).

The church in Ephesus wasn't as bad as the one in Laodicea. Jesus commended them for several things—their good deeds, their hard work, their perseverance and their refusal to tolerate false teachers. These are all good, but notice where they missed it:

Yet I hold this against you: <u>You have forsaken your first love</u>. [5] Remember <u>the height from which you have fallen</u>! Repent, and do the things you did at first. If you do not repent, I will come to you and remove your lampstand from its place.

Revelation 2:4-5

The Ephesians forsook their "first love." They steadily moved away from *relationship* with the Lord toward cold, mechanical *religion*. They maintained orthodoxy and performed good works, which is good, but they lost intimacy with God. They were just going through the motions. They had the outward veneer of Christianity but lacked its heart. Since Christianity at its core is a relationship with God and the first and greatest command is to love the Lord with all our heart, soul, mind and strength (Mark 12:29-30), this was a grievous offense, which is why Christ said they had fallen from a great height. Reflect on that: As far as Jesus was concerned they had fallen from a great height! In other words, it was no little transgression. They stumbled into the trap of legalism and the Lord's message was a stern warning to repent. If they didn't, he threatened to remove their "lampstand from its place." The "lampstand" represented the Ephesian church itself (Revelation 1:20) and therefore its removal meant that they would no longer be Christ's church. In short, the Lord was prepared to "pull the plug" on them if they refused to repent; in which case they'd be a church in name only.

Both the Laodicean and Ephesian churches made the mistake of substituting sterile religiosity for personal relationship and it resulted in a lifeless, go-through-the-motions spirit. The Laodiceans were further along on this dark road, which can be observed in their arrogant attitude and the fact that the Lord had *nothing* good to say about them, but the Ephesians were heading in this same direction.

A Church with a Sterile Spirit

Years ago I went to an assembly for nine months to fulfill my formal schooling in an internship program. The first thing I detected on my initial visit was a very sterile spirit. Everything was done in such a formal, ritualistic manner and the congregants participated in drone-like fashion. I'm not saying this to be mean or to suggest that I was looking down on these dear brothers and sisters in the Lord; I'm just giving my honest appraisal of the experience.

Needless to say, I did everything in my power to give this fellowship a spark of life while I was there. After nine months with no appreciable change—not to mention enduring some gnashing of the teeth by some of the congregants—Carol and I decided to leave. I couldn't stomach that lifeless spirit for one more service.

It dawned on me later that this sterile go-through-the-motions mindset was a form of legalism.

The pastor was a gentle soul, and—I believe—a sincere Christian man. Yet the whole time I was involved with his fellowship I saw him in the grip of some kind of quiet torture. This is the same person noted in **Chapter 2** who was, in essence, just putting on a show by functioning as a pastor. It was as if he was just playing the role of a pastor, just going through the motions, and his sermons and ministry reflected this. The entire time I was there I didn't hear a single moving, stimulating or life-changing teaching. It wasn't in him. Somewhere along the line in his decades of service he was infected by legalism in the form of religious formal death. It's a spirit of sterility.

I say this with sadness, not joy. I had zero hostility toward the pastor or any of his congregants; I just felt sad for them. They were in a rut and couldn't get out. The only way out was to break free of their "go through the motions" spirit. Unfortunately, they probably weren't even aware of the problem. Although they were obviously concerned that their church wasn't growing, I doubt they were aware of how utterly dead their gatherings had become. My wife and I could see it only because we were outsiders.

How did the pastor develop a "go through the motions" manner? I'm sure it was something that slowly developed over the years as he moved away from *relationship* with God to *working* for God. A spirit of familiarity settled in concerning the Almighty, the church, God's Word, pastoring, and the things of God in general.

A Spirit of Familiarity

We see this "spirit of familiarity" with Uzziah in the Old Testament. Uzziah was involved in moving the Ark of the Covenant to a different location, along with many others. If you're familiar with the Ark you know that it was a sacred chest filled with holy articles and that God's very presence dwelled on its lid—the Mercy Seat—between two gold-sculptured angels.[26] The oxen stumbled whereupon Uzziah reached

---

[26] The last time the Ark is mentioned in the Bible is during the righteous reforms of King Josiah (2 Chronicles 35:3). Within 22 years after Josiah's death Judah fell to the Babylonians due to their rebellion and the Ark has been lost ever since. The good news is that we don't need the [continued on next page]

out to grab the Ark and the LORD struck him down in righteous anger (2 Samuel 6:6-7). Why was God mad and why did he take Uzziah's life when he was only trying to help? Because only the Kohathites, a clan of the Levites, were permitted to carry the Ark and even they weren't allowed to touch it at the penalty of death (Numbers 4:15). There were some 30,000 men involved with moving the Ark on this occasion and they were all ripe for judgment because they were moving the sacred chest in a manner contrary to God's instructions. We see the LORD's great mercy in that he only struck down *one* individual in this fiasco, the person who came closest to disrespecting his holiness, Uzziah.

We know Uzziah grew up in the house where the Ark was stored for many years. It's conceivable that he became so *familiar* with the holy object that he no longer had a healthy reverence for it. This was a mistake that cost him his life.

Just the same, it's possible for believers in the New Testament era who grew up in church or have pastored for many years to become so familiar with the things of God that they take them for granted. It's easy for such people to cop a "go through the motions" attitude, especially if they've moved away from relationship with God to focus on performing tasks for him. God may not kill them, as he did Uzziah, but they'll experience death nevertheless in the form of this strain of legalism.

A Spirit of Stupor

I gave a total of four sermons while attending the aforementioned sterile assembly. The first sermon was on Sunday morning and it was one of the worst experiences of my life, as far as Christian service goes. I was very prepared for the teaching and gave it with vigor, but it was as if there was some unseen presence hindering the ministry of the Word that morning. The second sermon was at a Sunday night service and it actually went pretty well, but there weren't many

---

Ark in the New Testament era because Jesus Christ is the believer's Mercy Seat. John 20:12 is an amazing passage that shows Mary Magdalene looking into Christ's empty tomb after his resurrection whereupon she "saw two angels in white, seated where Jesus' body had been, one at the head and the other at the foot." (!!)

people there. The third one was on Sunday morning again and the Word just wasn't getting across to the people, except a few. They just sat there with blank faces in some sort of religious trance. I previously taught the same teaching at a couple of other churches and it was received well, so I know the problem wasn't the topic or my delivery. So what was the problem? This passage might shed some light on the matter:

> **As it is written: "God gave them a <u>spirit of stupor</u>, eyes so that they could not see and ears so that they could not hear, to this very day."**
>
> **Romans 11:8**

Paul was referring to the Israelites who hardened themselves to the truths of the Messiah's message. Since they rejected God's grace in Christ he gave them over to a state of stupor so that they couldn't see or hear spiritual truths. In other words, God *allowed* them to reap the harvest of their own bad choices. Don't misinterpret this, God will show his ways to *anyone* who humbly turns to him. As James put it: "Come near to God and he will come near to you" (James 4:8). But he will give a spirit of stupor to those who continually harden their hearts to his ways. Why would he do this? Simple: "God resists the proud, but gives his grace to the humble" (James 4:6). God actively *resists* or *opposes* the stubborn and arrogant, but gives his favor to the humble.

What is a spirit of stupor? It's a dazed condition of inertia and lethargy wherein the simplest of spiritual truths are unable to arouse, change or motivate. This is what I saw in that congregation; not all of them, but most of them. I could preach the most magnificent truths of God's Word until I was blue in the face and it would've had little or no effect on the bulk of them due to their foggy religious stupor.

This appears to have been the problem with the Sardis church in the late 1st century. Notice what Jesus said to these believers:

> **"I know your deeds; you have a reputation of being alive, but <u>you are dead</u>. ² <u>Wake up</u>! Strengthen what remains and is about to die, for I have not found your deeds complete in the sight of my God. ³Remember, therefore, what you have received and**

heard; obey it, and repent. But <u>if you do not wake up</u>, I will come like a thief, and you will not know at what time I will come to you."

Revelation 3:1-3

The church in Sardis was *dead*. They had a reputation for being alive only because of their legalistic airs, which undiscerning people confused as genuine Christianity. The Lord urged them to "Wake up!" Why? They had fallen into a religious stupor.

I experienced a similar condition in an old friend I saw this past week. I desperately wanted to minister to him the life-changing power of the LORD and his Word, but he kept chain-smoking and drinking beer after beer while blasting secular music. As a confessing Christian, these were things he should have dealt with over 25 years earlier, but here he was still in bondage, still in the baby-stage. I'm not saying this with arrogance, but with honesty and compassion—I truly *wanted* to help him. Unfortunately, although he admitted to being an alcoholic and that God was the ultimate answer to life's problems, he talked as if everyone else was to blame for the pit he was in and nothing I said could penetrate his dazed mindset. It's a spirit of stupor, although in this case it was a lawless stupor and not a religious one.

I haven't given up on him. I'm still praying for him and trying to reach him. He admitted to feeling "lost" recently and has expressed a desire to change. This is the most important thing because there's no hope of change without the *realization* of the need to change and, of course, the *desire* to change.

Needless to say, be careful of succumbing to a spirit of stupor, whether a religious stupor or a lawless stupor.

My First Experiences with this Lifeless Spirit

The first time I experienced this form of legalism was when I became a Christian in 1984. During my teens I lived the "party" lifestyle but was secretly dissatisfied with it. I collected quite a few Christian tracts during these years and was very interested in hearing the gospel on the rare occasion that a fellow student would bring it up. The Bible declares that the seed of God's Word will not return to him empty and so it was with me (Isaiah 55:10-11). I turned to the Lord less than two years after high school, but I didn't get saved in a church facility. The words sown in my heart through those tracts and the few witnesses at school did their work. The Holy Spirit enlightened me late one night while cleaning a woman's shower room at a fitness center. I *believed* and experienced this profound sense of peace and joy. It was like a huge weight was taken off my shoulders. The next morning I confessed my salvation to my mother and sister.

Of course, I needed a local church to hook up with so I decided to try my mother's traditional church, the Episcopal Church, which she seldom went to because it was so far away and she didn't drive (so she regularly attended a local Missionary Alliance church). My grandfather, who died long before I was born, was a minister in the Episcopal denomination and I naturally thought it would be proper to follow in his footsteps. I had experienced Episcopalian services a few times with my mother as a child or teen in two different states, but this would be the first time I experienced it with new spiritual eyes.

I went three times—once by myself, once with my mother, and once with a friend—and I was severely let down each time. Everything about the services was deadly dull—the worship, the sermons, the "fellowship." The latter was practically non-existent, except for shaking the minister's hand while leaving. When I went by myself I longed to connect with people after the service to share my incredible spiritual rebirth, but everyone quickly left or they were preoccupied with the Sunday affairs of the church. I consequently left without experiencing a real connection with *anyone*. When I visited the assembly with a friend it was just as sterile and forgettable, except I distinctly remember this good-looking blonde across the aisle who kept ogling me. Although it's always nice to be noticed, I wasn't there to pick up a hot date; I was there to experience God. Unfortunately, I didn't see him!

Roughly fifteen years later the Lord led my wife and me to a certain fellowship for a couple of years. This particular church's denomination started in the mid-1800s and my first impression was that it was very old-fashioned compared to the services we were used to attending. This assembly wasn't as bad as the Episcopal one in this regard but it definitely had a sterile vibe. On the positive side, the fellowship was good and we developed a few relationships that continued even after our departure a couple of years later. Regardless, the services were painfully dull. We never felt like we encountered God during the song service and were never inspired by any of the sermons or Sunday school teachings, although—of course—there was an occasional insightful moment now and then. Nevertheless, the fellowship was good. The people were very loving and hospitable. Obviously they weren't as infected by this form of legalism as the Episcopalian church, but they were still noticeably infected. The church building was always so quiet, empty and lifeless. There were very few visitors and I didn't see a single convert in the two years we were there. It had a sterile spirit, pure and simple.

Age is Conducive to the Sterile Spirit

Newer ministries are almost always livelier than older ones. Take that Episcopalian church as an example. The Episcopal denomination has historical ties to the Dark Age Roman Church. It's been around for centuries and this is obvious if you attend their services. The other assembly was part of a denomination that had been around since the mid-1800s. Both churches were infected by the lifeless go-through-the-motions spirit, but the Episcopalian church was definitely worse. At the other assembly we at least experienced God through the fellowship of the saints, but I didn't experience him at all in the Episcopal church.

Less than fifteen years after my final visit to that Episcopalian assembly the denomination decided to allow unrepentant homosexuals to be ordained as ministers. Please notice I said "unrepentant," which means there's absolutely nothing wrong with allowing *former* homosexuals to serve in ministry positions. When writing to the Corinthian church Paul listed numerous sins, including homosexuality, and then added "And that is what some of you *were*. But you were washed, you were sanctified, you were justified in the name of the Lord Jesus Christ and by the Spirit of our God" (1 Corinthians 6:9-11). There were many believers in the Corinth church who were once thieves, adulterers, drunkards, slanderers and homosexuals, but they had repented and been cleansed of all unrighteousness (1 John 1:8-9). Those who proved themselves mature enough were involved in important ministry positions. The point is that they *used* to walk in these sins in their former lives, but they didn't any longer. They had repented. They were washed and freed. Not so with the Episcopal Church in 1996. They decided to allow *practicing* homosexuals to serve in leadership positions. That would be no different than allowing unrepentant thieves, drunkards or adulterers to serve in ministry. It's absurd and goes completely against the teaching of Scripture. As always, there was a faithful remnant who rejected this corruption and broke off or, in some cases, stayed. Regardless, God figuratively "pulled the plug" on the Episcopal Church when they made this rebellious decision in 1996. If someone finds that judgmental and politically incorrect, that's too bad; it's the sad, awful truth.

The point is that there's definitely a correlation between a church or denomination's age and their vulnerability to this sterile limb of legalism. The individual believer's age can be a factor as well. This is only natural since, as years or generations pass, there's a tendency to accumulate experiences, traditions and rituals to the point where it becomes meaningless to the current generation, but the people continue to observe them and go through the motions because it's "the way it's always been done."

This doesn't mean, of course, that just because a church or denomination is old that it definitely has this sterile spirit; just that it's more susceptible to it.

Needless to say, if you belong to an aging ministry or sect, be on guard that it doesn't become infected by this religious spirit and rob you and your spiritual family.

Why "Religious Formal Death"?

Why do I describe this sterile spirit as "religious formal death"? I refer to it as "death" because that's what sterile means—absence of life, lacking inspiration or vitality.

I call it "religious" because ministries and people that are infected by this strain of legalism are religious, not spiritual. If they were spiritual they'd naturally produce fruit of the Spirit, like joy and power.

Galatians 5:22-23 lists nine fruits of the spirit—love, joy, peace, patience, kindness, goodness, faith, humility and self-control. This list is awesome and it gives a well-rounded sampling, but the fruits of the spirit are no more limited to these nine than the works of the flesh are limited to the fifteen cited in the previous three verses. Righteousness and truth are also fruits of the spirit, as shown in Ephesians 5:9 and Philippians 1:11. So is power. Jesus told his disciples that they'd receive power from on high when the Holy Spirit came upon them (Luke 24:49 & Acts 1:8). If they were to receive power when the Spirit came upon them it's obviously because power is a trait of the Spirit, a fruit of God's character. Power is also a fruit of the born-again spirit:

> **For God did not give us a spirit of timidity, <u>but a spirit of power</u>, love and self-discipline.**
> **2 Timothy 1:7**

The word 'power' comes from the Greek *dunamis (DOO-nah-miss)*, which is where we get the English dynamite. Does "dynamite power" sound dull and lifeless? How about joy? Peter described this spiritual fruit as "inexpressible and glorious joy" (1 Peter 1:8). Does that sound boring and deathly? No, it sounds full of life and vibrancy! Those who are spiritual naturally produce the fruit of the spirit, while those who aren't spiritual, don't. Obviously the more fruit a person produces the more spiritual he or she is. This is why Jesus said we can recognize those who speak falsely for God "by their fruit" (Matthew 7:15-23). If someone who ministers the Word doesn't show consistent evidence of the fruit of the spirit it's a big red flag. If they have an arrogant, abusive spirit and are unrepentant when they miss it, this tells you everything you need to know. They're false. Leave them!

Being deathly dull is a red flag as well. While dull, lifeless spiritual leaders are not abusive in an aggressive sense, they're certainly abusive in a passive sense. How so? An uninspiring minister who puts people to sleep is a living oxymoron since the very purpose of fivefold ministers is to build up, inspire and set a godly (*"like*-God") example, not bore to tears![27]

Keep in mind that 'religion' literally means "to bind back" and refers to the human attempt to bind back to God, that is, reconnect with him. Christianity, by contrast, is God connecting with humanity through the gospel of Christ and spiritual regeneration by the Holy Spirit. Putting it another way, religion is what people try to do for God in their own strength while Christianity is what God does for us through Christ. Religion is what people do for God in the flesh while Christianity is what God does for us in the spirit. Legalists are focused on their *own* attempts to connect with God when they should be focused on God's superior method of connecting with us. Man's way is of the flesh, God's way is of the spirit. As such, religionists lack the life, power and joy that only the Fountain of Life can give.

Jesus plainly pointed out the failure of religion when his disciples asked him who could be saved:

> **Jesus looked at them and said, "With man this is impossible, but not with God; all things are possible with God."**
>
> **Mark 10:27**

Salvation through the flesh—through religion—is impossible. But with God it's not only possible, it's available to all. That's Christianity—*real* Christianity, not the counterfeit legalism.

At the beginning of this book I shared an excellent saying that distinguishes religion from Christianity:

> **Religion says "do" while Jesus says "done"; religion says "slave" while Christianity says "son" (or daughter).**

Concerning the first part, religion stresses rules: "Do this" or "Don't do that," whereas Christianity stresses that the Law has been completed through Jesus Christ. As Romans 10:4 points out: "Christ is the end of the law so that there may be righteousness for everyone who

---

[27] See Ephesians 4:11-13 and 1 Peter 5:1-4.

believes." Before Jesus breathed his last on the cross he said, "It is finished," which literally means "Paid in full."

Regarding the second part, religion is all about making people slaves to the religious system, whereas Christianity is about making people a part of God's family through spiritual rebirth. The difference between the two is like night and day.

Why "Formal"?

I refer to this sterile spirit as "formal" because people infected by this strain of legalism are attached to the outward forms of religion rather than its core, namely YaHWeH.[28] As such, they get discombobulated when someone questions or disturbs these embedded forms.

'Formal' literally means "being in accordance with the typical requirements and marked by form or ceremony." While there are some formal activities in Christianity—like the Lord's Supper—and God should definitely be revered, this doesn't mean we have to be bogged down by a somber spirit of staunch formality in everything we do, whether gathering together, fellowshipping, praise & worship, teaching or feeding from God's Word.

Unfortunately, some Christians and churches are so encumbered by formality it's reflected in practically everything they do, at least everything they do that's church-related. In some assemblies the air is so thick with formality it's actually oppressive. For those sensitive to the things of the spirit, it's spiritually nauseating and prompts a compulsion to run away screaming, sometimes literally.

Let me share an example of this life-stifling formality. Years ago I was in the lobby of a church facility where I utilized a blow-up spear to "attack" a 12 year-old girl. This occurred well after the service. The girl fought back as best she could and we had a fun time without getting out of hand. Carol later informed me that she happened to see the pastor eying us with a scowl of disapproval. I met him later that week and decided to bring up the incident (without telling him what Carol said, of course). I did this because I wanted to explain my actions. Why did I have a balloon-sword "fight" with a girl in the lobby of the church?

---

[28] See the footnote on page 76 for an explanation of the divine Name.

Although I didn't word it like this to the pastor—and wisely so—I was trying to instill a sense of energy and levity into a dreadfully boring atmosphere. Think about it: What was this girl going to remember in years to come about her time at this church—the sleep-inducing services or the fun time she had with Dirk and his blow-up spear? Keep in mind that the service was over and most of the people had already left, not to mention we were in the lobby area and not the sanctuary.

How could this possibly upset the pastor? The answer is obvious: He was attached to the forms of religiosity and my actions were upsetting these forms. He and his ministry were so encumbered by a rigid spirit of formality that he couldn't bear to watch anything upset it. Yet it was something like this that his church needed to break out of its rut of religious formality. It was a **pattern interruption**.

Before you object, Jesus implemented "pattern interruptions" quite often. What do you think his radical cleansing of the temple was all about? What about when he called Peter "Satan"? How about when he performed a miraculous healing on the Sabbath even though the religious leaders objected? What about when Christ was invited to dine at a Pharisee's house and he deliberately didn't follow their customary rules of washing before the meal? He then proceeded to tell the Pharisees how foolish they were and that they were full of greed and wickedness! [29] What I did with the blow-up spear was tame by comparison.

"Having a Form of Godliness but Denying its Power"

A passage we touched on in **Chapter 2** ties into what we're talking about here:

> **having a form of godliness <u>but denying its power</u>.**
> **Have nothing to do with them.**
>
> > **2 Timothy 3:5**

---

[29] You can read these accounts in the Gospels as follows: Christ cleanses the Temple: John 2:13-17; Jesus refers to Peter as "Satan": Matthew 16:23; the Messiah performs a healing on the Sabbath: Mark 3:1-6; and Christ dines with the Pharisees, breaks their rule, and rebukes them: Luke 11:37-40.

This is a description of legalists who are only concerned with putting on the *appearances* of godliness, not true godliness.

Since 'godliness' means "to be like God" it's one-and-the-same as producing the fruit of the Spirit because these fruits are the fruits of God's character. Those who are truly godly are godly *because* they're living out of their spirits and therefore produce fruit of the spirit.[30] It's simple. As noted above, one of these fruits is *power*—**dynamite** power.

Now notice what the passage says about legalists: They only have a *form* of godliness, but deny its power. How so? Because their godliness is mere outward adornment; it has no depth. It's outward structure without inward substance. In other words, it's not real!

I've heard some teach on this passage and they wrongly interpreted it to mean that legalists deny the miraculous power of the Holy Spirit and charismatic gifts. But this is not what the text says. Read the passage closely. It says that legalists deny the power of *godliness*. The only godliness they have is superficial appearances because they deny godliness' power. What is the power of godliness that they deny? It's the power of spiritual regeneration and living out of one's "new self" rather than out of the "old self," which means being spirit-controlled rather than flesh-ruled:

> **You were taught, with regard to your former way of life, to <u>put off your old self</u>, which is being corrupted by its deceitful desires; [23] to be made new in the attitude of your minds; [24] and to <u>put on the new self</u>, created to be <u>like God</u> in <u>true righteousness and holiness</u>.**
>
> **Ephesians 4:22-24**

---

[30] Since there is no capitalization in the original Greek, translators have to discern whether "spirit" should be capitalized in reference to the Holy Spirit or not capitalized in reference to the human spirit (e.g. Matthew 26:41). I maintain that whenever a text contrasts flesh and spirit, like Matthew 26:41 or Mark 14:38, "spirit" obviously refers to the human spirit. It makes little difference, however, in light of the fact that the believer's human spirit is indwelt and guided by the Holy Spirit; hence, if we're living out of our human spirit (un-capitalized), we're automatically following the Holy Spirit and therefore living by the Spirit (capitalized).

Those who live by their born-again spirit and not the flesh will naturally produce the fruits of God's character, meaning they'll be "like God in true righteousness and holiness." This doesn't mean they'll be perfect, of course, because they still have a body of flesh as long as they're in this world, which is where 1 John 1:8-9 comes into play. Yet those who mature spiritually will become more and more freed-up from the flesh and be "like God," that is, godly. This is the awesome *power* of Christianity.

Paul spoke of this power when he noted the *treasure* we have in our earthen vessels:

> **For God who said, "Let light shine out of darkness," made his light shine <u>in our hearts</u> to give us the light of the knowledge of the glory of God in the face of Christis.**
> **⁷ But we have this <u>treasure in jars of clay</u> to know that this all-surpassing power is from God and not from us.**
>
> **2 Corinthians 4:6-7**

The "jar of clay" refers to your body. The "treasure" in your body is your reborn spirit, created to be like God in true righteousness and holiness. It's the "new creation":

> **Therefore, if anyone is in Christ, he is <u>a new creation</u>; the old has gone, the new has come!**
>
> **2 Corinthians 5:17**

Obviously your body isn't a new creation. Did your body change when you turned to the Lord in repentance and faith? No, this "new creation" refers to your re-born spirit. It's "Christ in you, the hope of glory":

> **God has chosen to make known among the Gentiles <u>the glorious riches of this mystery</u>, which is <u>Christ in you, the hope of glory</u>.**
>
> **Colossians 1:27**

How can your spirit possibly be "Christ in you, the hope of glory"? Through spiritual rebirth. Notice how Peter described it:

For <u>you have been born-again</u>, not of perishable seed, but <u>of imperishable, through</u> the living and enduring Word of God.

1 Peter 1:23

You've been born-again of the imperishable seed of the living, enduring Word of God, meaning Jesus Christ. 'Seed' in the Greek literally means "sperm," as a comparison to 1 John 3:9 attests. You've been regenerated through the imperishable sperm of Christ. As it is written, "Flesh gives birth to flesh, but Spirit gives birth to spirit" (John 3:6).

Why is all this important? I'm simply pointing out the *incredible power* that is within every believer, a *treasure* that is full of "glorious riches". All you have to do is learn to recognize the flesh and not feed it, put it off, which includes keeping your spiritual arteries clear of the build-up of unconfessed sin. Be transformed in your mind, in your thinking, through these Scriptures and many more (Romans 12:1-2). And simply learn how to put on the new man and be spirit-controlled as led of the Holy Spirit. If you do this, you'll experience the dynamite power and full-life Jesus promised in John 10:10. You'll be "like God in true righteousness and holiness." You'll be *godly*, Hallelujah!

Are you excited? Are you feeling encouraged and built-up within? Is there a *fire* of motivation burning within you? I hope so. Even mellow types should be feeling a blip of inspiration!

This is the *dynamite power* that's available to every believer; all you have to do is learn how to tap into it. If you do, you'll "reign in life," as the Bible promises (Romans 5:17); you'll *soar* on a spiritual level far above the carnal plane and the limitations thereof.

Legalists deny all this. They deny the power of this new life, the power of spiritual regeneration, the power of godliness. All they can do is put on a *form* of godliness, a useless garnishment. And that's why they're so dull, sterile and impotent. "By their fruit you will recognize them" (Matthew 7:16,20).

We'll address tapping into the divine nature in more detail in **Chapter 11**.

The Dos & Don'ts Rob Churches of the Gifts of the Spirit

The emphasis of legalists on religious law automatically robs ministries of the moving of the Spirit and miracles:

> **You foolish Galatians! Who has bewitched you? Before your very eyes Jesus Christ was clearly portrayed as crucified. [2] I would like to learn just one thing from you: Did you receive the Spirit by observing the law, or by believing what you heard? [3]Are you so foolish? After beginning with the Spirit, are you now trying to attain your goal by human effort? [4] Have you suffered so much for nothing – it if really was for nothing? [5] Does God give you his Spirit and work miracles among you because you observe the law, or because you believe what you heard?**
>
> **Galatians 3:1-5**

As you can see, Paul was quite upset that the Galatian believers allowed themselves to be "bewitched" by the legalists who infiltrated their assemblies. He was so upset that he calls them "foolish" outright. Paul then goes on to ask a series of questions, the essence of which is: Did you receive the Spirit by following a system of rules and regulations or simply by faith? Did you experience awesome miracles by observing the dos & don'ts or by believing what you heard?

You see, religious law cannot give the Spirit or the gifts of the Spirit, including miracles (1 Corinthians 12:7-11). Whenever charismatic churches rise up they're naturally marked by the moving of the Spirit and miracles. Unfortunately, as the years pass some of these assemblies get bogged down by religious dos and don'ts and what happens? No more mighty moves of the Spirit or miracles. Why? Because the emphasis on rules and regulations quenches the Spirit's fire. Simply put, legalism stifles the flow of God's power!

We observe this in Church history: The thrilling outpouring of God's spirit at the dawn of the 20th century produced many lively and miraculous Pentecostal fellowships and groups. But when some of these started deviating from God's Word in favor of preaching dos and don'ts, the miracles dried up. They got off track with silly rules and regulations about dress length, shirt length, men's hair-length, movie-going, card-playing, pool-playing and lipstick & jewelry-wearing that it cut off the power of God!

To get back on track such ministries have to switch to focusing on God's Word—sharing the full gospel and true gospel—the message of grace, freedom and power in the Holy Spirit. If they'll do this, the signs and wonders will follow. Praise God!

Some ministers fear the message of grace because they think if they preach freedom believers will get out of hand and "do whatever they want." Answer: Share the message of freedom and let God's people make up their own minds. It's amazing what the liberating gospel of Christ will do! Although there will always be some flakes who can't handle freedom, all legitimate believers will revel in their freedom and will ultimately discover that following the Spirit is what they really want to do.

The LORD's not a dictator but rather a liberator. He doesn't want his children obeying him because they're coerced from the outside by a religious system of dos and don'ts but rather because they're moved from within out of thankful, loving, transformed hearts! *That's* Christianity.

Beware the Deadly Dull

Beware! If the church assembly you're involved with is dreadfully boring and shows signs of just going through the motions, it's probably infected by this form of legalism. By all means, do your part to help free it through prayer and service, as detailed in **Chapter 9**, but if you see no positive results in the ensuing months it may be necessary to leave. Be led of the Holy Spirit.

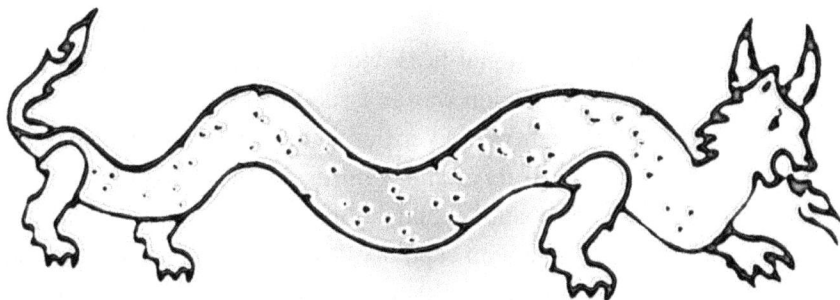

Bondage

Chapter 6

Limb Three:
The Spirit of
BONDAGE

The Bible emphatically declares:

> **It is for freedom that Christ has set us free.**
> **Stand firm, then, and do not let yourselves be**
> **burdened again by a yoke of slavery.**
>
> **Galatians 5:1**

The "yoke of slavery" Paul was referring to is the yoke of religious law. In this particular case, a group of legalistic teachers called the Judaizers infiltrated the Gentile churches of Galatia and taught that the requirements of Jewish religion—the Mosaic Law plus other traditions—were necessary for salvation and spirituality. This included physical circumcision, traditional fasts and observing various holy-days. How do we know? Circumcision was an issue as confirmed by Galatians 2:3 and 5:2-3, while the others are verified in 4:10 where Paul criticizes: "You are observing special **days** and **months** and **seasons** and **years**!" "Days" refers to strict Sabbath-keeping, "months" to the fast initiated by the Jews during their Babylonian captivity, "seasons" to the seven Jewish feasts, and "years" to the seven 7-year periods that culminated in the fiftieth year, the year of Jubilee.

Putting believers under such laws is a "different gospel," as Paul called it (Galatians 1:6)—a perversion of the true gospel.

The true gospel is that salvation comes simply by God's graciousness through faith in Christ's justifying death and resurrection, "not by works so that no one can boast" (Ephesians 2:9). True faith will produce good works (James 2:14-24) because "we are God's workmanship, created in Christ Jesus **to do good works**" (Ephesians 2:10). This occurs naturally as the believer learns to put off the old self—the flesh—and put on the new self—the spirit (Ephesians 4:22-24).

This is why it's so important for believers to *know who they are* in Christ. Those who aren't bearing fruit and doing good works aren't necessarily counterfeits. More likely they have an identity problem—they simply don't know who they are (a topic we'll address in **Chapter 11**). Counterfeits can be identified by a consistent *unrepentant* spirit; in other words, they stubbornly continue to walk in the flesh with no care of repentance, even *after* being exposed to these powerful life-changing truths (Matthew 7:15-23).

Legalists Want to Put You into Bondage

The Judaizers who infiltrated the Galatian churches were legalists. They had a spirit of bondage that made them obsessed with the yoke of religious law. A "yoke" is a device for joining together a pair of draft animals so they can be worked as a team, typically oxen. The beasts are shackled together for the purpose of *work*. That's what the yoke of religious law does to people; it shackles them together to perform religious works. It's religious bondage, which is the antithesis of the spirit of freedom and, as such, saps joy.

You won't see a lot of joy in those entrenched in religious bondage. The Judaizers were such people and they started to sap the Galatians' joy, which is why Paul asked them, "What happened to all your joy?" (Galatians 4:15).

Those who have a spirit of bondage *can't* set others free because they themselves don't have freedom. People can only give what they've got. Those who have a spirit of bondage can only give bondage. In fact, it's their primary objective—to make people slaves to religious rules. It's their *goal*. Here's an example:

> ...some <u>false brothers</u> had **infiltrated our ranks to spy on the freedom we have in Christ Jesus and <u>to make us slaves</u>.** [5] **We did not give in to them for a moment,**
>
> **Galatians 2:4-5**

In this passage Paul is talking about his second trip to Jerusalem where he shared his calling with the leaders of the Jerusalem church. His calling was to minister to the Gentiles. That's when some dyed-in-the-wool legalists infiltrated Paul's group to spy on them. We know they were hardcore legalists because Paul describes them as "false brothers." In other words, these weren't genuine believers who were stumbling into a system of rules and regulations, like the Galatians, but rather full-tilt legalists similar to the Pharisees who antagonized the Messiah. They weren't spiritual brothers *at all*. And notice what their goal was: *to make those who were walking in the freedom of Christ **slaves***. Make no mistake, legalists hate freedom; it goes against everything they are. Legalists are people in bondage to rules, which is why it's called legalism, meaning law-ism or rule-ism.

Paul stresses in verse 5 that he and his team didn't give in to these legalists for a moment. You can't parley with people infected by this spiritual disease. If you give 'em an inch they'll take the proverbial mile. Resist their legalism, pray for them, correct them through the Scriptures, and leave them when you must, as Jesus taught in Matthew 15:14, but never give in to them, not a single inch. The only exception would be if you're going into *their* territory to try to minister life to them. Paul expressed it this way: "Though I am free and belong to no man, I make myself a slave to everyone, to win as many as possible. To the Jews I became like a Jew, to win the Jews. *To those under the law I became like one under the law (though I myself am not under the law), so as to win those under the law...* To the weak I became weak, to win the weak. I have become all things to all men so that by all possible means I might save some. I do all this for the sake of the gospel, that I may share in its blessings" (1 Corinthians 9:19-20,22-23).

The legalistic spirit of bondage manifests in many forms. Let's start with the most obvious...

Bondage to Old Testament Law (Torah)

The Judaizers who infiltrated the Galatian assemblies wanted to put the believers back under the Old Testament Law, along with other religious traditions. A good modern example of this would be the legalists of the Hebrew Roots movement, who have infiltrated many churches and seminaries. Yet notice how clear the New Testament is about believers *not* being under the Mosaic Law, the Torah:

> **But if you are led by the Spirit, <u>you are not under the law</u>.**
>
> **Galatians 5:18**

> **For sin shall not be your master, because <u>you are not under law, but under grace</u>.**
>
> **Romans 6:14**

> **...<u>we have been released from the law</u> so that we serve in the new way of the Spirit, and <u>not in the old way of the written code</u>.**
>
> **Romans 7:6**

In the New Testament era **we've been released from the Law**— the Torah—to "serve in the new way of the Spirit, and ***not*** in the old way of the written code." We're "not under Law, but under grace," meaning we're under God's *graciousness*—favor—through the work of Christ wherein we obtain spiritual regeneration and are reconciled with the LORD & indwelt by the Counselor, the Holy Spirit.

What does being "under the law" mean? It means putting the Law in front of you and trying to force your flesh to comply. This never works. In fact, it will actually increase the sin problem. Why do you think Paul said, "The law was added **so that the trespass might increase**" (Romans 5:20)? This was the reason the Law was given to humanity—to increase the sin problem and drive us to the Savior in whom we can have spiritual regeneration. The Law "is holy, righteous and good"—no doubt—but God uses it to illustrate humanity's miserable sinful condition and drive us to Christ (Romans 7:12).

Since believers are justified in God's sight by faith we are no longer under the supervision of the Law:

> **So the law was our guardian <u>until Christ came</u> that we might be justified by faith. ²⁵ Now that this faith has come, <u>we are no longer under a guardian</u>.**
> **Galatians 3:24-25**

'Guardian' is translated as "tutor" in some translations and as "schoolmaster" in the King James Version. The original Greek word refers to a household servant or slave whose job was to tutor and oversee male children until they came of age whereupon they took on the responsibilities and freedoms of adulthood. Are you getting this? **Believers are no longer under the supervision of religious law.** Since we are spiritually regenerated and have the Holy Spirit we are liberated to function in the responsibilities and freedoms of spiritual adulthood.

While New Testament believers are not under the Mosaic Law, we *are* under **the law of Christ**:

> **Though I am free and belong to no one, I
> have made myself a slave to everyone, to win as many
> as possible. [20] To the Jews I became like a Jew, to win
> the Jews. <u>To those under the law I became like one
> under the law (though I myself am not under the
> law), so as to win those under the law</u>. [21] To those not
> having the law I became like one not having the law
> (though I am not free from God's law but am <u>under
> Christ's law</u>), so as to win those not having the law.**
>
> **1 Corinthians 9:19-21**

As you can see, the apostle Paul was "under Christ's law," not
under the Mosaic Law. He only became "*like* one under the law" on
certain occasions in order to "win those under the law," meaning he did
so to win Jews over to the superior New Covenant. We'll look at what
makes the New Covenant 'superior' momentarily.

So believers are not under the Old Testament Law, but rather
"under Christ's law." Here's another passage that verifies this:

> **Carry each other's burdens, and in this way
> you will fulfill <u>the law of Christ</u>.**
>
> **Galatians 6:2**

But what is the law of Christ? Neither of these verses defines it.
Yet this isn't a problem because Scripture interprets Scripture and the
rest of the New Testament shows us what the law of Christ is. Notice
how Jesus answers an Expert in the Law who sought to test him:

> **"Teacher, which is the greatest commandment in the
> Law?"**
>
> **[37] Jesus replied: "'<u>Love the Lord your God
> with all your heart and with all your soul and with all
> your mind.</u>' [38] <u>This is the first and greatest
> commandment.</u> [39] And the second is like it: '<u>Love
> your neighbor as yourself.</u>' [40] <u>All the Law and the
> Prophets hang on these two commandments.</u>"**
>
> **Matthew 22:36-40**

"The law and the prophets" is a reference to the Old Testament Scriptures; and, specifically, to the moral law since the dietary and ceremonial laws of the Old Testament were foreshadows of Christ and were **fulfilled** in Him:

> **Therefore do not let anyone judge you by what you eat or drink, or with regard to a religious festival, a New Moon celebration or a Sabbath day.** **¹⁷ These are a shadow of the things that were to come; the reality, however, is found in Christ.**
>
> **Colossians 2:16-17**

The passage is addressing the dietary and ceremonial laws of the Old Testament: "what you eat or drink" refers to dietary laws and the others refer to ceremonial laws. We are **not** to allow legalists to judge us negatively by these things. In fact, all of them—dietary laws, the Jewish festivals, the New Moon celebration and the Sabbath day—were mere **shadows** of what was to come, meaning Jesus Christ, the Anointed One. "A shadow" means a *foreshadow*, which is something that testifies to the reality to come. The real thing, however, is not the shadow. "The reality is found in Christ" and if you're a believer **YOU** are "in Christ." Are you following?

Everything in the Law and Prophets from Genesis to Malachi were types and shadows of the true reality, which is Christ and the spiritual rebirth that comes through his seed and the corresponding indwelling/empowerment of the Holy Spirit.[31] More than 600 laws were given to the Hebrews in the Old Testament and Jesus fulfilled every one of them; he completed or stopped each one of them, including the Sabbath. This is why Scripture blatantly says "Christ is the culmination [end] of the law so that there may be righteousness for everyone who believes" (Romans 9:4).

So the dietary and ceremonial laws were fulfilled in Christ and thus we are "released from" them (Romans 7:6). Of course, we are released from the moral law as well since the Messiah also fulfilled the moral law. As such, we're not *under* the moral law. Now, some dubious

---

[31] 'Seed,' again, is "sperm" in the Greek; compare 1 John 3:9 and 1 Peter 1:23.

believers might think that this gives them a license to sin, but Paul dealt with this same question in the 1ˢᵗ century and notice his response:

> **What then? Shall we sin because we are not under the law but under grace? <u>By no means</u>!**
>
> **Romans 6:15**

So, while believers are not under the moral law, we uphold it:

> **Do we, then, nullify the law by this faith? Not at all! Rather, <u>we uphold the law</u>.**
>
> **Romans 3:31**

How exactly do we uphold the moral law; that is, establish it and fulfill it? Observe...

> **so that <u>the righteous standard of the Law</u> might be <u>fulfilled in us</u>, who do not live according to the flesh but according to the spirit.**
>
> **Romans 8:4 (BSB)**

The "righteous standard of the Law" refers to the moral law, which is fulfilled in believers "who do not live according to the flesh, but according to the spirit." This means learning to live out of your new spiritual nature as led of the Holy Spirit:

> **So I say, walk by the spirit,[32] and <u>you will not gratify the desires of the flesh</u>.**
>
> **Galatians 5:16**

You see? **Walking in the spirit** is the key to fulfilling the moral law for the New Testament believer. This is one-in-the-same as

---

[32] As footnoted last chapter, since there is no capitalization in the original Greek text, translators have to determine if the word for "spirit," *pneuma*, refers to the human spirit (un-capitalized) or the Holy Spirit (capitalized). Either/or works in this case since the believer's spirit (un-capitalized) is indwelt and led by *the* Spirit (capitalized).

"**participating in the divine nature**" (2 Peter 1:4). It means being spirit-controlled rather than flesh-ruled and is the automatic result of loving God, which is the primary part of the law of Christ and includes "coming near to God" (James 4:8). If you are "near to God" that obviously means that you have a close *relationship*. So relationship with the LORD is key.

Let's get back to the Messiah's statement in Matthew 22:

> **Jesus replied: "'<u>Love the Lord your God</u> with all your heart and with all your soul and with all your mind.' [38] <u>This is the first and greatest commandment</u>. [39] And the second is like it: '<u>Love your neighbor</u> as yourself.' [40] <u>All the Law and the Prophets hang on these two commandments</u>."**
>
> **Matthew 22:37-40**

All the Old Testament moral laws can be condensed into two basic rules with three applications: **LOVE GOD** and **LOVE PEOPLE** as you **LOVE YOURSELF**. When you do this you automatically fulfill all the moral law of the Old Testament, which is verified by several passages:

> **"In everything, then, do to others as you would have them do to you. For <u>this is the essence of the Law and the prophets</u>."**
>
> **Matthew 7:12**

> **Let no debt remain outstanding, except the continuing debt to love one another, <u>for whoever loves others has fulfilled the law</u>. [9] <u>The commandments</u>, "You shall not commit adultery," "You shall not murder," "You shall not steal," "You shall not covet," <u>and whatever other command there may be, are summed up in this one command: "Love your neighbor as yourself</u>." [10] Love does no harm to a neighbor. Therefore <u>love is the fulfillment of the law</u>.**
>
> **Romans 13:8-10**

> **The entire Law is <u>fulfilled</u> in a single decree: "<u>Love</u>**
> **<u>your neighbor as yourself</u>."**
>
> >   **Galatians 5:14**

The law of Christ or **law of love** is also referred to as "the royal law" in Scripture:

> **If you really keep <u>the royal law</u> found in**
> **Scripture, "Love your neighbor as yourself," you are**
> **doing right.**
>
> >   **James 2:8**

By the way, loving others means walking in **tough love** when necessary just as much as it means walking in gentle love. There are several clear examples in Scripture of both Jesus and the apostles walking in tough love when appropriate (e.g. Matthew 23:13-35, Mark 11:15-18, Acts 8:17-24 & 13:8-12).

As noted earlier, the New Covenant that believers have with God is *superior* to the Old Covenant that the Israelites had:

> **They serve at a sanctuary that is a copy and shadow**
> **of what is in heaven. This is why Moses was warned**
> **when he was about to build the tabernacle: "See to it**
> **that you make everything according to the pattern**
> **shown you on the mountain." [6]<u>But in fact the</u>**
> **<u>ministry Jesus has received is as superior to theirs as</u>**
> **<u>the covenant of which he is mediator is superior to</u>**
> **<u>the old one</u>, since <u>the new covenant is established on</u>**
> **<u>better promises</u>...**
> >   **[13]<u>By calling this covenant "new," he has</u>**
> **<u>made the first one obsolete</u>; and what is obsolete and**
> **outdated will soon disappear.**
>
> >   **Hebrews 8:5-6,13**

The New Covenant is "superior" because we've been **released from** the Law—the Torah—as shown in Romans 7:6. We serve **in the new way of the Spirit** wherein we receive spiritual regeneration

(Ephesians 4:22-24) and not in the Old Covenant way of the written code, i.e. the Law. This is great because "the letter [the Law] *kills*, but the Spirit gives *life*" (2 Corinthians 3:6).

Humble **repentance and faith** are the conditions for entering into the New Covenant (Acts 20:21 & Hebrews 6:1) and the terms are **"faith working through love,"** which means faith is *activated* by love (Galatians 5:6 Amplified). When we walk out of love (1 Corinthians 13:4-7) we walk out of faith and thus negate it, which isn't good because faith is the foundation of our covenant. Why is "faith working through love" so important? Because **love is the fulfillment of the moral law**. It's the law of Christ, the law of love.

Needless to say, if you come across a church, a group or any Christian in general who advocates putting believers *under* the Old Testament Law—including observing the Saturday Sabbath—flee for your spiritual welfare. These types adhere to a "different gospel" (Galatians 1:6). Some obvious modern examples include: The Hebrew Roots movement, adherents of Armstrongism (e.g. the United Church of God and the Philadelphia Church of God) and the Seventh-Day Adventists.

For important details on this topic see my book *THE LAW and the Believer*.[33]

Bondage to the Mosaic Law is just one type of this form of legalism. Spiritual bondage can manifest in several different ways. Here's another example...

A Church with a Spirit of Bondage

Carol and I visited an assembly for a couple of months to consider joining. We went to every service for these two months, two a week, along with a special service at a linking fellowship as well. We walked in love and faithfully supported the church both financially and prayerfully. I had researched the group online and basically agreed with their doctrinal statement and general vision, but just because something looks good on paper doesn't mean it's good in reality. I've known

---

[33] Also see the article at the FOL site *LAW (Torah) and the Believer*.

women, for example, who married men claiming to own companies, yachts, vacation cabins, etc., but it all turned out to be untrue.

The first bad sign was that the pastor was consistently prune-faced and continually looked at us with a suspicious eye. Being prune-faced indicates a lack of joy (and I don't mean "prune-faced" solely in a physical sense, as there may be legit reasons for this; I'm talking about the sourpuss disposition *behind* a prune-face). The second bad sign was that the believers had to sign an attendance sheet at the beginning of each service and check whether they were a member or a visitor, which made us feel like we were back in grade school. The third bad sign was the requirement that believers had to have permission from the pastor to pray for other believers during services and, in fact, required authorized necklace tags. The fourth bad sign was that the apostle of the church was ridiculously aloof and unfriendly. The fifth bad sign was that the pastor compared joining the sect to a marriage contract. Carol and I couldn't help wondering: Did this mean "divorce" from the church was forbidden? Couldn't believers just leave if they no longer wanted to be a part of the group? Why not? The sixth bad sign was that the pastor described her submission to the apostle of the church in a disturbing manner. In a sermon she explained that she submitted *everything* in her life to this man, including her marriage. It sounded weird and even creepy. Does the Bible encourage this type of *extreme* submission between a pastor and an apostle? No, the Scriptures actually instruct us to "submit to *one another* out of reverence to Christ" (Ephesians 5:21). It's a *mutual* thing and healthy for unity in the body. The radical submission the pastor was talking about was the result of the apostle fostering it. She submitted to him in a bad way and, in turn, projected this same unhealthy submission on to her congregants. Bondage begats bondage.

We overlooked all this, however, since the praise & worship was good and some of the other believers were genuinely fruit-bearing, including the assistant pastor—the pastor's husband—whom we got along with well.

We realized that we'd likely have to go through some religious hoops to be part of this group even though I already had ministry credentials and a history of proven service, including numerous sermons and a couple self-published books. No problem. The first "hoop" was a series of orientation meetings with the pastor and the assistant pastor, her husband. These meetings included reading material from an introductory booklet and going over questions and answers with the pastors. Since Carol and I were seasoned believers with a long history of service we sort of rolled our eyes at this initiation "hoop," but we humbled ourselves and were willing to go through such formalities in order to join the group and get things moving.

I should add here that the New Testament certainly provides guidelines for those who want to be servant-leaders in the Church (e.g. 1 Timothy 3). This is simply a matter of wisdom. After all, those who serve in leadership positions *should* have proven character, humility being especially important in light of Proverbs 3:34, James 4:6 and 1 Peter 5:5. This is vital because Christian leaders have influence and their influence should be positive, not abusive. But wise guidelines for leadership are not what I'm talking about when I say this church had a spirit of bondage. I'm talking about such an obsession with rules that it smacked of bondage. Think about it, believers couldn't even pray for fellow believers unless they had an authorized neck-tag! And merely joining the church was likened to Marriage! (I'm of course talking about joining *their* assembly since believers are already a part of *the* Church). This is the textbook definition of "legal-ism"—obsession with laws to the point that it squeezes out all life and sense of freedom.

Getting back to the story, Carol and I received the booklet and were instructed to go over it before the first meeting; this included answering numerous questions in the booklet. It didn't take long for us to conclude that we weren't going to be able to go through with it. The booklet was ridiculous. The questions went on and on and, frankly, many of them were nosy. It was so bad we half-expected to be asked to list every sin we had committed in the last five years and then be told to openly confess them in front of the congregation! (Lol). Quite a few of the questions concerned things that were no one's business, including the pastors. We'd be willing to answer some or all of them, as long as we were allowed to ask the pastors the same questions. After all, why should we divulge our entire history and private lives to these relative strangers, unless they were willing to do the same? Aren't leaders in the Church commissioned to be *servants*—even *slaves* in a figurative sense—to those they're called to *serve*? See Mark 10:42-45. The intimate questions were an obvious attempt to acquire power over any believer who was considering joining their church.

So I called the assistant pastor and said I'd like to talk with him personally, not just about the absurd booklet, but also about the other bad signs we observed. He tried to get me to elaborate on the phone but I insisted that we get together face-to-face since this was serious stuff that should be discussed in person. He said he'd get back to me, but never did. I was pretty sure he wasn't going to anyway. His wife, the pastor, obviously told him not to meet with me. I'm sure she concluded that I was "of the devil" when, in fact, I simply wanted to share some things from the viewpoint of an outside observer and mature believer, things that would benefit their ministry. It's called constructive criticism and it's a biblical principle (Proverbs 27:17).

Needless to say, we had no intention of going back to this particular fellowship.

Unjust Ostracizing

About eight weeks later my wife ran into a couple from that assembly while we were shopping at a department store (Carol & I were separate in the store). We were friends with this couple during our two months at this church. Carol immediately recognized them, gave a cheerful greeting, and asked how they were doing. Incredibly, all she got in return was dead looks and uncomfortable silence—they totally snubbed her! If you know my wife, Carol, you know that she's the quintessence of sweetness and doesn't deserve this type of legalistic mistreatment. It pained me when I met up with her shortly later because she was obviously shaken by the encounter and just wanted to leave the store. After we got into the car and drove away she told me what happened and I encouraged her to just laugh it off. You can be sure this couple didn't treat Carol this way merely because we decided their church wasn't for us; more likely the pastor slandered us to the congregation. I'm sure she told them we were "of the devil" or something to this effect. How sad. We prayed for the couple and their church, and let it go.

If you've experienced this type of unjustified treatment be encouraged because Jesus said you're blessed when people falsely accuse you and mistreat you (Matthew 5:10-12). Great is your reward in Heaven! This is why I encouraged Carol to laugh it off.

Fifteen months later, we ran into the pastor and her husband at a restaurant, but they refused to acknowledge us even though it was clear they recognized us. This was another overt snubbing.

Now, think about it, what did we do to deserve this type of treatment? We went to their church for two months and attended every service, including the mid-week service and a special one at another assembly. While we were there we walked in love, we prayed for the people regularly, we generously supported the church financially and we didn't cause trouble in any way. Our last communication with them was when I called the assistant pastor after reading their introductory booklet; all I asked was if we could get together to discuss a few things. That's it. I never said what it was and *never criticized their fellowship*. I was going to wait to offer constructive criticism in a loving manner when we sat down together face to face.

My point is that Carol & I did nothing to deserve being ostracized by the pastors and their congregation members. Unless, of course, it's a sin to attend every service for two months, walk in love, regularly intercede, financially support and not cause trouble! Think about how absurd this is. Something is direly wrong with a church when believers are mistreated like this. It's Christianity gone wrong!

Also consider this: The pastors' decision to denounce us to their congregants and to ostracize us when meeting in public actually *proved* that our decision to not plant ourselves in their church was the right one. Thankfully, the Lord moved us to leave after discerning the red flags. This prevented us from getting entangled and wasting our time and support. This is important because the more you get entangled in a group like this one the harder it is to get out.

Again, this ministry may have looked fine on paper but, in practice, they had a serious spirit of bondage, at least this particular assembly did. And a spirit of bondage screams legalism. It's the antithesis of the spirit of Christ, which is a spirit of *freedom*.

Unfortunately, unjust ostracizing like this happens way too often in the Church. I listened to an audio sermon yesterday and the minister was teaching on what to do when people decide to leave a church. He shared how he and his family went to a large fellowship in the Midwest, USA, where he was an associate pastor. The company he worked for offered a better position in another city and, after seeking the Lord, he took it; but this meant his family would have to leave the assembly. The church leaders laid hands on them and prayed during a brief ceremony, but he discerned that their hearts really weren't in it. The reason the ceremony was so cold and mechanical was the church's undercurrent mentality on occupational transfers: It was wrong to take a job offer that would take you and your family away from *their* church. This was all verified in the ensuing months as all relations with the members of their former fellowship ceased. It hurt because these people were spiritual family and close friends for many years. They grieved for a period, but the Lord healed their hearts and blessed them with close relationships in their new location. It wasn't until *five years later* that a brother from their former assembly contacted them and sought fellowship—*five years*.

Another minister shared in a sermon how, years prior, he informed the senior pastor of his church that he had decided to leave and pursue other ministerial endeavors. He had been serving as an associate at this fellowship. The pastor sternly told him that it wasn't God's will for him to go and, if he did, he'd "come back crawling on his hands and knees!" Can you believe it? Understandably, he decided right then and there that—even if he were reduced to crawling on his hands and knees—he certainly wasn't going back to that church!

Yesterday I read an email from a brother who shared his testimony. He grew up in a sect steeped with tradition. When he was in the Navy in his late teens some Evangelical believers would invite him to revivals or church services, but he couldn't go because his denomination viewed any such activity as a mortal sin worthy of condemnation to hell!

Bondage to a Church or Freedom in Christ?

The problem with this type of mentality is that it's religious bondage. The threats come in different forms, which may be subtle or pronounced, but the objective is the same: To keep believers shackled to the assembly or sect in question. In some churches prophecies are given stating that the individual has to stay at the fellowship. The reason legalistic leaders resort to these kinds of tactics is to prevent "their sheep" from leaving, but congregants aren't really *their* sheep, they're *God's* sheep. Jesus is the Chief Shepherd and pastoral leaders are actually *under*-shepherds. Notice what the Bible says in this regard:

> **To the elders among you, I appeal as a fellow elder, a witness of Christ's sufferings and one who also will share in the glory to be revealed:** [2] **Be shepherds [pastors] of <u>God's flock</u> that is <u>under your care</u>, <u>serving as overseers</u>—not because you must, but because you are willing, as God wants you to be; not greedy for money, but eager <u>to serve</u>;** [3] **<u>not lording it over those entrusted to you</u>, but being examples to the flock.** [4] **And when <u>the Chief Shepherd</u> appears, you will receive the crown of glory that will never fade away.**
>
> **1 Peter 5:1-4**

Pastors who fall into legalism mistakenly think that the believers at their church are *their* flock when, in reality, they're "God's flock" who are merely entrusted to the pastor's care for a season. When ministers fall into this mentality, they naturally start "lording it over" the congregants. They'll use threats to prevent individuals from leaving and they'll ostracize those who do. Again, the threats come in different forms and may be subtle or overt.

But why do they ostracize those who leave? One reason is immaturity and insecurity. When believers leave, these types of pastors feel rejected and their ego is hurt, so they lash out through ostracizing. This includes denouncing them to their remaining congregants and snubbing them if they meet in public. I wouldn't believe this type of thing happens if I hadn't seen it with my own eyes, but it does.

The problem with this mentality—other than the fact that it's fleshly and abusive—is that it starts to create a closed community. Churches that cop it become like gated communities where people aren't free to come and go as they choose. As such, the very thing the legalistic leaders fear starts to come to pass and the congregation becomes spiritually inbred because there's little flow of new blood, if any.

God has blessed humankind with the power of volition and respects our decisions. The LORD provided the Israelites with two options—life or death. He encouraged them to choose life and warned them of the consequences of choosing death, but he didn't force them to make the right decision. He does the same thing with all humanity in the New Testament (Deuteronomy 30:19 & Romans 6:23). Just as God respects our power of decision so we must extend this freedom to our fellow believers. If we think they're making a mistake we can tell them so and explain why. We can even issue a warning *in love* if we feel compelled by the Spirit. But we have to ultimately give people the freedom to decide for themselves.

A popular pastor said he refuses to make people feel like they're in bondage to his fellowship. He gives people the freedom to leave and the freedom to come back, if they choose.[34] This is precisely what Jesus did with his disciples. After giving a hard teaching many of his disciples decided to stop following him and he refused to say anything to pressure them to stay. He simply turned to his remaining disciples and asked, "You do not want to leave too, do you?" (John 6:60-67). That's it. Jesus refused to "lord it over" people. He gave them the freedom to *choose*—to follow him or leave.

The aforementioned pastor said the most he'd do in cases where he felt believers were making a mistake was to tell them so and leave it at that. Furthermore, when some of them eventually decided to come back he refused to arrogantly say, "I told you so." Amen.

---

[34] I'm obviously not talking about cases where believers are excommunicated due to unrepentant sin *a la* Matthew 18:15-17. Yet, even in those circumstances the individual should be warmly welcomed back into the church if he/she *decides* to repent, as illustrated in 2 Corinthians 2:5-11.

How Do the Leaders of Your Assembly Talk About Previous Members?

This is a good question to ask: How do the ministers and elders of your fellowship speak of past members? I'm not talking about people who were dismissed due to an unwillingness to repent of a certain sin— although they shouldn't talk about that either—I'm talking about brothers and sisters who simply decided to leave for one reason or another. The reason is irrelevant. How do the leaders of your fellowship talk about these people? Do they badmouth them? Do they put a negative spin on everything about them? Do they say things like they were "of the devil" or imply that they were walking in secret sins? If so, it's not good. It bespeaks of **1.** spiritual immaturity, **2.** fleshliness, since malice, gossip and slander are serious sins, and **3.** a rigidly sectarian mentality that automatically discredits or denounces others who are not part of their group. All three of these reasons are somewhat interconnected and they all convey the spirit of bondage: People are in bondage to the church or ministry in question and anyone who chooses to leave must be punished. Thus the leaders justify maligning them.

This is very legalistic behavior. Luke 7:33-34 shows that the Pharisees and Teachers of the Law automatically tried to discredit and denounce Jesus and John the Baptist because they both operated outside of their circles and the legalistic mindset thereof. Consequently, they slandered Christ as a glutton, drunkard and friend of "sinners" while they maligned John as demon-possessed! This is spiritual tunnel-vision. It's pathetic really.

The way spiritual leaders talk about genuine ministers and believers who function outside of their accepted circles speaks volumes. Take heed.

Bondage to the Pastor's Limited Understanding of Scripture

I went to a charismatic "mega-church" for a decade, which involved most of my 20s. The pastor and much of his staff hailed from a Bible college of a well-known charismatic minister who has since passed on. The church was exemplary on almost every level—the teaching of the Word, the praise & worship, God's presence, and the flow of gifts of the Spirit. It was an outstanding church. Since the pastor was hooked-up with this ministry he naturally adhered to their doctrinal mindset. This is the way it is at most churches. Even so, it didn't smother the spirit of freedom. Yes, there were doctrinal parameters set and the congregants weren't advised to go beyond them but, at the same time, there was a sense of freedom and believers were very much encouraged to explore the Bible and its many topics. We were encouraged to be thorough, balanced and honest in our studies. We were also free to leave the fellowship if we wanted, without any threat of ostracizing.

Needless to say, this was a healthy assembly and well worthy of investing one's time, even if you didn't happen to agree with every jot and tittle. (Who agrees with anyone about everything anyway? Is that even healthy?).

Another church my wife and I went to for seven years had even more of a spirit of freedom. The pastor was one of those scatterbrained preachers who wasn't really able to teach, but he allowed qualifying individuals the opportunity to teach, as long as they could support what they taught by the Scriptures. I taught there often, typically every other week. There were two or three praise & worship leaders and it was very lively. Although I disagreed with the pastor in some areas—usually because he hadn't studied the particular topics in detail like I had—it didn't matter. The saying "In essentials, unity; in non-essentials, liberty; in all things, charity" was our unofficial creed and practice. There was such a spirit of freedom and Carol & I literally *loved* going to the gatherings.

These two churches comprised 17 years of my Christian walk. I mention them to point out that you can be hooked-up with a church where there are general doctrinal parameters and you don't necessarily agree with every jot and tittle, but there's still an air of liberty in Christ, which is the way it should be.

Unfortunately, some assemblies aren't like this. In many fellowships the congregants are pretty much in bondage to the pastor's understanding of the Scriptures. Questioning what the pastor teaches from the pulpit or the doctrinal parameters of the sect is strongly discouraged. This rule may be unofficial and unwritten, but it's still there. It pervades the atmosphere. Those who merely question the pastor's belief system are marked and not allowed into the inner circle of the governing structure. Such people eventually leave and understandably so.

What's so bad about this type of environment? It's bad because it tends to produce robotic "yes men," but it fails to produce believers who are free to *know* the Lord and grow in knowledge, understanding and wisdom through their *own* pursuit of God and truth.

Unless you want to become a mindless automaton, beware of this type of bondage.

The Bondage of Pastoral Dependency

Some pastors encourage a spirit of dependency in their congregants, which simply isn't healthy. For instance, I've been in some churches where the believers are never taught how to pray effectively. Instead, they're encouraged to have the pastor or other speaker pray for them at the end of the service. The Bible encourages this to some degree (James 5:14-15), but it shouldn't become a *lifestyle* of dependency where the *same* people come up for the *same* things on a regular basis. Why is this wrong? Because it discourages believers from developing their *own* prayer life and utilizing their *own* faith to receive answers, healings and miracles. It fosters an unhealthy dependency on the pastor and pastoral staff. In short, it encourages spiritual immaturity.

Why would pastors want to cultivate such a spirit in the believers entrusted to their care? Likely because they enjoy feeling needed and it feeds their ego to have people dependent on them. It's also a security issue. If believers are *dependent* on the pastor they're less likely to leave. Thus, to all intents and purposes the people become in bondage to the pastor.

What kind of minister would cultivate such an unhealthy dependency? Those who fall into legalism. This doesn't mean they're *wholly* infected, of course, but any amount of legalism is too much.

Wise and godly ministers, by contrast, would never cultivate such an environment in their churches. Notice what the Bible says about ministers and their purpose in the body of Christ:

> **It was he [Jesus] who gave some to be <u>apostles</u>, some to be <u>prophets</u>, some to be <u>evangelists</u>, and some to be <u>pastors</u> and <u>teachers</u>, [12] <u>to prepare God's people for works of service</u>, so that the body of Christ may be <u>built up</u> [13] until we all <u>reach unity in the faith and in the knowledge</u> of the Son of God <u>and become mature</u>, attaining to the whole measure of the fullness of Christ.**

> **Ephesians 4:11-13**

These five positions or callings comprise the "fivefold ministry"—**apostles, prophets, evangelists, pastors** and **teachers.** All five are important and have their specific place and function in the body of Christ. Yet notice that they all have the same general fourfold purpose: **1.** To prepare God's people for works of service, that is, works of ministry; **2.** to build up God's people and not tear them down; **3.** to feed a balanced diet of God's Word in a way that cultivates unity in faith and knowledge; and **4.** to help bring the believer into *maturity.*

All four are important, but I want to stress the fourth function. One of the main purposes of fivefold ministers is *to facilitate maturity in the believer*, not foster a spirit of dependency!

All believers are dependent to varying degrees on their pastors while growing up spiritually, but it's unnatural for them to *stay* dependent. In a sense, fivefold ministers are spiritual parents, which is why Paul referred to himself as the father of the believers at Corinth (1 Corinthians 4:15).[35] He started the church and pastored it for a couple years, feeding them God's Word, so he was in essence their spiritual parent. Don't physical children eventually leave home to go to college, work, get married and start families? Wouldn't it be absurd for a child to grow into full adulthood and still be in a crib with a pacifier, completely dependent upon his or her parents? Of course it would. Yet this happens too often in the Church in a spiritual sense. It shouldn't. Believers need

---

[35] This doesn't mean that "father" should become a title, as in "Father Thomas." Paul was the spiritual father of the Corinthian church but the believers didn't call him Father Paul. Jesus denounced this type of practice in Matthew 23:7-11.

to move on to maturity, not be locked-up in the spiritual nursery all their lives!

In healthy churches the congregants are encouraged to grow to spiritual adulthood and bear forth fruit; they're not hampered by dependency to fivefold ministers. One minister put it to me like this: "My job is to become unnecessary in the life of the believer." He wasn't saying that believers no longer need to go to church gatherings once they reach spiritual maturity, but rather that they should come to the point where they're no longer dependent on pastors for every little thing. Say if a neighbor or someone at work needs prayer, the believer should handle it instead of calling the pastor. If a family member is in the hospital, the believer should go and visit instead of asking the pastor. If the believer feels led to do something important, like take a new job or move to another location, the believer should pray about it and get a confirmation from the Holy Spirit rather than requiring the pastor to instruct him/her. Etcetera.

This is the way it should be when believers grow properly.

Take an honest look at your church assembly. Does it cultivate a spirit of dependency in the congregants? If so, it's not good. Do your part to help set it free from this infection of legalism. If they're stubborn and refuse to change you may have to leave. Be led of the Lord.

Beware of the Spirit of Bondage

Needless to say, if the group you're involved with, or thinking about getting involved with, seems obsessed with rules to the point that being a member feels more like bondage than freedom it's a huge red flag. Are the leaders prune-faces? Are they more interested in lording it over you than serving? Do they require you to answer a bunch of nosey questions but show offense if you desire to ask them the same? Is being part of their group likened to a marriage contract and you can't just leave if you want? Do they unjustly denounce and shun believers who simply decided to leave the fellowship? Do you feel like you're boxed-in or trapped by the pastor's limited understanding of the Bible? Do you feel pressured to believe everything that's taught from the pulpit without question? Is questioning discouraged? Is seeking truth discouraged? Is everything figured out to a 'T' with no room for mystery or variation? Do you feel like you can't legitimately disagree without being shut out in some manner? Does the assembly encourage unhealthy dependency to the pastor and associates rather than fostering spiritual maturity? Beware!

Remember, Christ came to set people free from the yoke of religious bondage. Groups that develop an environment of bondage are the antithesis of the true Christian spirit.

Stand Firm in Your Freedom!

Take another look at this important verse:

> **It is for freedom that Christ has set us free. <u>Stand firm, then, and do not let yourselves be burdened</u> again by a yoke of slavery.**
>
> **Galatians 5:1**

As pointed out at the beginning of this chapter, Paul was talking about freedom from the bondage of religious law, the system of rules and regulations that can only give an appearance of spirituality by imposing restraints, but has no real power to set people free and change them. God wants believers to be totally free, not just from the works of the flesh—which Paul also addresses in Galatians 5—but from the bondage of religious law.

"It is for *freedom* that Christ has set us free." Let that soak in— freedom, freedom, freedom, freedom. Make it a soothing meditation throughout the day—freedom, freedom, freedom, freedom. Shout it from the rooftops—*"freedom, freedom, freedom, freedom!"*

If you think I'm getting carried away, you're wrong. The message of freedom is something every believer needs to understand. It's foundational to walking in the abundant life that Jesus Christ offers.

Notice in the above passage that there's something we need to do in order to walk in freedom—we have to "stand firm." We have to be careful not to allow legalists to bog us down with their religious burdens.

'Stand firm' is translated as "stand fast" in other versions. It's a military expression meaning to hold one's ground.

Our freedom in Christ was bought at a great price—the humbling, suffering and crucifixion of Jesus Christ, the Son of God, sent by the Father to reconcile the world to himself and grant us everlasting life. Freedom didn't come easy and we won't keep it without effort; we must continually be on our guard.

Political freedom comes at a great price and citizens have to be vigilant to guard it. Citizens of the kingdom of God must be every bit as vigilant to preserve and protect our spiritual freedom. There are enemies to both political and spiritual freedom who would want nothing more than to enslave us, but they can only do it if we allow it. We must be on our guard, constantly.

Don't think the threat of legalism can only come from some peculiar group outside your normal Christian circles. As previously stressed, legalism can infect anyone, anywhere, anytime, regardless of sectarian tag or belief system. It could infect a respected colleague like it did Peter in Antioch when Paul had to openly correct him for giving in to the legalists (Galatians 2:11-14). In fact, legalism can infect you or me, which is why we must regularly examine ourselves and purge as necessary (2 Corinthians 13:5).

Expect Persecution

Lastly, any believer who's walking in the true freedom and abundant life of Christ should expect some of the mistreatments described in this chapter, like slander and shunning by people of former churches. Why expect it? Because the Bible promises that "everyone who wants to live a godly life in Christ Jesus will be persecuted" (2 Timothy 3:12). 'Persecuted' means mistreated or abused.

Speaking of mistreatment by those from former assemblies, don't expect all your persecution to come from those in the world. After all, Jesus' main enemies were *religious leaders who knew the Scriptures like the backs of their hands!* A lot of the unjust persecutions you will face will be from people who say they're believers and are even leaders in churches. Why? Because religionists will not stand idly by while you live free in the Lord and strive to set others free. As soon as they see the light of liberty in your eyes and your actions they'll rise up and try to snuff you out with great sourpuss zeal.

You can bank on these types of experiences now and then because we're in the midst of a spiritual war. When legalists brush shoulders with liberated believers it's like death clashing with life. It may take some time for their true colors to show but they will always eventually gnash their teeth in unreasoning religious hostility. It's like mixing oil with water; they don't gel. Not that there's no hope for them; there's hope for everybody. Continue to intercede for them in the hope that the truth may set them free. Amen.

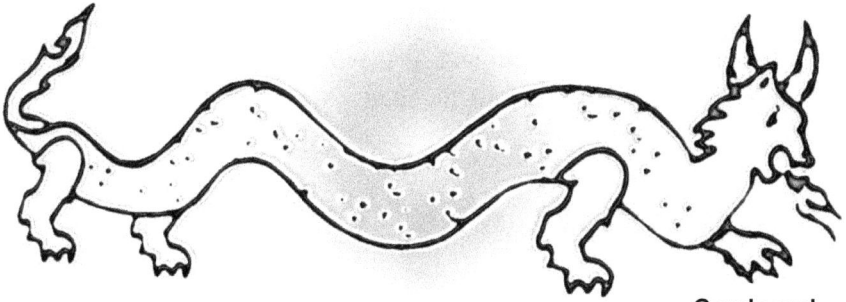

Chapter 7

Limb Four: CONDO and Authoritarianism

Condemnation can be referred to as 'condo' for short, as in "the minister heaped on the condo in his sermon."

What is a spirit of condemnation? It's when a minister regularly tears down and beats up a congregation, which is an abuse of the pulpit. Such ministers tend to motivate others based on shame. For example: "You're not reading the Word of God like you should! And you call yourself a Christian?" You could insert any number of spiritual activities here, like evangelizing, praying, church attendance or giving.

The root of this type of wicked spirit is arrogance, which is a superiority complex. When these types of ministers tear down others they automatically elevate themselves. Its fleshly pride, impure and simple, and it's truly sad when ministers fall into such a religionist rut. Sometimes they never get out and, if they do, it's either due to intense intercession or because someone dared to walk in tough love and openly correct them, or both.[36]

Building Up, Not Tearing Down

The spirit of condo is at odds with the true ministerial spirit, which Paul summed up nicely when he spoke of the authority ministers have for building believers up and not tearing them down (2 Corinthians 10:8 & 13:10). He also stressed this in Ephesians 4:11-13 where he detailed the purpose of all fivefold ministers: "to prepare God's people for works of service, so that the body of Christ may be **built up**".

You don't have to be a spiritual Einstein to recognize a spirit of condemnation. Years ago my sister, Jennifer, was looking for a church in Southern California and ended up visiting one for three Sundays in a row, but she decided not to stay. Why? Because after all three services she left feeling beat up and condemned rather than inspired and encouraged. Needless to say, only a glutton for punishment would stay in such a church. This isn't to suggest that there's no place for denouncing sins and encouraging repentance at church services. Skilled ministers who are led of the Spirit will bring about a spirit of repentance through the ministry of the Word, but will also remove the burden of guilt, instill the Lord's peace and motivate individuals onward. In other words, even though they denounce sin and spur repentance their ministry is encouraging and inspiring. This is the minister's job.

A good example of such an inspiring spirit can be seen in Jesus after his resurrection. Christ appeared to two of the disciples who were understandably discouraged after his unjust crucifixion. The Messiah met up with them as they were walking along the road and they talked for a bit, but they were prevented from recognizing him. After Jesus departed, the two disciples reflected on the encounter:

---

[36] See the teaching *Gentle Love and Tough Love* at the FOL site for details, also available in chapter 5 of *The Believer's Guide to FORGIVENESS & WARFARE.*

"Were not our hearts burning within us while he talked with us on the road and opened the Scriptures to us?" **Luke 24:32**

This is the effect Christ-like ministers should have on believers. You know you're at a healthy assembly when you leave a service with your heart burning with inspiration and you see things in God's Word you never saw before.

Luke 24 goes on to show us what Christ did on the day he ascended, which was weeks later: "he lifted up his hands **and blessed them**. While he was **blessing them**, he left them and was taken up into heaven" (verses 50-51). Even as Jesus was leaving this Earth he was blessing people—it was the last thing he did before going to the Father! This is how Christ-like ministers should be—constantly blessing people and building them up, not condemning them and tearing down.

The Arrogance of Authoritarianism

Since the spirit of condemnation is rooted in arrogance (tearing others down to build oneself up) it's also a spirit of authoritarianism. This is when a "minister" leads by trying to lord it over people, which is plainly condemned in Scripture:

To the elders among you... [2] **Be shepherds of God's flock that is under your care, serving as overseers—not because you must, but because you are willing, as God wants you to be; not greedy for money, but eager to serve;** [3] **not lording it over those entrusted to you, but being examples to the flock.**
1 Peter 5:1-3

Authoritarianism is demagoguery where the Christian leader tries to dominate others through intimidation and manipulation. But this is an oxymoron since 'minister' literally means "servant" and it reveals how Christian ministers are to minister—with a servant's heart. This isn't to say, of course, that ministers have to be perpetually sugary sweet as there's a time and place for Spirit-led rebuke and radical righteousness, like when Paul openly reprimanded Peter for his legalism (Galatians 2:11-14) or when Jesus boldly cleared the temple of fools (Mark 11:15-18).

Verses 1-2 of the above passage show that Peter was specifically addressing "elders"—mature believers who were called to serve as "shepherds," that is, pastors. He goes on to say that they should be eager to "serve," meaning minister. This is important because pastors who regularly tear down their subordinates are essentially grumps who have lost the joyful eagerness of serving as shepherds of God's flock and all that goes with it. In such cases, pastoring has become more of a job than a joy. This can always be seen on their faces; instead of the joy of serving there's the scowl of forced labor.

Verse 3 says point blank that pastors are not to lord it over the people entrusted to their care. The word "lording" here means to control, subjugate or rule in the sense of being the final authority. Pastors are not to be like this! Although pastors are certainly the authority of the fellowships they oversee, Yeshua is the final authority of the Church. Pastors simply have no business "lording it over" believers as if they are the supreme and final authority in their lives.

Beating the Sheep

Jesus spoke of ministers who have a fleshly tendency to "beat up" the members of the congregation when he said:

> **"Who then is the faithful and wise manager, whom the master puts in charge of his servants to give them their food allowance at the proper time? [43]It will be good for that servant whom the master finds doing so when he returns. [44] I tell you the truth, he will put him in charge of all his possessions. [45] But suppose the servant says to himself, 'My master is taking a long time in coming,' and <u>he begins to beat the menservants and maidservants</u> and <u>to eat and drink and get drunk</u>."   Luke 12:42-45**

The "manager" that the "master" puts in charge of his "servants" refers to a minister that the Lord puts over a congregation of believers, a pastor. Jesus points out that the main job of the pastor is to give the believers their "food allowance at the proper time," meaning feed them God's Word appropriately (Matthew 4:4). In verse 43 Christ says that it will be good for the pastors who faithfully feed the sheep and build them up. They will be rewarded in the age to come. But in verse 45 Jesus points out a different kind of minister. This is one who forsakes his calling and, instead, beats the believers and lives a lifestyle of gluttony and revelry.

Christ goes on to say that such "ministers" will be held accountable for their abuse and punished accordingly; in fact, verse 46 suggests that they well be assigned the fate of unbelievers, which indicates they were fakes. This is supported by Matthew's account where Jesus says the unfaithful "minister" will be severely flogged and assigned "a place with the hypocrites" (Matthew 24:51). Remember, a 'hypocrite' literally refers to a stage actor—someone who pretends to be who they are not.

What can we conclude from all this? Three things: **1.** Jesus himself made it clear that there will be people in pastoral positions who misuse their power by "beating up" the believers who are entrusted to their care and setting a bad example of fleshly indulgence. **2.** So-called pastors who abuse the people in this way will be held accountable and punished accordingly. **3.** Such "ministers" have proven themselves to be counterfeits by their very actions.

As far as the third point goes, Jesus was obviously referring to authoritarian "ministers" who consistently beat on believers and live out of the flesh and therefore aren't likely even saved. He wasn't referring to legitimate pastors who fall into a spirit of condemnation or authoritarianism and then repent.

Three Examples of Condo

Let me share three examples of the spirit of condemnation that I've personally observed...

Years ago I was at a home-styled fellowship on a week night. This fellowship typically attracted guys in their early 20s or thereabouts. One night the main pastor decided to ream them for not reading their Bibles. He sternly said, "You're not reading the Bible like you should; you need to read the Word; you need to hit the book!" There's nothing wrong with a stern correction when it's called for, like when Paul openly corrected Peter for his hypocrisy in Galatians 2:11-14. The Bible says "Better is open rebuke than hidden love" (Proverbs 27:5). Such reprimands are sometimes necessary, but it wasn't fitting in this case. Let me explain.

The pastor felt that these potential disciples weren't reading the Bible like they should've been, so he scolded them and tried to get them to read it by shaming them. This never works because the best condo can do is *coerce* people into doing something by making them feel bad. What's wrong with this approach? The youths may have picked up their Bibles, but it wouldn't have been because they wanted to; it would've been because they were shamed into doing it. How effective or exciting would their time in the Word be, if at all? Who enjoys doing something they don't really want to do? Don't get me wrong here because the flesh never wants to do any type of spiritual activity and we are instructed in the Bible to put it off in favor of putting on the "new self," that is, walk in the spirit. But the job of fivefold ministers is to motivate believers to spiritual activities, like reading the Word and prayer, through *spiritual inspiration*. This means that the believers are so inspired, spiritually speaking, that their lower nature is overruled. When believers are stirred in this manner they'll do the activity in question because they're excited about doing it and not because some angry preacher told them they were bad for not doing it. Are you following?

I ministered the Word at this same fellowship once or twice a month and I remember one gathering where I taught on the nature of eternal life and God's Word itself did its work with zero condo on my part. At the end of the meeting the believers—mostly young guys—were clearly excited about the material we went over. The light of the Lord was in their eyes and joy on their faces! Many of them went over the main passages in their personal time. They didn't do this because they were pressured to, but because they were *excited* about the incredible truths of God's Word and *wanted* to do it.

Obviously the same applies to any spiritual activity and not just reading the Scriptures, things like prayer and evangelism. For instance, Carol and I were at a week night service of a church and the pastor lined the small group up and asked us each to pray, one at a time. No problem, right? I started it off by praying for a few minutes and the rest of the people followed in line. Now, I was a minor teacher at this fellowship and had no problem praying in public, even though I prefer to pray in private. But most of the other believers were understandably shy about praying in public and so their prayers were rather quiet and simple. As soon as the last person finished, the pastor went on a loud tangent stressing that "God doesn't hear namby-pamby prayers!"

Although he wasn't referring to me, I was righteously angry because he was abusing most of the others with his scathing denouncement. Why was I upset? Because, like with the other example, this wasn't the proper way to motivate believers to produce spiritual works. If the pastor truly didn't think the believers were effectively praying then what should he have done? Certainly not tear them down and condemn them! What did Christ do when his disciples asked him how to pray more effectively? Did Jesus rebuke them for not knowing how to pray? Of course not. He proceeded to teach them *how* to pray! (Luke 11:1-13). What a concept, huh? The fact that the believers at this weeknight service didn't know how to effectively pray—at least in public—was actually a discredit to the pastor. After all, if he had been doing his job by teaching them how to pray in the months prior to this meeting there wouldn't have been a problem. In short, *he* was the one who deserved reproved, not the growing disciples!

One last example: Carol and I were attending a church where the pastor was teaching a series on the nine fruits of the spirit, one sermon per fruit. A wonderful topic, right? Unfortunately, three Sundays in a row the pastor slipped into condo mode. With a noticeable scowl, he yelled at the believers for this and that, including not bringing enough new people to the church. Seriously, how could anyone take an awesome subject like the fruit of the spirit and morph it into condo? Someone infected by legalism could, very easily. How? Because it's *in* them. They've been poisoned by a hideous spiritual disease.

One of this pastor's main problems was that he felt the believers weren't evangelizing like they should. He based this on the fact that there was very little new blood in the congregation. Okay, so this was a legitimate problem, but *condemning the people was not the answer!* What he needed to do was to teach the believers how to produce the fruit of the spirit because anyone who consistently produces the fruit of the spirit will automatically be a light to the lost in this dark, dying world (Matthew 5:13-16). He could have also taught on effective verbal witnessing and took groups out to share the gospel, etc. Regardless, beating up the congregation wasn't the answer. As with the previous example, the pastor was projecting his anger on the wrong party because, when it came down to it, *he* was the one responsible for teaching the believers how to be effective witnesses, as well as set the example.

Needless to say, trying to get people to do spiritual activities based on shaming and condemning is from the legalistic school of counterfeit Christianity. If you come across it, beware; it's not a good sign.

Examples of Authoritarianism in the New Testament

In **Chapter 2** and **3** we went over some examples of authoritarian abuse by the religious leaders of Israel in the 1st century, so let's focus our attention here on the early church.

Paul founded the Corinthian church on his second missionary journey. He stayed in Corinth for at least a year and a half feeding the believers the Word of God before venturing off to other areas (Acts 18:11). Two or three years later Paul heard some disturbing news about the church so he wrote them a few letters of instruction, encouragement and correction. The epistles known as 1 Corinthians and 2 Corinthians are the two surviving letters.

Notice Paul's comments in this passage:

> **You gladly put up with fools since you are so wise!** [20]
> **In fact, you even put up with anyone who enslaves**
> **you or exploits you or takes advantage of you or**
> **pushes himself forward or slaps you in the face.** [21] **To**
> **my shame I admit that we were too weak for that!**
> **2 Corinthians 11:19-21**

During Paul's absence some arrogant authoritarians rose up and were abusing the believers. As you can see, he blatantly calls these corrupt leaders "fools".

Paul then details five ways in which the authoritarians were abusing the believers:

"Enslaves you". This refers to a general atmosphere of bondage, including excessive rules that quench the spirit of freedom in Christ. This was covered in the previous chapter.

"Exploits you". 'Exploit' means "to use selfishly for one's own ends." This likely refers to excessive demands for financial support in light of the fact that the same Greek word is used in Luke 20:47 to describe Jesus' denouncement of legalists' "*devouring* widows' houses".

"Takes advantage of you". This refers to all manner of manipulation, including intimidation and social pressure.

"Pushes himself forward". This refers to lording it over people with an authoritarian spirit, something which fivefold ministers *aren't* supposed to do. We'll address this further in the next section.

"Slaps you in the face". Apparently the legalists resorted to physical abuse to humiliate the believers, but this could also be a figurative reference to humiliating abuse in general. Either way, both are wrong. Abuse is the misuse of power.

Paul then points out in verse 21 that he never resorted to these types of fleshly tactics when he established the church. Why didn't he? Because Paul was a *godly* minister and not one poisoned by legalism.

All five of these practices are typical of authoritarians and are condemned in Scripture. Please be aware of each and don't tolerate it if any should surface in your fellowship.

Pastors (and Other Leaders) are NOT Supposed to "Lord it Over" People

Concerning "lording it over" believers, let's revisit an important passage we observed last chapter and the beginning of this one:

> **To the elders among you, I appeal as a fellow elder, a witness of Christ's sufferings and one who also will share in the glory to be revealed: [2] Be shepherds [pastors] of <u>God's flock</u> that is <u>under your care</u>, <u>serving as overseers</u>—not because you must, but because you are willing, as God wants you to be; not greedy for money, but eager <u>to serve</u>; [3] <u>not lording it over those entrusted to you</u>, but being examples to the flock. [4] And when <u>the Chief Shepherd</u> appears, you will receive the crown of glory that will never fade away.**
>
> **1 Peter 5:1-4**

As you can see in verses 2-3, the Bible condemns the practice of pastors "lording it over" others outright. Earlier this chapter we saw that "lording it over" means to try to control or subjugate people in the sense of being the ultimate authority. The passage says that pastors are to serve as "overseers" and not lord it over those entrusted to their care. In light of this, whatever else 'oversee' means, we can be sure that it does *not* mean to lord it over people. This applies to spiritual leaders of all types, whatever tag they go by in their particular camp (bishop, elder, reverend, associate pastor, overseer, prophet, teacher, deacon, etc.).

It's important to understand how spiritual leaders are supposed to oversee others so we don't allow those who are over us to oversee us in the wrong way. Genuine ministers are to oversee believers in two ways—in a *protective* sense and in a *directive* sense:

> ➢ **Ministers are *protective*** in the sense of guarding people from false teachers and their false doctrines, not to mention wolves in general, whether legalists or libertines.
> ➢ **Ministers are *directive*** in the sense of directing the affairs of the fellowship and giving people their God-given vision for the ministry. This includes providing believers the encouragement and opportunity to excel in their gifting & calling within the framework of that vision.

Needless to say, overseeing in these senses has nothing to do with lording it over people.

Lording it over people is authoritarianism and this can be both obvious and subtle. Here's an obvious example: I was at a restaurant with someone who was technically over me in the Lord, although he wasn't my pastor. Out of nowhere he started an argument by saying I needed to pursue getting a ministerial license so I could start marrying and burying people. He added that I needed to stop "pissing around" with the teaching ministry I was regularly giving at two local churches. His manner was rude and uncalled for, not to mention dictatorial. I happened to know that he was frustrated at the time about something and he was clearly projecting this frustration on me, the nearest person available. I told him that I had no interest in marrying or burying people and, in fact, the New Testament doesn't even mention these works, at least as far as ministerial duties go. I then told him that I was doing precisely what I was called to do—teach God's Word. I also relayed how I had been more involved in ministry in the previous two years than he was and very much so. In other words, if either of us were to correct the other for wasting time and not being diligent in ministry, it should've been the other way around. I didn't feed his argumentative spirit, of course; I merely shared the facts. If someone who is over you in the Lord abuses you in this manner I encourage you to do likewise. Don't feed the contentiousness, but be sure to tell him/her the facts of the matter and convey that you're not going to tolerate bullying of any kind. Be as covert or overt as you need to be.

Here's a more subtle example: A friend of mine visited a church in California where the pastor brought up a movie that was about to be released in theaters. The pastor instructed the congregation not to see this movie because he intended on viewing it and would inform them if they should. My friend couldn't believe his ears and neither could I when he told me. This is an example of Christianity gone wrong. It is one thing for believers to ask their pastors for their opinion of a movie, but it's quite another for a minister to tell believers not to see a film because he's going to watch it first and then *tell them* if they can see it. This may not be hardcore authoritarian abuse, but it's still authoritarianism and it's just not healthy. It's behavior like this that encourages a *dependent* and *immature* spirit in believers. It cultivates weakness, not strength. Strong believers—maturing believers—don't need their pastor's permission to watch a movie or do anything else along these lines. They make their *own* decisions. If they make a mistake and discover that they've exposed themselves to unhealthy material or a bad environment they simply make a 180, just like their pastor would. But they would never learn to do this if their pastor always made these kinds of decisions for them.

There was a big church in my area in the 80s where the pastor had an overtly authoritarian spirit. I know because I heard many of his sermons on radio and cassette. This pastor had an overwhelming air and it was easy to see why people would follow him, but I didn't sense any love or joy in his words. I later developed a friendship with someone who attended this church for a season. Some of his relatives and friends were members, but they were so wowed by the pastor's natural leadership qualities that they failed to see his potentially harmful spirit. My friend, on the other hand, wasn't so wowed. He said he visited the church many times before deciding not to stay. He told his relatives and friends, "He's a charismatic speaker and all, but I just don't see any love or joy there." It wasn't much later that the church had two mass exoduses over a period of about a year.[37] By this point the church had a bad reputation in the community and it never really recovered. The pastor died prematurely less than fifteen years later.

Before the breakdown and decline of this church there were red flags of authoritarianism everywhere: congregants had to get the pastor's approval for large purchases, like a refrigerator; if someone left the assembly his or her relatives and friends were instructed to cut all ties; people were encouraged to quit their well-paying jobs and start their own businesses; men with longer hair were pressured to cut it and maintain shorter hair length; the entrance gates were closed and the doors locked during services; believers were discouraged from going to the restroom during the ridiculously long Sunday services; individuals were literally screamed at in front of the congregation if the pastor thought they were going astray; etc. If you ever saw the excellent 1980 film *Guyana Tragedy: The Story of Jim Jones*, this church was bordering on being that authoritarian.

---

[37] Not splits, since a split is when those who leave an assembly start their own church. An exodus is when believers leave and disperse to other fellowships.

Since the Bible plainly teaches that pastors are not to "lord it over" believers, they have no business telling congregants where to work, how to wear their hair, what kind of car to buy, what kind of clothes to wear, what style of music to listen to, what kind of movies to watch, etc. The only exception would be if any one of these elements is causing the believer or others to slip into immorality (e.g. a woman is wearing apparel that incites lust). Pastors and other ministerial leaders are not the final authority in believers' lives, God is. The believer should simply be fed the Word of God and encouraged to develop a relationship with the Lord. This includes teaching them important principles like how to guard their hearts as the wellspring of life (Proverbs 4:23). As they grow they'll develop wisdom and naturally make their own decisions about these types of things.

Respecting Ministers

The converse is true as well. Congregants have *no business whatsoever* judging and criticizing fivefold ministers on these types of neutral issues. These things are a matter of taste and personal opinion, not moral absolutes. If a minister is walking in unrepentant sin, like adultery, then—by all means—confront and rebuke him or her. This would be an example of using the Law lawfully, as shown in 1 Timothy 1:8-11, which we examined in **Chapter 3**.[38] Otherwise please shutteth thy mouth and keep your opinions of taste to yourself. I'm not being mean; I'm just saying this for your protection and blessing. How so? The Bible says point blank that believers shouldn't pass judgment on other believers in regards to disputable matters, which includes matters of taste (Romans 14:1,10,13). Not to mention, Jesus plainly said that if we unjustly judge others we ourselves will reap judgment (Matthew 7:1-5), how much more so if we judge hardworking ministers who we're *supposed* to esteem highly? As the Bible says:

---

[38] See the section *Law is Made Not for the Righteous*.

> **Now we ask you, brothers, to <u>respect those
> who work hard among you</u>, who are <u>over you in the
> Lord</u> and who admonish you. ¹³ <u>Hold them in the
> highest regard in love because of their work</u>. Live in
> peace with each other.**
>
> **1 Thessalonians 5:12-13**

This is talking about respecting those who are "over you in the Lord" and refers to fivefold ministers, like pastors and teachers (Ephesians 4:11-13). The reason it says to respect those who "work hard among you" is because it's impossible to respect lazy ministers. For instance, it's impossible for me to respect ministers who are obviously lazy when it comes to the teaching and preaching of God's Word. Think about it, roughly 50% of every church service is devoted to the ministry of the Word, which is necessary for the feeding, inspiration and growth of believers (Acts 6:2). As such, you would think that ministers would be *prepared* before they teach or preach and that they'd serve with *all their hearts* (Colossians 3:23), but sometimes—too often—I observe ministers just winging it, and you can always tell. This is laziness and it's impossible to respect ministers who give lazy sermons, whether at a home-styled fellowship, a mega-church or anywhere in between.

By the way, I'm not suggesting that ministers should write-out their teachings verbatim and read them word-for-word, which is dullest form of sermonizing. Generally speaking, ministers should have a topic with a mental or physical outline while simultaneously relying on the Holy Spirit for unction and spontaneity.

While on the subject, please be careful not to judge whether a minister is hardworking or lazy in regards to things that aren't his or her assignment. Although all fivefold ministers are to be effective in teaching or preaching God's Word, they each have different callings and therefore different assignments. For instance, my calling is to teach the Word of God in varying formats—books, internet, public speaking, etc. This is the area I'm obliged to focus and work at diligently, and I do. Please don't judge me for things I'm not called to focus on, like marrying and burying people or visiting folks in the hospital. Unless God moves me to do these types of things I won't do it. Don't get me wrong; of course I visit people in the hospital who are close to me, but it's impossible to visit every person I know and their family members who are in the hospital or sick at home and—at the same time—carry out my God-given assignment effectively.

One of the problems with the modern Church is that believers don't realize the Church is a *body*, which means *every member has their place and their part*. If YOU feel moved to visit someone who's sick and minister to them, then—by all means—do it. Don't kick back and denounce so-and-so for not doing it. Don't expect the pastor of your fellowship to run around like a headless chicken doing every task of the church and *then* expect him to be prayed-up, Worded-up and anointed of God. If his (or her) sermon is lousy it's certainly not because he's lazy, but rather because he unwisely spread himself too thin by trying to do everything for the church, which is partially his own fault. This is precisely why the apostles of the early Church in Jerusalem gave the responsibility of food distribution over to other individuals so they could *focus* on their specific assignment—"prayer and the ministry of the Word" (Acts 6:1-4).

Getting back to 1 Thessalonians 5:12-13, this passage is talking about respecting ministers who work hard and are "over you in the Lord." These people are over you *in the Lord*. They're over you at the fellowship you're a part of, but they're not over you in matters of style and taste, like clothing, hair styles, food, romantic interests or types of music, movies and recreation. They're over you *spiritually*, not over you in areas of personal taste.

Lastly, the passage says to hold hard-working ministers in the highest regard "because of their work." Respect them for *their work*— their calling and anointing from God—and not in regards to items of personal taste. If you think a minister has bad taste in women, too bad, it's his choice. If you don't like her choice of vehicle, it's none of your business. If you don't like the way he prefers to dress at church, at home or when he's out and about, too bad, mind your own beeswax.

Amen.

"Obey Your Leaders and Submit to their Authority"

While on the subject of the believer's attitude toward spiritual leaders, it's necessary to bring up this passage:

> **Obey your leaders and submit to their authority. They keep watch over you as men who must give an account. Obey them so that their work will be a joy, not a burden, for that would be of no advantage to you."**
>
> **Hebrews 13:17**

The verse instructs us to "obey" those who are over us in the Lord and "submit to their authority." Does this mean to obey and submit in the absolute sense? If your spiritual leaders told you to jump off the roof of a building, should you do it? Of course not. If they instructed you to do something immoral, should you do it? Clearly not. So these instructions have obvious parameters or limitations. Such limitations can be observed throughout the rest of the New Testament. The exhortation here to obey spiritual leaders is akin to other appeals in the Epistles for wives to obey husbands, children to obey parents and believers to obey governing authorities. Such instructions are only applicable when the authority gives good or neutral commands. Otherwise "we must obey God rather than human beings" (Acts 5:29).

One rule of Bible interpretation is that we must "interpret Scripture with Scripture," meaning our interpretation of a passage must gel with what the rest of Scripture teaches on that topic, as long as it's relevant.[39] In other words, the Bible itself is the ultimate context of every passage and, therefore, every passage must be interpreted within *that* context. Clearer and more detailed passages obviously trump the more ambiguous and sketchy ones. This encourages balance and keeps believers from taking one or two passages and going to extremes.

---

[39] For instance, dietary laws for Hebrews under the Old Covenant are decidedly *irrelevant* to New Testament believers (see Mark 7:18-19, Colossians 2:16-17, Romans 14:17,20 and 1 Corinthians 10:25).

Consider the above verse. Authoritarian pastors could take it and implement a spirit of domination over their congregants. They could say, for example: "As a believer you are obligated to obey God's Word and God's Word says that you *must* obey me and submit to me." They might say it in a more subtle manner, but — whatever the case — it fosters an unhealthy dictatorial environment.

We know for a fact that this passage doesn't give ministers a license to be authoritarian because, as already stressed, 1 Peter 5:1-4 plainly states that spiritual leaders are to "serve" and *not* "lord it over" believers. Christ himself repeatedly rebuked the arrogance of the religious leaders of 1st century Israel. Matthew 23 is a great example.

Notice what Jesus plainly taught about Christian leadership to his 12 disciples:

> **"You know that the rulers of the Gentiles <u>lord it over them</u>, and their high officials <u>exercise authority over them</u>. [26] <u>Not so with you</u>. Instead, <u>whoever wants to become great among you must be your servant</u>, [27] and <u>whoever wants to be first must be your slave</u> — [28] just as the Son of Man did not come to be served, but to serve, and to give his life as a ransom for many."**
>
> **Matthew 20:25-28**

This doesn't mean, of course, that Christian leaders are to be spineless milksops; Jesus, Peter and Paul were anything but, yet it does reveal the style of leadership believers are to have—an attitude of a servant or slave. Do servants or slaves "lord it over" others? Obviously not. Do they "exercise authority" with a dictatorial air? Again, the answer is obvious. Jesus taught that Christian leaders are not to be like this, period.

With this understanding, never feel obligated to obey or submit to ministers who have an arrogant, authoritarian bearing. If you do, I guarantee you'll be abused in some manner down the road. As for those who have proven their godly character and sound doctrine, please submit to them so that their work will be a joy and not a burden. If their work is a joy they'll obviously serve better and you'll be blessed because of it.

This is just a matter of common sense. Submit to their vision for the local church and do your part to help it manifest. If you can't do this, please leave and find a fellowship with whose vision you can agree. After all, two opposing visions create di-vision.

As far as *obeying* spiritual authorities goes, we've already established that this doesn't mean to obey them in an absolute sense, but—by all means—be sure to obey what they've proven to be true from God's Word as confirmed in your own study time (1 John 2:27). Amen.

The Diotrephes Spirit vs. the Davidic Spirit

The most fascinating example of authoritarian abuse in the New Testament can be found in the shortest "book" of the Bible, the Epistle known as 3 John, which John wrote to his friend Gaius (*GAH-ee-os*). Notice what John says about a certain authoritarian individual:

> **I wrote to the church, but Diotrephes, who loves to be first, will have nothing to do with us.** [10] **So if I come, I will call attention to what he is doing, <u>gossiping maliciously about us</u>. Not satisfied with that, he <u>refuses to welcome the brothers</u>. He also stops those who want to do so and <u>puts them out of the church</u>.**
>
> **3 John 9-10**

John was referring to a leader of one of the churches he oversaw—Diotrephes[40]—who decided to stop welcoming John and other godly ministers in his assembly and even ran a smear campaign against them (!). Furthermore, those in the congregation who objected to Diotrephes' fleshly tactics were swiftly excommunicated! This indicates that Diotrephes was likely the head pastor. After all, who else but the pastor would have the authority to prevent leaders of John's stature from coming and ministering? Who else but the pastor has the power to excommunicate?

---

[40] Pronounced: *dye-OT-rah-feez*.

John readily understood Diotrephes' root problem—he loved to be first (verse 9). In other words, Diotrephes was an arrogant control-freak who wasn't interested in serving others, but rather desired others to serve him. Such an attitude is, of course, in direct opposition to Jesus & the apostles' teachings and example of servant-leadership (Matthew 23:1-11, 2 Corinthians 10:8, 13:10 & 1 Peter 5:2-3).

John may have been renowned for his loving spirit, but he wasn't about to overlook such abuses in the name of peace and niceness; no, he was fully intent on exposing and correcting the man (verse 10). In fact, John's third epistle was/is a public judgment and exposal of Diotrephes' error to every person who has read it ever since! This includes *you* right now.

Sadly, there are ungodly "ministers" in the Church today just like Diotrephes. Mature Christians need to boldly rise up and call attention to the abuses of these selfish control-freaks whenever such abuses occur, like John did—even at the threat of excommunication or losing one's ministry gig. After all, evil thrives when good people do nothing! (Speaking of which, there's nothing more pathetic than weak 'yes men' or 'yes women' who condone corruption in the name of meekness or due to idolization of a relationship, position or sect).

Strong leaders, by contrast, are able to utilize strong people and properly integrate them in their work. Take the example of David, "a man after God's own heart." The Bible goes into quite a bit of detail about David's "mighty men," which were some 53 individuals who helped David become king of Israel (2 Samuel 23:8-39 & 1 Chronicles 11:10-47). These powerful men formed David's inner circle of leadership and were more skilled than David in their areas of expertise (!). Yet David knew his calling and strengths, and was therefore secure and unthreatened. He also knew his limitations. He realized he wasn't going to make it alone because no one makes it alone—no one. All great men and women embrace the help and skills of others. Consequently, David enlisted a formidable group to assist him in fulfilling God's assignment. In short, David didn't automatically view gifted people with an eye of evil suspicion and chase them away. No, he wisely recognized their uniqueness & greatness and released them to operate in their strengths on his team. Thus David became the greatest king of Israel. Oh, that there were more leaders like David in the Church today!

Intimidation

Another clear sign of authoritarianism is intimidation. Let me give a couple examples...

Carol & I visited a church for two months and were considering joining it. This was the same church discussed in the previous chapter. The pastor was a woman and her husband was the assistant pastor; they were basically a pastoral team, which is often the case regardless of who's the head pastor. Carol & I got along with the husband well, but the pastor always seemed to eye us suspiciously, not to mention she often had a sourpuss expression. Every time I was around her I got this feeling like I was a 9 year-old boy who needed direction from his Mommy. I would just shirk it off, of course, but it happened every time I tried to have a conversation with her. Carol said she felt the same thing and told me about a women's meeting at the fellowship: There were about a dozen ladies present. The pastor sat at one end of the long table with her assistant by her side while, strangely, all the other women sat at the other end—as far away from her as possible! Was this just a coincidence or did it confirm what Carol and I were already sensing? The woman projected an intimidating air that was adverse to loving fellowship.

Here's another example: Back when I first became a Christian in 1984 I was reading the Bible voraciously and developing a prayer life. I was setting a sound doctrinal foundation through my Bible studies and the works of quality ministers like Hal Lindsey,[41] but I hadn't found a regular church yet. One Summer Sunday a friend invited me to his family's Nazarene church, so I decided to go and asked my older sister to join us. Although the service was too old-fashioned for my tastes, it was lively enough and full of people. They had a visiting evangelist who obviously knew the pastor well and was familiar with the assembly. At the end of his sermon he conducted an altar call that went on for what seemed like forever. A handful of people went up, evidently regular members of the church, but this didn't satisfy the evangelist. He kept

---

[41] I'm referring to Hal's books that are conducive to spiritual growth—like *The Liberation of Planet Earth* and *There's a New World Coming*—and not his dubious predictions concerning current events at the time he made them. These were predictions, *not* prophecies. He's a teacher, not a prophet.

trying to get people to come up to the altar to get saved, rededicate their lives or whatever. Although I was struggling a bit in certain areas like any young man, I didn't go up because **1.** I was already saved, reading the Word intensely and developing a real walk with God, and **2.** I didn't need to rededicate anything since I was already following the Lord with my whole heart, as best as I knew how. I didn't need to become saved and I didn't need to rededicate my life, so I didn't go up; it was that simple. Although my sister wasn't pursuing the Lord as heartily as I was, she was a Christian, and whether she decided to go up or not wasn't my affair.

Since we didn't go up the minister got increasingly more specific in pinpointing us in the crowd. Although he wasn't able to cite us by name, he kept looking right at us with his piercing gaze. He eventually called out, "There's a young man and a young woman in the back who need to come up here." Subtle he wasn't. Although my sister and I would've appreciated prayer and blessing, neither of us felt comfortable about going up, so we didn't go. Maybe it was because the evangelist made it seem like the altar call was for pathetic backsliders and not legitimate believers who simply needed prayer and blessing. I just didn't feel right about the situation. It was like going up there would've been a surrender to this man's demands rather than a surrender to God, particularly since *I was already surrendered to God.*

At any rate, he gave up and the service ended. I talked briefly with the friendly pastor in the sanctuary and proceeded to walk out by myself. As I walked toward the big opening room, there was a short hallway with a few steps. The evangelist was standing at these steps with his back to the banister. As I walked toward him he looked at me with the same grim visage he had during the altar call, all the while tapping his fingers on the railing. I humbly greeted him and walked past while he stubbornly maintained his stern, intimidating persona.

Now, you tell me, was it right for this minister to treat me like this? It's likely that he thought I was unsaved or backslidden since I wasn't a regular member and I had a "hip" haircut. If so, he was wrong on both counts. Regardless, whether or not I went up to the altar at the end of the service shouldn't affect the way I was treated.

This is ministerial intimidation—making people feel inferior and trying to coerce them to do something through social pressure. I saw it way back then, the very first year I was saved, and you'll see it today in ministers infected by legalism. It has no place in any legitimate ministry.

While neither of these examples is that big a deal, they're not good either. Arrogant manipulation of any kind simply has no place in Church ministry or Church leaders.

Beware of this type of intimidation. If you see it at your fellowship or one you're visiting, it's a big red flag. Don't succumb to it. Don't allow these legalists to make you feel inferior and, please, refuse to do anything that's encouraged through their intimidation.

Legalistic "Accountability"

A minister who preferred small-group churches criticized pastors of large churches on the grounds that it's impossible to be an example to people you can't spend quality time with because the church is so big. It's true that fivefold ministers and elders are called to be examples to younger believers (spiritually speaking),[42] but does this mean that spending considerable time with them is the only way to be a good example? If so, how much time does this require? How much privacy is a fivefold minister or elder allowed? Didn't Paul say strong believers need to keep some things private to prevent those with weak consciences from stumbling? (Romans 14:22). How far do we take this?

I've functioned in both small group settings and mega-churches and I've seen God work in both. There's nothing wrong with preferring one over the other, but it's wrong to condemn the one you don't favor because **1.** a solid scriptural argument can be made for both and **2.** the LORD is big enough to minister in either setting, and everything in between. Remember, God's not one-dimensional.

Consider Yeshua, who was a daily example to the 12 disciples & friends who traveled with him for three years, and also to the other 72 disciples to a lesser degree (Luke 10:1,17). Yet how much of an example was he to the *thousands* who came to see him minister? There's *no way* he could regularly spend time with all these people and maintain a tight relationship with the Father and minister effectively. What Christ did was spend quality time with those within his inner circle—particularly

---

[42] See, for example, 1 Peter 5:3, 1 Corinthians 11:1 and 1 Timothy 4:12.

Peter, James and John—and they would, in turn, set a similar example with those within their sphere of influence. It's the domino effect of positive social impact. This is precisely how legitimate pastors of big churches set the example for their hundreds or thousands of members.

Getting back to the minister's criticisms, he chastised pastors of huge churches by accusing them of having some sinful practice on the side that they were supposedly hiding. He claimed that this was the real reason they weren't interested in being examples to the flock. Wow, what an accusation and what a blanket statement. Surely no pastor of a small fellowship would ever do this! (Obvious sarcasm). If this were true, then consider the pastor of a church I used to go to that had less than 20 members: he fell from the ministry after being caught with his hand in the money jar, amongst other fleshly activities. Simply put, to accuse *all* pastors of big churches of not setting a proper example and enjoying some wicked sin on the side is ridiculous. It also smacks of legalism (see *Legalists are Unreasonably Judgmental* in **Chapter 3**).

Such reasoning stems from a legalistic understanding of accountability. It assumes that believers are all a bunch of weak fools just waiting to rush into sin and hypocrisy, even seasoned fivefold ministers. As such, we need to protect our brothers and sisters by snooping around in their houses and nosing into their personal affairs. In fact, this is the main reason we need "accountability partners." After all, without the watchful eye of some prying elder we're all doomed to going astray. What a sick mentality. Sure, there will always be believers we need to keep an eye on in a protective sense, but we have to be careful that it doesn't become a form of bondage or authoritarianism. It's better to give people the freedom to make a mistake and learn from it than to eye them overbearingly like some mother hen. The former fosters independence while the latter cultivates a dependent, immature spirit. We don't need domineering authoritarians or moronic accountability partners, we need gatherings of warriors and warrioresses!

As for those "believers" in our midst who can't seem to do anything remotely spiritual without someone hovering over them and twisting their arm, isn't it possible that they're not believers at all? Perhaps they're goats in sheep's clothing, so to speak. Let 'em go! The Church is better off without counterfeits. If they're truly genuine they'll come back at some point of their own accord.

This will come as a shock to those with a legalistic understanding of accountability, but there are numerous areas of believers' lives—including fivefold ministers—that are no one's business. Unless a serious sin is involved, what I do in the bathroom or what I do when I go out with my wife or what I enjoy for recreation is no one's business but mine, Carol's and the Lord's.

Here's something else to consider on the issue of accountability: Who oversees the pastor? Usually someone higher up in the pastor's organization that doesn't regularly attend his assembly. It may also be pastors from other fellowships in the area. How closely do these people oversee the pastor? How often do they communicate? Not all that closely or often, right? Furthermore, who oversees those who oversee the pastor? My point is that at some point in spiritual growth close oversight becomes unnecessary. Why? Because the believers have matured. They've established a relationship with God; they walk in the spirit and not in the flesh; and they're quick to repent when they do miss it; etc. This is in line with what a pastor friend told me, which I shared before: "My job is to become unnecessary in the life of the believer." This should be the goal of *all* ministers—disciple people to the point where they walk with God of their own accord and have no need of close pastoral oversight. Unfortunately, too many pastors foster a dependent spirit with their congregants because—consciously or subconsciously—they don't want to lose them and, in some cases, they enjoy having people dependent on them. This is an unhealthy and unscriptural attitude to say the least.

Be on your guard against legalistic forms of "accountability."

Never Condone Condo and Authoritarianism

If you're hooked up with a church where the pastor regularly tears down the congregation, and is stubborn and unrepentant about it, head for the hills! Never submit to a spirit of condemnation. Same thing with a "lord it over" spirit. The two go hand-in-hand. Pray about it, boldly confront it, as led of the Spirit, and disassociate from it if necessary. Make no mistake, if you unwisely opt to tolerate this type of disposition you'll be poisoned one way or another because "Bad company corrupts good character" (1 Corinthians 15:33). It's an axiom.

Beware of Authoritarian Prophets

Before closing this chapter it's necessary to address New Testament prophets because of misunderstandings about this gift. For instance, I've heard it taught that when a prophet prophesies over a believer the believer is obligated to obey the prophecy to the letter and that church leaders are to hold him/her accountable to it. Here are a couple examples: If the believer feels she wants to leave the church—for whatever reason—but is informed she must stay because it was prophesied that she *belonged* to that church. Or if the believer intends on going to college or start a career but he's told he can't because the prophet prophesied that he was to be a missionary to Africa. Absurd, you say? It's been known to happen, typically in Pentecostal churches that adopt an authoritarian spirit.

This is a case of using the gift of prophecy to manipulate people, which is condemned in the New Testament. It's a form of bondage. As such, this topic could've been addressed in the previous chapter, but I decided to cover it here because it's also a form of authoritarian abuse where the prophet's words are viewed as the spoken Word of God in which the believer cannot disagree.

First, I want to stress what a wonderful gift prophecy is to the Church. Prophecies are very encouraging and are able to touch believers in that specific area where they need ministered. For example, Acts 15:32 points out that "Judas and Silas, who themselves were prophets, said much to encourage and strengthen the brothers." This is the purpose of the prophetic gift in the Church and reveals why it is so necessary—it *encourages* and *strengthens* believers. The original Greek word for 'encourage' in this passage means "to cause to move forward." In other words, a prophetic word will inspire believers and provoke them to go forward and fulfill God's call on their lives. Have you ever been in the spiritual doldrums where you're not necessarily walking in sin, but you just seem to lack that spiritual drive and passion for the Lord and your calling? The gift of prophecy has the ability to wake believers from such a stupor and spark them onward. It's an awesome gift and a needed gift. So the office of the prophet should be valued and esteemed in the Church. Unfortunately, too many churches and sects are ignorant of it or the gift lies dormant for various reasons.

While the word of prophecy is important and necessary in the Church this doesn't condone the abuse of it wherein people are made to feel like they're in bondage to a prophetic word that may, in fact, be off or even completely wrong. Nor does it condone the dictatorial antics of prophets who think their prophecies are the Word of God which must be blindly accepted and obeyed to the letter.

The reason such abuse exists is because believers are largely ignorant of the gift of prophecy in the New Testament era. They confuse the office of the Old Testament prophet with that of the New Testament prophet. This shouldn't be done because they're very different. In the Old Testament, what the prophet said was equal to the Word of the LORD and kings made extremely important decisions at their word, like going to war. The primary purpose of the Old Testament prophet was to lead and guide Israel through the Word of the LORD and, in fact, a lot of their words became Holy Scripture, which we know today as the prophetic books of the Old Testament.

For this reason, the words of a prophet had to be 100% accurate. If their words were proven to be false they were to no longer be regarded as prophets and, in fact, were to be put to death (Deuteronomy 18:20-22). If an Old Testament prophet missed it *just once*, they were done. This, of course, didn't happen in cases where the king and other leaders were corrupt and actually *wanted* false prophets to comfort them with lies, which occurred all too often in Israel and Judah.

Jesus Christ has replaced the Old Testament prophet in the New Covenant (Hebrews 1:1-2). In fact, he's *The* **Prophet** that the Hebrews had been expecting for almost 1500 years (Deuteronomy 18:15, John 6:14 & 7:40).

The New Testament prophet is different than the Old Testament prophet. The gift of prophecy was not given to the body of Christ for the purpose of leading and guiding God's people because believers are born-again spiritually and have the Holy Spirit *within them* for this very purpose. As Jesus said: "But when he, the Spirit of truth, comes, he will guide you into all truth. He will not speak on his own; he will speak only what he hears, and he will tell you what is yet to come" (John16:13).

Since it's the Holy Spirit's job to guide believers in the New Testament era, we don't need the gift of prophecy for this function, as was the case in the Old Testament. So when a prophet prophesies over you and says you're to do this or that or go here or there, don't receive it unless the Spirit has *already* been leading you in that direction. In other words, prophecies in the New Testament are to *confirm* what the Holy Spirit has *already* been leading you to do. You could say it's an external source to confirm or compliment the believer's internal source of direction from God. I suppose it's possible that the order could be reversed, particularly in cases where the believer isn't sensitive to the moving of the Spirit, but both external and internal should match up.

How do you know if the Holy Spirit's leading you to do something or not do something? The Bible says we are to "let the peace of Christ rule in your heart" (Colossians 3:15). In the Greek "rule" means govern. Say if you have a decision to make and you've prayed about it, as shown in Proverbs 3:6. How do you know what God wants you to do? Simple: What do you have a peace about doing? Which course of action do you have a 'good feeling' about? That's the direction you should take. You'll naturally become better at this as you grow in the Lord.

There may be times, of course, when this is somewhat inapplicable because the prophet may warn you of a *forthcoming* negative situation, like a job loss or a disaster. The purpose of this type of prophecy is to prepare you and encourage you to get through the negative situation. This was the function of Agabus' prophecy to Paul when he warned him of the severe persecutions he was going to face in Jerusalem, which we'll look at momentarily. With these types of prophecies, if the event doesn't come to pass then the prophet obviously missed it and I'd be a little leery the next time he or she gives such a word.

Why am I bringing all this up? Because in the New Testament era you are *not* in bondage to the words of some prophet who likes to throw his or her weight around. You're to be led and guided by the Holy Spirit, not a prophet. So if some prophet prophesies over you and it doesn't bear witness with your spirit, throw it out! Never allow yourself to be manipulated into doing something you don't have a peace from God about doing!

Judging Prophecies

I want to prove to you beyond any shadow of doubt that you are not obligated to accept any prophecy that you don't have a peace about in your spirit. In fact, the New Testament *repeatedly* instructs believers to *judge prophecies* before embracing them.

Let's look at three such passages, starting with this one:

> **Dear friends, do not believe every spirit, but
> test the spirits to see whether they are from God,
> because many false prophets have gone out into the
> world.   1 John 4:1**

As you can see, the topic is false prophets and their false prophesies, which is why John encourages believers to "test the spirits," which means to try or examine the prophecy. If you have to test the prophecy then there's a possibility that it might be wrong.

How do you test prophecies? **1.** By the Word of God and **2.** by the leading of the Holy Spirit in your spirit. If a prophet says to a married woman, "You are to attend to my sexual needs" it can be thrown out as a false prophecy because it violates the morality of the Bible; in fact, the "prophet" himself should no longer be considered a prophet since his "fruit" has exposed him as false (Matthew 7:15-23). If a prophet tells you to quit your job in order to do such-and-such for the church and you don't have a peace about it then don't accept it.

My wife, Carol, was at an assembly where a pastor exhorted her to do secretarial work for the church, even though they already had a secretary who didn't work outside the church. This was to free-up the secretary to concentrate more on worship, etc. Carol rejected this "word from the Lord" right away because she already had her hands full with a full-time job as a general manager. More importantly, she didn't feel any moving of the Spirit to do secretarial work in her spare time. None. She didn't have a peace about it (Colossians 3:15). The pastor who gave this word may have been a sincere man of God, but he missed it on this occasion because the Spirit wasn't speaking to the other person (in this case, Carol). The Holy Spirit never brings confusion and conflict, but rather comfort and peace (although the Spirit will convict, of course).

Let's look at another passage:

> **Be joyful always; [17] pray continually; [18] give thanks in all circumstances, for this is God's will for <u>you</u> <u>in Christ Jesus.</u>**
> **[19] Do not put out the Spirit's fire; [20] <u>do not treat prophecies with contempt.</u> [21] <u>Test everything.</u> <u>Hold on to the good.</u>**
>
> 1 Thessalonians 5:16-21

The reason I include verses 16-18 in this quote is to show that Paul was addressing *all believers* in Thessalonica and, as such, his words apply to *all believers* today.

With that understanding, he says that we are not to treat prophecies with contempt, meaning we should never look down on the gift of prophecy. Why would a believer be tempted to look down on prophesying? Because they're not always 100% correct. You heard me. They're not always completely accurate. Let me explain.

New Testament prophets speak by unction, that is, by spiritual influence. They pick something up in the spirit and speak by faith from there. Everything in our covenant is by faith. Since those with the gift of prophecy are human beings and human beings are imperfect, it's always possible for a person who's prophesying to be inaccurate in some ways, even though they're legitimately picking something up in the spirit. It might simply be a matter of immaturity or inexperience where they have not yet fully learned to distinguish the vile (flesh) from the precious (spirit).

For instance, some with the gift of prophecy may legitimately pick something up in the spirit but wrap their prophecy in their pet doctrine or conviction. They might say, for instance, "Yea, I the LORD love thee and you are greatly blessed; now go out and witness door-to-door in your neighborhood." In this case the prophet had an encouraging word from the Lord, but then he throws in his *own* conviction.

This explains why Paul added "Test everything. Hold on to the good" after instructing believers not to hold prophecies in contempt. Why? Because it's possible for the prophecy to be partially right-on and partially off. Keep in mind that there were no verse numbers in the original text; verses 20 and 21 go together. In verse 20 Paul's talking about prophecies and then instructs the believers in verse 21 to test or judge every prophecy with the conclusion that they are to hold on to the good, that is, what is accurate.

Say a prophet gives you a personal prophecy but only half of it bears witness with your spirit. The rest of it doesn't apply, and you know it. Should you discard the entire prophecy? No. Paul says to hold on to what is good. The rest of it should be thrown out or, at most, put on the shelf until you have a peace about it. Are you getting what God's Word is saying? Don't despise prophecies just because people with this gift miss it in certain ways now and then. The prophetic word is good because it encourages believers to move forward and fulfill their calling. But don't blindly embrace every jot and tittle prophesied over you; only accept what you have a peace about, as confirmed by the Holy Spirit. Put the rest aside or throw it out entirely, if necessary. But please don't throw out the person who prophesies or their ministry, unless of course their "fruit" has exposed them as false (Matthew 7:15-23).

Let's look at one final passage on this matter:

> **Two or three <u>prophets</u> should speak, <u>and the others should weigh carefully what is said</u>. [30] And if a revelation comes to someone who is sitting down, the first speaker should stop. [31] For you can all prophesy in turn so that everyone may be instructed and encouraged. [32] The spirits of prophets are subject to the control of prophets. [33] For God is not a God of disorder but of peace**
>
> **1 Corinthians 14:29-33**

This passage specifically addresses the New Testament prophet. It's not talking about someone in the body who gives a prophecy, but rather those who are in the office of a prophet, which is part of the fivefold ministry (Ephesians 4:11-13). Like the two other passages above, this one stresses that believers should weigh carefully what the prophet says, meaning examine and judge it.

Some have suggested that "the others" refers to other prophets, as if the only valid people who can test the prophecy of a prophet are other prophets. This isn't so for four reasons: **1.** The other two passages above say that *believers in general* are to examine and judge prophetic words. Why would this passage change that? Scripture interprets Scripture. **2.** The natural reading of the passage shows that "the others" refers to the same people Paul was addressing in verse 26 where he said, "What then shall we say, *brothers*? When you come together, *everyone* has a hymn, or a word of instruction, a revelation, a tongue or an interpretation." **3.** Since Paul was clearly addressing all believers in verse 26 he would have naturally specified who "the others" were in verse 29 *if* he was referring only to prophets, but he didn't. **4.** The notion that only another fivefold prophet can judge a prophet's words just doesn't make sense and creates all kinds of obvious difficulties. What if there's no other prophet present at the church gathering, which is often the case? Would the believers have to blindly embrace what the prophet says, including the pastor? Even if there are other prophets present, wouldn't it be silly for the pastor to have to turn to another prophet and ask, "Is what he said true?" What if two or three prophets got into cahoots and agreed to agree with one another's prophecy? The notion that only another prophet can judge a prophet's prophecy opens the door for authoritarian abuse.

In summary, it's the believer's responsibility to examine and judge prophecies based on God's Word and the leading of the Holy Spirit within, hold on to the good and throw out the bad. This is a good thing— a wise thing—because it protects the believer from abuse, including manipulation to do things that aren't God's will for their lives.

The Example of Agabus the Prophet

All this information is good, but it helps to see an actual example from the Scriptures, so let's look at Agabus. Agabus was a New Testament prophet; a good and respected prophet. Notice how he successfully predicted a famine:

> During this time <u>some prophets</u> came down
> from Jerusalem to Antioch. [28] <u>One of them, named
> Agabus</u>, stood up and <u>through the Spirit predicted
> that a severe famine would spread over the entire
> Roman world</u>. <u>(This happened during the reign of
> Claudius.)</u> [29] The disciples, each according to his
> ability, <u>decided to provide help</u> for the brothers living
> in Judea. [30] This they did, sending their gift to the
> elders by Barnabas and Saul.
>
> Acts 11:27-30

As you can see, Agabus was a prophet. He came to Antioch from Jerusalem with some other prophets and prophesied a famine that would negatively affect the people of Judea. The great historian, Josephus, documented this famine as occurring around 46 AD when Claudius was the Roman emperor. So Agabus was right about the famine and it was good that the Christians at Antioch believed his prophecy and compassionately sent an offering to Judea.

Agabus was obviously a highly respected prophet otherwise the believers wouldn't have sent aid to Judea. Think about it: If some Joe Blow off the street wandered into your fellowship and said there was going to be a famine in a bordering nation would you blindly accept it and dish out the cash? Not likely, and wisely so. This indicates that Agabus was a renowned and respected prophet. Also notice that the believers "decided to provide help" (verse 29), meaning no one commanded them to give with a dictatorial air. Furthermore, this gives the impression that they *decided* after weighing the prophecy and discerning the leading of the Holy Spirit. They had a peace about it so they generously gave. We should do likewise if someone prophesies something along these lines in our circles, but if you have a bad gut feeling about it I wouldn't go along with it.

I mention this passage to show that Agabus was a good prophet, a respected prophet, and an accurate prophet. However, this doesn't mean he was perfect. If he and other New Testament prophets were 100% right 100% of the time the Scriptures wouldn't instruct us to examine and judge their prophecies and hold on to the good. As a matter of fact, Paul had to do just this with another one of Agabus' prophecies:

> Leaving the next day, we reached Caesarea and
> stayed at the house of Philip the evangelist, one of the
> seven. [9] He had four unmarried daughters who
> prophesied.
> [10] After we had been there a number of days,
> <u>a prophet named Agabus</u> came down from Judea.
> [11]Coming over to us, <u>he took Paul's belt, tied his own
> hands and feet with it and said, "The Holy Spirit
> says, 'In this way the Jews of Jerusalem will bind the
> owner of this belt and will hand him over to the
> Gentiles.' "</u>   Acts 21:8-11

Agabus obviously picked up something in the spirit about Paul
and proceeded to speak in faith. Notice the impact this prophecy had:

> When we heard this, we and the people there
> <u>pleaded with Paul not to go up to Jerusalem.</u> [13] Then
> Paul answered, "Why are you weeping and breaking
> my heart? I am ready not only to be bound, but also
> to die in Jerusalem for the name of the Lord Jesus."
> [14] When he would not be dissuaded, we gave up and
> said, "The Lord's will be done."
>   Acts 21:12-14

The other believers unwisely accepted Agabus' prophecy at face
value and took it in a negative sense, that is, they assumed that it *wasn't*
God's will for Paul to go to Jerusalem. They consequently tried to
discourage the apostle from going, even to the extent of weeping! Yet
notice that Agabus never said it *wasn't* God's will for Paul to go to
Jerusalem, he merely informed him of the intense persecutions he would
experience by going there. Acts 23:11 verifies beyond any shadow of
doubt that it *was* God's will for the apostle to witness for Him in
Jerusalem. With this understanding, the obvious purpose of Agabus'
prophecy was to warn Paul of the troubles he was going to face so that
he'd have the grace to trust God and persevere when it happened.

After hearing the prophecy and being discouraged by the others
who took Agabus' prophecy the wrong way, Paul practiced precisely

what he taught: He weighed Agabus' prophecy carefully, held on to the good, and made the decision to go to Jerusalem based on the leading of the Holy Spirit. In other words, Paul had a peace about going to Jerusalem despite Agabus' warning and despite the discouraging antics of the believers.

But there's more: Agabus' prophecy was good in that it prepared Paul for the severe persecutions he would face in Jerusalem, but the details of his prophecy weren't wholly accurate. Agabus said that the Jews in Jerusalem would bind up Paul's hands and feet and deliver him to the Roman government, but this isn't what happened. Nine days after arriving in Jerusalem the Jews apprehended Paul for the purpose of murdering him, not to turn him over to the Romans; furthermore, the Romans actually saved Paul from the Jews. The soldiers then bound him with chains and took him into custody, but as soon as they found out Paul was a Roman citizen they released him. This is all detailed in Acts 21:30-33 and 22:25-30.

As you can see, Agabus was a respected prophet and rightly so. He accurately predicted that Paul was going to suffer great persecution in Jerusalem and he was right that the apostle was going to be bound hand and foot. This warning helped prepare Paul for his mission and gave him the grace to persevere when persecuted, but—clearly—some of the details of Agabus' prophecy were off.

What this indicates is that Agabus legitimately picked up something from the Spirit, something Paul needed to hear, but as Agabus spoke in faith he missed some of the details. Frankly, these details are insignificant in the grand scheme of things because it was enough that Paul was warned of the troubles he was about to face. And, remember, Agabus never told Paul not to go to Jerusalem; it was the other believers who mistook his words and tried to stop him from going.

This information is important because it proves that New Testament prophets can miss it even while they legitimately pick something up in the spirit. This is why believers must test prophecies by the Word of God and the leading of the Holy Spirit. This is what Paul did and he was blessed because of it. Amen.

Chapter 8

The Hideous Beast and Its Four Limbs

We've covered a lot of material in describing general legalism and its four "limbs," possibly more detail than any other book on the subject, but this was necessary so that believers can readily discern this spiritual disease—in themselves and others. After all, legalism cannot be dealt with and eliminated unless it's first recognized. The most dangerous enemy is a hidden enemy.

The reason I segmented legalism into five basic strains is because this disease is such a hideous behemoth. Dissecting it into five main parts makes it convenient to ingest the material. Furthermore, learning to differentiate the five strains will help you recognize the form of legalism with which you're dealing and will also assist in eliminating it through spiritual warfare, which we'll address next chapter.

As you probably noticed, my descriptions of the five categories of legalism are based on both Scripture and decades of experience. I discerned these different strains in some of the ministries that Carol & I have been involved with, as well as the numerous Christians I've known over the years. Of course, I've had to deal with legalism rearing its ugly head in my own life.

I'd like to reemphasize that just because people show signs of one or more of these forms of legalism it doesn't automatically mean that they're dyed-in-the-wool legalists. It simply indicates that they're infected to some degree. Again, there are levels of infection. I've only experienced light levels of infection in my own life, so it was easy for me to purge the disease once I discerned it. Others are more deeply infected because it's something that has built up over time, sometimes decades. In such cases it will naturally take more for them to walk free, whether more time, more prayer, more Word, more insight, more anointing, or what have you. Some people, on the other hand, are so direly poisoned that they're essentially modern-day Pharisees or Teachers of the Law. Such legalists will be arrogant, hostile, stubborn, self-deluded and unrepentant, just like the Pharisees and Teachers of the Law were during Jesus' earthly ministry.

Recapping Legalism and its Four Limbs

Let's briefly summarize the five basic strains of legalism:

General Legalism refers to legalism in general. It's an obsession with legalities and could just as well be described as law-ism or rule-ism. It's the emphasis on the outer at the expense of the inner. As such, outward conformity to the letter of the law is what's most important to legalists. For instance, as long as you go to multiple church services each week, wear the "right" clothes and say the right things you're good to go; it doesn't matter that you're a practicing liar, gossip, slanderer, abuser, thief, drunkard, druggie or porn addict the rest of the week. Why? Because legalism is a spirit of religious hypocrisy. It's only concerned with the *appearances* of godliness, not godliness itself. It's *fake* Christianity.

Rigid Sectarianism refers to an unhealthy devotion to one's sect or group. People infected by this strain accept or reject others based on whether or not they're part of *their* group and how devoted they are to *their* sect's distinctive doctrines and rules. All pseudo-Christian groups are, of course, steeped in this, like the Jehovah's False Witnesses and Mormons, but Evangelical, Charismatic and Mainline groups can be infected just as easily. Legalism is no respecter of church, ministry or denominational boundaries. It can infect anyone, anywhere, anytime, but only if you're unaware of it and allow it.

The Spirit of Religious Formal Death is a sterile "go through the motions" disposition. The older a sect or person is, the easier it is to fall into this legalistic rut. Groups that veer toward formality and ritualism naturally have a greater tendency of being infected by this strain. Don't get me wrong here as there's a time and place for formality and ritual,[43] but each must be kept in check; they shouldn't spill over into every area of life. If you're a spiritual believer and the church services you're experiencing are dreadfully boring you can be sure the assembly is infected by this strain.

The Spirit of Bondage is a sourpuss spirit that's obsessed with numerous religious rules. You'll observe many peculiar rules and sense a suffocating vibe of bondage rather than freedom. Becoming an elder or teacher is more involved than flying to the moon; sometimes merely becoming a member of the congregation. Contrast this to what Paul simply taught in 1 Corinthians 14:26 (and, no, I'm not suggesting that people of very questionable character should be allowed to serve at churches). To leave such groups is tantamount to getting a divorce and disobeying the LORD because these types seek to keep you in bondage to them. They'll even cite prophesies to wield power and prevent you from leaving. Groups that try to put New Testament believers under the yoke of Old Testament Law are steeped in this form of legalism, like the Hebrew Roots movement.

The Spirit of Condemnation and Authoritarianism refers to those who typically tear down believers rather than build them up. Since the Bible clearly teaches that ministers are supposed to build believers up, those who tear them down are actually doing the opposite of their purpose as ministers! The teachings of those infected by this

---

[43] Ritual will take you further than desire because it's habitual—it's something you do no matter what because it's a *disciplined* activity. Desire, by contrast, is whimsical.

strain aren't about setting believers free but rather tearing them down. It's all about power, intimidation, fear and manipulation. These types love to dominate others with a "lord it over" disposition rather than serve or lead by example. As such, they're not truly ministers because 'minister' means "servant."

The Beast of Legalism

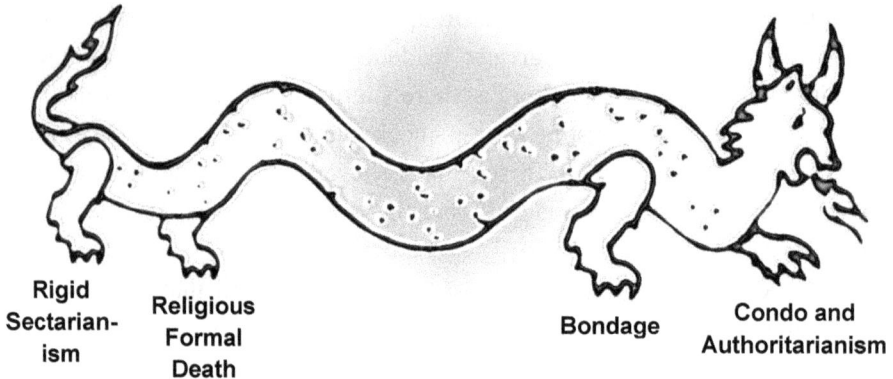

Rigid Sectarian-ism

Religious Formal Death

Bondage

Condo and Authoritarianism

A Quintessential Example of Legalism

Now that we have a detailed biblical understanding of legalism and its many manifestations, allow me to share a fascinating brush with legalism I had twenty years ago.

It was late June, 1993. My aging mother wanted to see Colonial Williamsburg, Virginia, so I took her. We went south from Northeast Ohio into the heart of West Virginia where we stopped to eat. We observed a large framed photo on the wall of the restaurant, which we discovered was a picture of the New River Gorge Bridge in South Central WV. The bridge was so spectacular we decided to take the detour to see it.

When we arrived at the bridge the park was full of visitors. I had driven over five hours and it was a real hot one so I immediately took off my muscle shirt. After unleashing some pent-up energy—dashing around and taking pictures—my mother and I climbed down the lengthy wooden stairs that culminated in a scenic overlook. Mom immediately sat down at the overlook while I proceeded to get some shots of the bridge.

I only half noticed a well-dressed family on the overlook platform. The family consisted of a young couple and maybe three little kids. They were done sightseeing and started to climb back up. While enjoying the view and snapping pictures, I observed that the husband turned around and came back down the stairs to hand my mother a pamphlet. Curious, I joined them and discovered that it was an evangelistic tract.

A smile beamed on my face as I said to the young man, "Oh, you're a Christian, so are we!" He looked at me with an utterly dead countenance, turned around and walked back up the stairs, saying nothing. We were dumbfounded by this peculiar reaction but didn't give it much thought and certainly didn't let it ruin our visit to the park.

At the time, I belonged to a thriving church that had a spirit of life and grace (my mother too, albeit a different assembly) so this was a relatively new experience for me. In other words, even though I was almost ten years old in the Lord, I wasn't used to run-ins with sourpuss religionists.

Over the many years since this experience the Lord has repeatedly brought me back to it. It's sad, but the man was clearly a prisoner of legalism. How so? Think about it, he couldn't even enjoy an afternoon at the park with his family without feeling compelled to "witness" to two individuals who had no need of his evangelistic efforts. My mother and I were solid churchgoing Christians and I was in the Word and prayer daily, serving the LORD.

Consider his response when I said, "Oh, you're a Christian, so are we!" He looked at me with a dead visage, turned around and walked away. This indicates a few obvious things: **1.** He had no joy; **2.** what he was *really* saying by this rude response was, "There's no way on God's green earth that you're a Christian"; and **3.** he condemned us—or rather me—based on appearances alone. How do I know? Because, unless smiling and being friendly are heinous sins, my mother and I did nothing to suggest that we were lost sinners. This indicates that he judged me by appearances alone. Now, at the time, my hair was sort of long in the back but the rest of it was rather short; my ears weren't covered and neither was my face. In short, I didn't look like Charles Manson. It's true that I had taken my muscle shirt off and all I had on were shorts, socks and tennis shoes, but this was entirely appropriate apparel for a park in the middle of a hot summer day, even more so for vacationers, which many of the people were. For whatever reasons, my appearance and free-spirited manner offended his religious sensibilities and he deemed me a diabolical heathen when nothing could've been further from the truth.

Interestingly, the man showed signs of all five of the main strains of legalism as follows:

General Legalism: He clearly focused on the outer at the expense of the inner. I spoke to him with a spirit of joy and kindness and all he could see was that I didn't have a shirt on and my hair was kind of long in the back (*the horror, the horror*). Apparently, he felt that true Christians should dress to the nines when they visit a park in the heat of the summer. And, by golly, they'd better have a close-shaven 50's-styled haircut!

Rigid Sectarianism: Why didn't this man accept that I was a fellow believer? Likely because I didn't *look* like someone from his church. Simply put, I wasn't one of them, so I must've been a desperately lost soul. After all, a truly saved person would look and dress exactly like the people in his congregation. Why sure!

The Spirit of Religious Formal Death: Like I said, he and his family were dressed to the nines without exception—ties, long white dresses and the like. Of course, there's nothing wrong with this. Some people dress up more than others. I enjoy dressing up when appropriate. Yet it did seem strange that they were so spit and polished for a frolic in the park on a hot summer afternoon. Then again, it might have been a Sunday and they were simply visiting the park after their church service (I can't remember what day it was). The point is that the man was all tight-wound and formal, way too much for the occasion. Apparently, my utter lack of formality offended him, possibly my spontaneity as well. God forbid that someone should have fun at a park in the heat of a summer day!

The Spirit of Bondage: As noted above, the man couldn't even enjoy an afternoon at the park with his family without feeling compelled to "boldly minister" to a couple of people who had absolutely no need of his evangelism. One thing's for sure, he wasn't led of the

Holy Spirit since we were already devout believers. However, even if we weren't believers his efforts would have been worthless because he had no joy and was inexplicably rude to boot. Needless to say, no one in their right mind would want to be like him and serve his God! The man was like a lifeless robot merely following his programming. I can just see the pastor of his church ranting during a sermon: "You're not witnessing enough! You need to go out there and boldly witness! I know you're not evangelizing because there aren't any new people here! And you call yourself a Christian?!" This type of shame-based "preaching" may manipulate some to go out and pass out tracts or what have you, but they won't have any life or joy doing it. They'll be miserable because they're stuck in a miserable church that has a spirit of religionist bondage. Bondage always brings misery and this guy was clearly miserable, at least that day at the park he was.

The Spirit of Condemnation: It's true that the man didn't speak a word to me, but his expression and actions spoke volumes. Communication is more than verbal. By looking at me with contempt and silently walking away he was most certainly condemning me. He was basically saying, "There's no way that *you* are a Christian!" Legalism doesn't extend love and grace because it has neither. Legalism unjustly condemns because that's its nature: "the letter kills."

I don't share this story with carnal anger or hatred toward this man. I didn't feel hostility toward him then and I don't now. At the time, I was simply perplexed by his actions, but not any longer. I now understand what went wrong in his spiritual walk. He was infected by legalism. I feel sad for him and people like him. For whatever reasons, they're stuck in a legalistic rut. They're prisoners. What's sadder is that they don't even know it, which is something we'll address in the next chapter—deception. They sincerely *think* they're walking according to true Christianity when nothing could be further from the truth.

Although I don't feel anger or hatred toward this man I DO feel anger and hatred toward legalism itself—*righteous* anger and *righteous* hatred. The Bible emphatically declares "To fear the LORD is to hate evil" (Proverbs 8:13) and legalism is thoroughly evil. In a way it's even more dangerous than conventional fleshly antics like sexual immorality, theft and drunkard-ness because legalism always hides under a mask of religious respectability, like the warden in the popular film *The Shawshank Redemption*. The Bible also says "The righteous hate what is false" (Proverbs 13:5) and legalism is false to its rotten core. It's *phony* Christianity.

The whole reason I wrote this book is because I loathe legalism in all its ugly forms and I'm righteously angry that so many have been deceived by it; not just those infected by legalism, but all the innocent believers in their midst who have experienced so much legalism that they start to think it's real Christianity when, in fact, it's the express opposite.

So what's the answer? How do we keep legalism from infecting ourselves, other believers and our churches?

Chapter 9

How to Purge Legalism

We've gone over a lot of biblical data to unmask legalism. How should you and I deal with this spiritual disease if we observe it in ourselves or others? What should we do if we see it taking root in our churches? Here's a 5-point plan of action:

1. Knowledge is Power

The book of wisdom says: "A wise man has great power, and a man of knowledge increases strength" (Proverbs 24:5). If knowledge is power then ignorance is the opposite—weakness and limitation. Jesus said "the truth will set you free" (John 8:31-32). "Truth" refers to *accurate* knowledge; and accurate knowledge that's understood and applied naturally sets free. Freedom is the purpose of this book— freedom from the yoke of religious bondage (as well as freedom from lawlessness, which we'll tackle next chapter).

So acquiring knowledge is the first step to freedom because people can't very well walk free of legalism if they don't even know what it is. Knowledge will *empower* you. So go over this book and the numerous scriptural passages as necessary until you master the material, particularly the parts that really register. Seek the LORD for understanding and insight, as encouraged in Proverbs 2:1-7.

Remember, knowledge is power whereas ignorance is weakness, limitation and even ruin.

2. Examine Yourself Regularly and Be Honest about It

The Bible instructs us to honestly look within and examine our actions and motives in view of God's Word with the help of the Holy Spirit, who guides us into all truth (2 Corinthians 13:5, John 14:26 & 16:13). This should be done regularly. It's the answer to any flesh problem or legalistic corruption; it's also the answer to deception, including self-deception.

Think about it: When people are deceived *they **don't know** they're deceived*. For instance, the Pharisees are the quintessential example of legalism in the Bible. They sincerely believed they were God's children, but Jesus squarely told them that they were children of the devil (John 8:41,44). Was Jesus being mean? No, he was walking in "tough love" because the first thing deceived people need is the truth since only the truth counteracts lies and sets free. I said that they "sincerely believed" they were God's children, but sincerity by itself isn't good if what you sincerely believe is a lie. They may have been sincere in their belief but their belief was sincerely wrong.

Think of all the deceived people who grow up in cultish quasi-Christian groups or false religions. They've been indoctrinated to believe that their group is the one true sect or religion, just like the Pharisees. Such people don't know they're deceived because that's the nature of deception.

Mainline, Evangelical, Charismatic and other Christian groups are not exempt from such deception. There's enough false teaching, legalism and lawlessness to go around.

The answer to deception is truth. How do people who are deceived in one or more areas get set free if they don't realize they're deceived? Simple: When you regularly examine yourself, be honest about it. Be honest with yourself, be honest with the LORD, and be honest with his Word. Ask something like: "Heavenly Father, if I am deceived in any area; open my eyes to the truth through your Word by the guidance of the Holy Spirit. May the truth continually set me free!"

You can be sure that any believer who regularly does this will move steadily forward, becoming more and more spiritually mature, walking in greater and greater insight, truth and freedom (Proverbs 2:1-6).

Consider this passage:

> **For with you is the fountain of life;**
> **in your light we see light.**
>
> **Psalm 36: 9**

God isn't just the Creator of life; he's the Fountain of Life! He gushes forth life constantly like a fountain or geyser gushes water. This is why the Bible constantly encourages believers to get close to God and stay close—because there's LIFE in his presence. This is why David emphasized the incredible JOY in His presence (Psalm 16:11 & 21:6)! There's no depression or sterility in God's presence—there's JOY and LIFE!

The passage states that when we experience the light of God's presence we'll naturally "see light." Spiritual light is the opposite of spiritual darkness and parallels truth, life and freedom. This is the answer to any type of deception—getting close to God and staying close. *Religion* will always deceive you one way or another but a *relationship* with the Fountain of Life will enlighten you and set you free. That's why Christianity is a relationship with God and not just another religion.

3. Repent as Necessary

It's important to keep in repentance whenever you discern deception or error in yourself or your belief system.

Although 'repentance' has a negative connotation in modern times it's actually a very healthy attitude and practice; it simply means to change your mind—your thinking—for the positive. For instance, if you're currently believing something that you discover is false or partially false then stop believing the lies and embrace the true belief and mindset (at least as "true" as you *presently* can fathom it). Thinking is linked to behavior. This is why Paul instructed believers to *count* themselves as dead to sin but alive on to God in Christ Jesus (Romans 6:11-12). Paul then went on to relay the **law of displacement**: If your behavior is in error, immediately stop the behavior and start implementing the right action. This is true repentance, not mere words. The law of displacement works in a spiritual sense just as it does in the physical, which is why it's vital that you replace the false belief with true belief (or, at least, more accurate belief) and the erroneous behavior with righteous behavior.

Continually changing for the positive—repentance—is literally *the way to* **life:**

> **the corrections of discipline**
> **are the way to life**
> **Proverbs 6:23**

> **Reproofs of instruction are the way of life**
> **Proverbs 6:23** (NKJV)

Regularly give yourself a spiritual examination and be honest about it; seek the Fountain of Life through His Word and the help of the Holy Spirit. Keep with repentance, as John the Baptist put it (Matthew 3:8 & Luke 3:8), and the Lord will continually purify you from all unrighteousness (1 John 1:8-9). This will keep you spiritually healthy and free from the poison of legalism.

4. Examine Believers Near You, Including the Church and Sect to which You Belong

You should only do this if you're freed-up of legalism yourself through applying the three previous points, otherwise you'll be guilty of hypocritical judging, something Jesus squarely condemned in Matthew 7:1-5. "Hypocritical judging" is when a man judges and condemns another person for something he himself is doing. Christ concluded this passage by saying that the believer with a figurative plank in his eye can help the believer with a speck once he removes his plank and can "see clearly." Only then is he able to help the other with his speck. This is just common sense since we can only give what we have; if you don't have freedom you can't give freedom.

It's important to stress that the Lord meant "Do not judge" only in this hypocritical sense, as there are numerous examples of *righteous* judging in the New Testament. For example, Christ condemned the legalists for wanting to stone an adulterous woman because they were just as guilty (John 8:1-11). Yeshua rightly condemned their hypocritical judging but proceeded to righteously judge the woman by telling her, "Go now and leave your life of sin." You see, Jesus made a righteous judgment about her immoral lifestyle and didn't hesitate to instruct her to repent, i.e. change for the positive.

Paul did the same thing when he judged an unrepentant fornicator at the Corinth church and encouraged the believers to expel him (1 Corinthians 5:1-5, 9-13). The good news is that the man later repented whereupon Paul readily instructed the believers to welcome him back into their fellowship (2 Corinthians 2:6-11).

It's important to point out from Matthew 7—the very chapter where Jesus said "Do not judge"—that **he also instructed believers to judge the fruit of those who propose to speak for God** (7:15-23). Christ stressed: "By their fruit you will recognize them," referring to those who falsely speak for God (verses 16 & 20). Why is this important? Because not everyone's genuine; there are false prophets all over. A "false prophet" is anyone who falsely speaks for God, usually people in positions of spiritual authority, whether pastor, teacher, elder, prophet or what have you. Christ pointed out that they can be easily recognized by their fruit. Do you see consistent fruit of the spirit in their lives or do you see works of the flesh, as detailed in Galatians 5:19-23? Not that anyone's perfect and even Christian servant-leaders miss it now and then (1 John 1:8-9), although they should certainly be mature enough that they're freed-up from major flesh issues (1 Timothy 3:1-6). After all, if someone in a leadership position has major flesh problems that tells you he or she is not a worthy servant-leader.

The difference between genuine believers and counterfeits is that genuine believers have a humble spirit and therefore readily confess and repent when they miss it, while counterfeits are stubborn and proud. The latter refuse to admit their error and turn from it, even when legitimately corrected; in fact, they'll *hate you* for correcting them (Proverbs 9:7-9). This is how you discern the genuine from the disingenuous. Do you see an elder or pastor who has an arrogant, stubborn spirit that refuses to repent, even when corrected in love? You can be sure that he or she is false or, *at the very least,* unworthy of following at the present time. Leave them! They are blind guides; if the blind follow the blind they will both fall into a pit (Matthew 15:13-14).

5. Implement Spiritual Warfare

As a faithful "fruit-watcher," if you discern legalistic qualities in others, including those in servant-leadership positions, you must implement spiritual warfare ASAP. "Spiritual warfare" means to overcome evil with spiritual activities. Here are some powerful warfare tactics that are 100% scriptural:

Prayer. This is where you'll always want to start because prayer is the vehicle that literally releases God's will and his kingdom to reign in people's lives and situations for which you intercede. If someone somewhere doesn't pray and "loose" God's will and kingdom on the scene, his will won't be done and his kingdom won't reign in the situation for which you're praying. Someone might understandably argue: "Well, why doesn't God just do it? Why does someone have to pray?" Because, although God is sovereign and reigns supreme, the kingdom of darkness has authority on this Earth until the end of this age, which is why this current era is called "the present evil age" in Galatians 1:4. Thankfully, the kingdom of darkness has no authority over members of the Church. 'Church' is *ekklesia (ee-KLEE-see-ah)* in the Greek and means "called-out ones." Believers are called out of this present darkness and have the authority to bind the kingdom of darkness and loose God's will and kingdom.[44]

Again, prayer is the vehicle that releases God's will and power into people's lives and situations on Earth. Why do you think Christ said we need to pray for our enemies? Because if someone is attacking you without cause you can be sure that he/she is walking in the flesh and God's kingdom is *not* reigning in his/her life. Praying for the individual is the antidote.

If people are walking in overt legalism they may not be a personal enemy, but they *are* an enemy of the kingdom of God, whether they know it or not, just as the Pharisees and Teachers of the Law were enemies of Christ. Pray for them regularly; pray in the spirit, which is the seventh piece of the armor of God, even though it's not given a figurative description (Ephesians 6:18); I call it the *artillery* or *missiles* of praying in the spirit because you can effectively pray for people miles away or on the other side of the planet.

Teaching/Preaching. This doesn't refer to just sermons but any occasion where you might have the opportunity to give a "word of instruction" (1 Corinthians 14:26), like when you're out for coffee or emailing. It simply refers to sharing the truths of God's Word. As such, teaching/preaching isn't limited to pulpit ministers who hail from respected cemeteries, I mean seminaries. Keep in mind that in the early Church believers normally met in houses where the groups were relatively small and there were no literal pulpits, nor were there any seminaries as we understand them. Ministers were raised up and trained in the churches.

Teaching or sharing biblical insights is important because it provides the opportunity to sow God's Word into others' lives. If someone is infected by legalism, the Word of God is the antidote because

---

[44] For details and scriptural support see the article *Spiritual Warfare—The Basics* at the FOL site, particularly the section *Binding & Loosing through Prayer*. Also see the article *Do You Know What You're Fighting For?*

it *is* the truth and has the power to set free (John 8:31-32 & 17:17), assuming of course it's "rightly divided," i.e. properly interpreted.

Setting a Godly Example. Some may scoff at this one because it's so simple, but it's a powerful principle nevertheless. Why else do you think Peter included it in his list of the four main duties of pastors, along with feeding the Word, overseeing and serving? See 1 Peter 5:1-3.

Consider these examples: If you observe an authoritarian spirit, counteract it by setting an example of humble service. If you see some believers getting overly technical with religious rules, set an example of the spirit of the law in question, as well as the spirit of grace. If you see condemnation, set an example of building others up. If you see greed, set an example of cheerful generosity. If you see an unbalanced emphasis on appearances, set an example of inward godliness. If you see an attitude of rigid sectarianism, set an example of openness to believers outside your group. If you see a sourpuss spirit, set an example of joy. If you witness stifling bondage, illustrate true freedom in everything you do. If you witness dreadfully boring formality, set an example of spontaneity and passion. Etcetera.

Setting an example is often more effective than verbal confrontation because actions speak louder than words.

Confront as Led of the Holy Spirit, Gently or Sternly. If prayer, teaching, and setting a godly example fail to produce positive results you may have to confront and offer correction. The Holy Spirit may even lead you to do this immediately when encountering legalism in one form or another, as was the case with Paul's open rebuke of Peter in Galatians 2:11-14. Provoked by the Spirit, Paul sought to nip Peter's blatant display of legalism in the bud because so much was at stake at that critical juncture in history. Paul loved the Lord and people too much to allow the gospel of grace to be poisoned by legalism. Had he not acted decisively at that moment the positive worldwide impact of Christianity would have suffered.

Open correction is necessary in such cases. Paul was walking according to biblical wisdom:

Better is open rebuke than hidden love.
Proverbs 27:5

This kind of correction need not be unnecessarily stern since "a gentle tongue can break a bone" (Proverbs 25:15), but sometimes you'll have to take a stricter approach. Paul was stern with Peter in the above confrontation but he certainly wasn't radically stern. I encourage you to be as gentle as possible with confrontations since gentleness "turns away wrath" (Proverbs 15:1); only take a severer approach when mandatory, as led of the Spirit, whether mild sternness or heavy sternness. Jesus took the mildly strict approach when he called Peter "Satan" in Matthew 16:23 and he obviously took the radically stern route when he openly called the legalists "hypocrites," "blind fools," "snakes," "brood of vipers" "full of wickedness" in Matthew 23.

The only type of people I know who seem to enjoy such confrontations are those with strong Type A personalities. These are people who typically throw their weight around, so to speak. No one else enjoys confrontation, but sometimes it has to be done, as Jesus taught in Matthew 18:15-17 and Luke 17:3-4.

Although I don't mind confrontation and correction when it comes to mild things, I hate it when it concerns serious issues. I'll only do it when there's no other recourse or if I'm seriously provoked by the Holy Spirit. Here's one occasion:

Years ago, about 15-20 believers were hanging out in the opening room of the church facility that Carol and I were attending. One group consisted of the pastor, two associates and a couple others. I was about 10 feet away talking with other believers but I couldn't help overhear some of the conversation of the other group because it was so loud and biting. Headed by the pastor and assistant, they were slamming a ministry couple from a different church who organized and implemented special concerts at our assembly once a month. I tried to ignore their conversation and concentrate on the people I was with, but their gossip went on and on. Not only were they overtly gossiping, they were fault-finding. What a great example to set for others, huh? After about twelve minutes I just couldn't take any more and so turned to them and shouted, "Will you chill out; they're not THAT bad!" This is not my typical manner but I couldn't stand idly by another second while church leaders behaved in such an ignoble fashion. The associate pastor turned to me with anger and corrected me for having the audacity to confront elders. He was much older than me and I respected him in many ways, so

I kept my mouth shut. This is what the Spirit led me to do. I even said I was sorry, but I didn't apologize for what I said—since what I said was right and I was provoked of the Spirit—I simply apologized for having to say it.

So, by keeping mum and apologizing I ate humble pie, but I didn't mind because the confrontation and correction immediately stopped the juvenile backbiting. In other words, it accomplished its purpose. Except for the brief knee-jerk response of the associate, they were all stunned to silence and clearly ashamed. The gossip stopped and no one ever discussed the occasion again, at least not in the open community.

The moral of the story is that sometimes the Spirit will compel you to open rebuke even if it's not your forte. It's a powerful principle that brings positive results, as long as the people receiving the correction are truly godly (Proverbs 9:7-9). But please don't misuse this principle by using it to dominate others, which is arrogance. Always strive for humility and a servant's heart; humility attracts God's grace whereas arrogance repels Him (James 4:6, 1 Peter 5:5 and Proverbs 3:34).

Victory over Legalism

To recap, these five factors are essential to purging legalism in yourself and others:

1. **Acquire knowledge** about legalism.
2. **Examine yourself** according to that knowledge and be honest.
3. **Repent as necessary** and keep in repentance.
4. **Examine the fruit of others** near you, particularly spiritual leaders; but also relatives, friends, people at work, government bureaucrats, etc.
5. **Implement spiritual warfare** whenever you observe legalism—pray, share the truth, set a godly example and confront when necessary.

If you keep a tight relationship with the LORD and implement these warfare tactics you'll surely incur the wrath of legalists, but don't be concerned. All they can do is reject you, slander you and prevent you from ministering in their circles. Jesus said to rejoice when people persecute you in this way (Matthew 5:11-12). As was the case with Christ, these persecutors will often be "God's people." In other words, those attacking you will put on the appearances of being godly and devout when nothing could be further from the truth. They're legalists and therefore fake. Again, don't be concerned. They can't stop someone who's anointed of God. They can't win.

The legalists of 1st century Israel tried to find a way to murder the Messiah "yet they could not find any way to do it" (Luke 19:47-48). Many times they tried to apprehend him and kill him, but they *couldn't* achieve it.[45] The only time they were able to apprehend him was when they captured him in order to crucify him. Of course, this was according to *God's will* so he could die for our sins, which opened the door to eternal salvation for humanity.

To Cut Ties or Not to Cut Ties?

What do you do when hardcore legalists refuse to repent even after implementing the above strategies with much patience? The Lord advised departing from so-called spiritual leaders who are dyed-in-the-wool legalists (Matthew 15:14). This would include pastors and the assemblies they shepherd. In such cases, simply seek the Lord about finding a new fellowship, obviously one that's spiritually healthy. But, if it comes down to having to do this, keep your former assembly in prayer. Who knows? Yahweh is a miraculous God who changes people's hearts—*if* they're willing—and the door may open one day to go back to

---

[45] Examples include: Luke 4:28-30 where the offended people of Nazareth attempted to throw Christ off a cliff but he escaped by mysteriously walking "right through the crowd"; John 7:30,44 where those who wanted to seize the Messiah couldn't lay a hand on him "because his time had not yet come"; John 8:59 where the offended religionists picked up stones to slay Yeshua but he miraculously hid himself and slipped by them; and John 10:31,39 where a group tried to murder him in Solomon's Colonnade and he "escaped their wrath."

a former fellowship or, at least, restore relations with people there. Whatever you do, don't allow bitterness and hatred to take root in your heart.

What if the legalist in question is a family member, relative, friend or someone at the work place? How do you "leave" such people when you're bound to run into them now and then? You can "leave" them in the sense of not being close to them. Don't buddy around with them. If possible, don't eat with them (1 Corinthians 5:11). Of course, continue to walk in love toward them when you inevitably brush shoulders, including walking in *tough* love when appropriate. But don't hate them or become bitter; and please don't gossip about them. Keep 'em in prayer. One day the LORD may break 'em, so to speak. If so, the door will be open for you to cultivate a closer relationship. Amen.

Chapter 10

Libertinism: The Other Side of the Coin

No study on legalism would be complete without addressing libertinism.[46] Legalism and libertinism are two sides of the same coin. Both are forms of counterfeit Christianity, albeit contrasting forms. How do you distinguish the two sides? Whereas legalists put on airs of religiosity while hiding their sins, libertines claim to be Christians while openly walking in the flesh and encouraging others to do so also (by their example and what they teach). Both are corrupt and neither solves the sin problem.

Libertinism should not be confused with libertarianism. A libertarian[47] is a person who advocates liberty in thought or conduct, whereas a libertine is a person who is morally unrestrained and therefore given to immoral or improper conduct. In short, libertines are hedonists.

---

[46] Pronounced *LIB-er-tee-niz-uhm*.

[47] Please don't confuse libertarian here with Libertarian (capitalized), a member of the Libertarian Party, the third largest political party in the USA.

Libertarianism doesn't have the negative connotation of libertinism. This doesn't mean, of course, that libertarians are all moral.

Christianity and Freedom

In a sense, authentic Christianity is the truest form of libertarianism because Christianity's all about liberty (please notice that I said "in a sense"). The Bible says that freedom is actually a quality of God's being:

> **Now the Lord is the Spirit, and <u>where the Spirit of the Lord is, there is freedom.</u>**
> **2 Corinthians 3:17**

The Scriptures also emphatically declare:

> **It is <u>for freedom</u> that Christ has set us free.**
> **Galatians 5:1**

And the Messiah said:

> **"So if the Son sets you free, you will be free <u>indeed</u>."**
> **John 8:36**

You see, **Christianity is all about freedom**—freedom to know God, freedom from the flesh, and freedom from the yoke of religious law. Yet notice that the freedom Christianity offers is freedom *from* the flesh, not freedom to engage the flesh. This is why Paul stressed, "You, my brothers, were called to be free. But do not use your freedom to indulge the sinful nature"; and Peter emphasized, "Live as free men, but do not use your freedom as a cover-up for evil" (Galatians 5:13 & 1 Peter 2:16). In other words, believers shouldn't pervert the freedom Christianity offers into a license to sin.

I've come across confessing Christians who say things like, "I'm totally free" or "I'm a freethinker" when what they really mean is, "I'm totally free and can indulge my sinful nature all I want." This is libertinism. It's a perversion of the doctrine of eternal security[48] and twists God's grace into an excuse to sin. Notice what Jude said about people who adopt this mentality:

> **For certain men whose condemnation was written about long ago have secretly slipped in among you. They are <u>godless men</u>, <u>who change the grace of our God into a license for immorality</u> and deny Jesus Christ our only Sovereign and Lord.**
>
> **Jude 1:4**

Jude was addressing believers and told them that libertines had slipped into their midst. What these libertines advocated, in essence, was this: "We're saved and have God's grace and can therefore sin all we want without care of repentance. The Lord won't reject us." Although these people didn't literally deny Jesus Christ, they denied him by using God's grace as a license for immorality. What deception!

If you're a believer and you're struggling with a certain sin, the answer to your problem is to learn to walk in the spirit and be spirit-controlled rather than flesh-ruled. Paul said in Galatians 5:16 that if we live by the Spirit we will not gratify the desires of the sinful nature because, again, "Where the Spirit of the Lord is, there is freedom." This is why you need to learn how to put off the "old self"—the flesh—and put on the "new self" (Ephesians 4:22-24). This means living out of your spirit as led of the Holy Spirit, which is easy as pie to learn. The result is that you'll be spirit-controlled rather than flesh-ruled. The more you learn to do this the more freedom you'll experience and the more fruit of the spirit you'll produce (Galatians 5:19-23).

Libertinism perverts these wonderful truths and makes freedom out to be an excuse to live in sin. It actually subjects people to the *bondage* of the flesh, which means it's not freedom at all, but rather

---

[48] The doctrine of eternal security refers to the fact that believers are eternally secure in Christ as they continue in faith (John 10:27-30). This isn't to suggest, however, that a believer is saved if they no longer have faith. After all, if it takes faith to be saved, how can an individual be saved if he or she no longer has faith? The very word "believer" means that the individual *believes*. See the article *Once Saved Always Saved?* at the FOL site.

bondage to the limitations and negative consequences of the flesh, the lower (base) nature. Christianity, by contrast, sets people free from captivity to the sinful nature to **soar in the spirit!**

So, while it could be said that Christianity is the *purest* form of libertarianism, it's totally against libertinism.

Libertinism, Lawlessness and Licentiousness

Libertinism is one-and-the-same as lawlessness and licentiousness (or 'license' for short); the terms are interchangeable. Hedonism is another synonym.

As the word implies, 'lawlessness' is the disregard of divine law. It's the attitude that says, "I don't care what God says about moral absolutes; I'm going to live however I want to and do whatever I want." On the surface this sounds like freedom, but it's really just bondage to the lower nature because the thing the person wants to do is of the flesh. It's like a husband or wife saying, "I don't care if God's Word says adultery is wrong and I don't care that I vowed to be faithful, I want to have an affair and I'm going to do it!" This is lawlessness—the disregard of divine law. Years ago I was at a friend's house and his wife was on a weight-loss regimen. Although she was a confessing Christian, she declared, "When I lose 15-20 pounds I'm going to have an affair." She said this in front of her husband and I wasn't sure if she was kidding. It was definitely an uncomfortable moment. In the months to come she did exactly what she said!

Or take the popular topic of "gay marriage." Homosexuals who want to redefine marriage to include people of the same sex are essentially waving their fists at their Creator in defiance. They don't care that their sex organs don't line up. I don't mean to be crude, but the truth about sexuality is obvious. Just look at the sex organs: Tab 'A' fits into Slot 'B.' It's really no more complicated than this. Those who rebel against this axiom are rebelling against their Creator and nature itself. They're embracing a lie. It's lawlessness. They may not be lawless in every area, very few people are, but they're lawless in regards to sexuality.

In light of this self-evident truth, the whole concept of "gay churches" is an oxymoron. Those who want to practice homosexuality and also be a Christian are practicing lawlessness. Please notice I'm referring to those who *practice* homosexuality. It's perfectly okay for a person who *repents* of homosexuality to be a Christian and function as a minister just as it's okay for people who repent of other sins to be Christians and minister. Notice what the Bible says:

> **Do you not know that the wicked will not inherit the kingdom of God? Do not be deceived: Neither the sexually immoral nor idolaters nor <u>adulterers</u> nor male prostitutes nor <u>homosexual offenders</u> [10] nor <u>thieves</u> nor <u>the greedy</u> nor <u>drunkards</u> nor <u>slanderers</u> nor <u>swindlers</u> <u>will inherit the kingdom of God</u>. [11] And that is what some of you <u>were</u>. But you were washed, you were sanctified, you were justified in the name of the Lord Jesus Christ and by the Spirit of our God.**
>
> **1 Corinthians 6:9-11**

As you can see, Paul lists an assortment of fleshly activities and then tells the Corinthian believers: "And that is what some of you *were*." It's past tense because the believers were no longer *practicing* these sins as a lifestyle. I'm not saying that some of them didn't stumble or fall now and then but they were willing to confess and repent when they did, which means God would forgive them and cleanse them (1 John 1:8-9). This is "keeping with repentance" (Matthew & Luke 3:8).

Notice that homosexuality is put on par with sins like adultery, thievery, greediness, drunkard-ness, slandering and swindling. This indicates two things: **1.** homosexuality is a sin, and **2.** believers are expected to repent of it just like any other fleshly behavior.

Discard Legalism & License
in Favor of True Godliness

Many Christians understandably flee to libertinism because they had bad experiences with churches tainted by legalism. Flawed "holiness" teaching is often part of these bad experiences. They instinctively want to vomit out the legalism, but they make the mistake of running to libertinism for succor. But, again, just as legalism puts people in bondage to religious law and the resulting hypocrisy, so libertinism puts people in bondage to the flesh. Since legalism and lawlessness are two sides of the same coin, switching from one side to the other is not the answer because it's still the same bad coin! Both are equally bad. The coin must be tossed out altogether in favor of a new coin, a priceless coin, which is genuine Christianity.

What is "genuine Christianity"? It's reconciliation with God through spiritual rebirth, putting off the flesh, and learning to live out of one's spirit as led of the Holy Spirit, which requires a new way of thinking. This is what Christianity is in a nutshell. It includes cultivating and maintaining a *relationship* with the Living LORD. Developing a relationship with God is important because the best way to become "like" someone is to spend time with him or her. If you want to be "like God" the first step is to spend time with your Creator. After that, being godly comes naturally. It'll come *from within* and not from without because it's who *you are* in your spirit and you've *decided* to be spirit-controlled rather than flesh-ruled.

I'm not saying that it won't take some discipline and perseverance on your part, but you'll be working *with* the Lord as a team and not without him. True holiness is not following a list of rules by trying to force your flesh to comply, it's discarding the way of the flesh altogether in favor of living out of your reborn spirit by the Holy Spirit. We'll look at this in detail next chapter.

An Example of Libertinism

Years ago I was part of a home-styled Bible study/fellowship where the teacher taught on the corruption of legalism and how his experiences with it made him reject the concept of holiness all together. Although he only taught about once every three weeks, it soon became clear that he was advocating lawlessness.

The group was mostly males in their early 20s or thereabouts. One day the subject of alcohol came up and this teacher told these impressionable guys that he regularly drank "and not just the light stuff." In other words, he regularly drank hard liquor. Now, I'm not one to believe that merely drinking a sip of alcohol is a sin,[49] but is this a good message to send to young Christian males in hedonistic modern America? One of them later said he saw the teacher at some function a year or so earlier where he was passed out in a lawn chair due to excessive drinking. Is this appropriate conduct for a pastor or any supposedly mature believer? Is it a good example? Of course not. The youth lost respect for him and understandably so.

This pastor escaped the bondage of legalism only to fall into the error of licentiousness. His negative experiences with legalism caused him to reject the concept of holiness altogether. He threw out the proverbial baby with the bathwater. It goes without saying that this is not the answer to legalism!

Years later he unsurprisingly joined a lawless sect.

A Biblical Example of Libertinism

Are there examples of so-called believers walking in lawlessness in the New Testament? Absolutely. Consider the church of Thyatira and what the Lord said to the believers of this fellowship:

---

[49] See, for example, Deuteronomy 14:26 and 1 Timothy 5:23. Such passages must be balanced out by other clear verses, like "Do not get drunk on wine, which leads to debauchery, but be filled with the Spirit" (Ephesians 5:18), as well as passages which teach that we shouldn't do anything that would make a fellow believer stumble in a weak area (Romans 14:21 & 1 Corinthians 10:31-32). Still, it's clear that merely drinking an alcoholic beverage isn't *by itself* evil. Keep in mind, however, that dealing with hardcore legalists is different that dealing with genuine believers. As such, Christ was known to break the rules of stubborn legalists for the purpose of provoking a reaction, like when he failed to wash his hands before a meal with staunch religionists, which opened the door for a much-needed open rebuke (Luke 11:37-44).

"**Nevertheless, I have this against you: You
tolerate that woman Jezebel, who calls herself a
prophetess. <u>By her teaching she misleads my servants
into sexual immorality</u> and the eating of food
sacrificed to idols.** [21] <u>**I have given her time to repent
of her immorality, but she is unwilling.**</u> [22] **So I will
cast her on a bed of suffering, and will make those
who commit adultery with her suffer intensely, unless
they repent of her ways.** [23] **I will strike her children
dead. Then all the churches will know that I am he
who searches hearts and minds, and I will repay each
of you according to your deeds.**"

Revelation 2:20-23

Christ was clearly ticked off and rightly so. This woman,
"Jezebel" (which is a symbolic name and not her real name), was
functioning in the role of a prophet in the Thyatiran church and she
misled some of the believers whom Jesus referred to as his "servants."
The Lord mercifully gave her time to repent, meaning he corrected her in
various ways, but she remained stubborn and unrepentant. As a result,
Christ was going to strike her and her followers with sickness unless they
repented of her ways (verse 22). Verse 23 mentions "her children,"
which is a reference to her followers who were mimicking her example.
Yeshua even said that he was going to strike them dead if they didn't
repent. What a far cry from "gentle Jesus meek and mild"!

The Thyatiran fellowship was a real church in Asia Minor
(modern-day Turkey) in the late 1st century. The situation in this
assembly provides a picture of what happens to people in leadership
positions when they succumb to libertinism. They'll spread their
lawlessness by encouraging others to walk in their unclean practices, just
like "Jezebel." They'll call it freedom when it's really just bondage to the
flesh.

What can Christians today get from this? Don't be misled by
libertines, even if they're in a leadership position in the church and go by
titles like "Pastor," "Prophet" or "Apostle." As this passage shows, the
Lord will show mercy to those who fall into libertinism and give them
time to repent, but if they stubbornly refuse they will face severe

discipline, just as "Jezebel" and her followers did in Thyatira. When God's mercy is repeatedly spurned his judgment inevitably falls.

Five Facts about Libertines

Paul was referring to libertines when he made this statement:

For, as I have often told you before and now say again even with tears, many live as enemies of the cross of Christ. [19] Their destiny is destruction, their god is their stomach, and their glory is in their shame. Their mind is on earthly things.
Philippians 3:18-19

There are four facts about lawlessness that we can extract from this passage:

Libertines worship fleshly indulgence with no concern to repent. We see this in Paul's statement, "their god is their stomach," which means libertines make an idol of the appetites of their flesh. This is different than a believer who struggles with sin or those who stumble into one area of the flesh or another. The struggler hates the sin but is in bondage to some degree; he or she doesn't want to commit the transgression but falls and repents again and again. Because such people humbly repent, God forgives them over and over. This is struggling with the flesh. Yet even mature Christians who are freed-up from life-dominating sins, like sexual immorality or substance abuse, are perfectly capable of missing it in less noticeable areas, like arrogance, gossip, envy, legalism, rivalry and mental lust. This isn't struggling but rather stumbling. The fact that even mature believers can miss it now and then explains why John the Baptist instructed his hearers to "produce fruit in keeping with repentance" (Matthew & Luke 3:8). If we want to be close to God and effective in his service we have to be diligent to keep our spiritual arteries clear of the build-up of unconfessed sin. Why? Because it'll block the flow of God's grace. Needless to say, be quick to repent whenever you feel even a tinge of conviction. This keeps your heart soft and unhardened.

The people Paul was talking about in this passage were neither struggling with the flesh nor stumbling. They made the appetites of their flesh an idol that they worshipped; in other words, they gave their hearts over to the flesh with no concern to repent. It's the difference between struggling or stumbling and outright rebellion, the latter being tantamount to what the Bible calls falling away (Hebrews 6:4-9). This isn't merely falling down, but falling *away*. Someone who stumbles can fall down if they're not careful, but those who fall away have abandoned the road and have even set a whole new course! Such people are in danger of being cut off from salvation altogether if they choose to persist in their stubborn folly.[50]

Paul instructed that we shouldn't even eat with someone who calls himself/herself a brother or sister in the Lord if they're practicing sin with no concern to repent (1 Corinthians 5:9-11). And it doesn't matter what the sin is. Paul listed six examples on this occasion—sexual immorality, greediness, idolatry, slander, drunkard-ness and swindling. If someone claims to be a Christian and is walking in these sins or others without concern to repent we are not to associate with them. This doesn't mean we can't greet them or minister to them as the Lord leads, but as far as close relations go—like dining together—we need to cease associations until they turn for the positive. This shows what a serious offense libertinism is.

A passage we looked at earlier, 1 Corinthians 6:9-11, clearly shows that those who practice sin as a lifestyle with no concern to repent will ***not*** *inherit the kingdom of God!*

I want to stress, however, that this is not referring to those who struggle with sin or stumble into sin and repent. All believers miss it, even mature believers, but God expects us to humbly 'fess up and he'll forgive us—dismiss the charge—and cleanse us of all unrighteousness (1 John 1:8-9). Praise God!

---

[50] See the teaching *Once Saved Always Saved?* at the FOL site for details. While the doctrine of "once saved always saved" naturally appeals to libertines, the opposite extreme—"sinless perfection"—is favored by hardcore legalists. Those who embrace the latter suggest that any minor sin causes the immediate loss of salvation, which they never apply to themselves because they self-righteously deem themselves perfect.

Libertines are proud of what they should be ashamed of. We see this in Paul's statement, "their glory is in their shame." Libertines will exalt a fleshly desire or behavior and make it an object of admiration or idolization, like alcoholism, drugs, pedophilia or homosexuality. They'll start organizations, movements or pride marches for the sin of their choice.

Libertines are focused on the here and now and not eternity. We observe this in Paul's statement, "Their mind is on earthly things." Indulgence of their fleshly desire is of such eminent importance that they are blinded to the eternal repercussions of their licentiousness.

The destiny of unrepentant libertines is destruction. Paul made this clear when he said, "Their destiny is destruction." He was talking about the "everlasting destruction" of the "second death" (2 Thessalonians 1:9 & Revelation 20:11-15). The Mighty Christ described it like so:

> **"Do not be afraid of those who kill the body but cannot kill the soul. Rather, be afraid of <u>the One who can destroy both soul and body in hell</u>."**
>
> **Matthew 10:28**

Why is everlasting destruction the penalty for unrepentant sin? Because "the wages of sin is death, but the gift of God is eternal life in Christ Jesus our Lord" (Romans 6:23).

Does this mean that any believer who dies with unrepentant sin will suffer everlasting destruction? No, but since they didn't repent of the sin in question God couldn't forgive it and therefore they'll have to answer for it at the judgment seat of Christ:

> **For we must all appear before the judgment seat of Christ, that each one may receive what is due him <u>for the things done while in the body, whether good or bad</u>.**
>
> **[11] Since, then, <u>we know what it is to fear the Lord</u>, we try to persuade men.**
>
> **2 Corinthians 5:10-11**

The "judgment seat of Christ" is the judgment believers will face (see also Romans 14:10,12). We will all stand before the Lord and give an account of our lives and receive what is due us, whether good or bad. This indicates rewards and penalties. The "bad" *cannot* refer to penalties for sins that were repented of since the believer already confessed them and God forgave him or her. So it must refer to sins of which the believer failed to repent in which God must justly hold the individual accountable.

A function at play in these situations is the conviction of the Holy Spirit. If the Spirit has not been convicting an individual of a sin then that person has less culpability than if the Spirit had been convicting him or her and quenched it.

How much unrepentant sin would it take for a believer to lose their salvation? Jesus' Parable of the Vineyard in Luke 13:5-9 reveals God's great patience and mercy in dealing with fruitless servants. It also shows that when his patient mercy ends his judgment begins.

The message we get from all of this should be loud and clear: DON'T BE A LIBERTINE! Always keep in repentance by honestly confessing sin when you miss it and God will forgive you. This keeps your heart soft and your spiritual arteries free of the clogging of unconfessed sin.

Libertines Have Allowed the Flesh to Master them

Notice what Peter taught about libertines:

For they mouth empty, boastful words and, by <u>appealing to the lustful desires of sinful human nature</u>, they entice people who are just escaping from those who live in error. [19] <u>They promise them freedom, while they themselves are slaves to depravity</u>—for <u>a man is a slave to whatever has mastered him</u>. [20] If they have escaped the corruption of the world by <u>knowing our Lord and Savior Jesus Christ</u> and are again entangled in it and overcome,

they are worse off at the end than they were at the beginning. [21] **It would have been better for them not to have known the way of righteousness, than to have known it and then to turn their backs on the sacred command that was passed on to them.** [22] **Of them the proverbs are true: "A dog returns to its vomit," and, "A sow that is washed goes back to her wallowing in the mud."**

2 Peter 2:18-22

Libertines focus on the desires of the flesh above all else and thus they entice immature believers with their licentiousness. They promise freedom when they themselves are slaves to the flesh, which is absurd. You can't give freedom if you don't have it. The only thing libertines can give is what they have—bondage to the flesh.

The latter part of verse 19 is important: "for a man is a slave to whatever has *mastered* him."

In an earlier chapter I mentioned how I stopped over an old friend's place recently; I hadn't seen him in years. The whole time I was with him he chain-smoked cigarettes and drank beer after beer, admitting that he was an alcoholic. He also said he regularly smoked pot. I knew he struggled in these areas in the past, but I wasn't sure of his current condition, although I suspected it wasn't good. As a friend and a minister I wanted to help him, if he was willing. I gave him a Christian book and we talked for a while, but any discussion about the Lord or the Bible was cursory at best. After about 40 minutes I was getting seriously smoked-out by his chain-smoking. When I dismissed myself he asked me to drive him to the store a mere two blocks away. I took him under the impression that I was doing a good deed and he came out with a 12-pack of beer! Do you see the problem here? I stopped by his apartment to share God's love and freedom with him and he *used me* to take him on a beer run. My purpose is to deliver people from addictions and bondages, not enable them, but he was so consumed with this addiction that he couldn't see this. All he cared about was getting his alcohol-fix. What bondage, what blindness, what utter folly!

This man was a confessing believer, but he was addicted to things that he should have dealt with over *25 years earlier*. This is where his fleshly bondages have taken him at close to 50 years of age—no job, no vehicle, no church and total dependency on the government for his basic needs. He only had one family member who was willing to associate with him. This is where his addictions have brought him. I say this with sadness, not Pharisaical arrogance, but he has no one to blame but himself. He had access to God, his Word, strong brothers & sisters in the Lord and excellent churches, but he forsook them all because he allowed the deceitful desires of his flesh to *master* him.

God told Cain, "sin is crouching at your door; it desires to have you, but you must master it" (Genesis 4:7). The root of sin is the flesh—the sinful nature—the hideous beast within us all. The LORD said we must master it, not allow it to master us, as was the case with this old friend of mine. The Bible refers to the desires of the sinful nature as deceitful (Ephesians 4:22). Why? Because the flesh promises satisfaction and happiness, but it doesn't deliver. It can't. It won't. All it can give is bondage and the resulting emptiness. It's deceitful.

I haven't given up on this man. I'm still praying for him and willing to minister as the Lord directs. I'm hoping and believing that he'll come to his senses and come out of this self-made pit of libertinism, like the prodigal son did. In fact, I've recently seen positive signs that he'll do just that. Praise God!

Needless to say, don't allow yourself to become mastered by the deceitful desires of your flesh. Your lower nature wants to have you but you must master it through Christ by counting it dead and participating in the divine nature, that is, walk in the spirit as led of the Holy Spirit.

I encourage believers to pray for the grace to walk free of sinful bondages as David did:

Keep your servant also from <u>willful sins</u>;
  <u>may they not rule over me</u>.

Psalm 19:13

Direct my footsteps according to your word;
  <u>let no sin rule over me</u>.

Psalm 119:133

Why did David pray like this? Because he knew that if he allowed a "willful sin" to master him and rule over him it would severely limit his life, even ruin it, as was the case with this friend of mine.

You'll see people who allow a sin or bad habit to rule over them all the time. For instance, gossips who spread slander and wonder why no one with an ounce of character wants to spend time with them; pathological liars who can't figure out why no one believes a word they say; the overweight glutton who can't enjoy a walk in the park because he/she is too heavy and out of shape; the millions who define their very lives by their sexual lusts; etc.

It goes without saying, refuse to let the flesh rule over you. Next chapter we'll go into detail about how to walk free of the flesh and its deceitful desires. It is *for freedom* that Christ has set you free!

"Everything is Permissible for Me"

As already established, libertines have the mindset that they're totally free in Christ and can therefore indulge the sinful nature anytime they feel like it. There were libertines in the church at Corinth who embraced this attitude so Paul brought up the topic *twice* in his first letter to the assembly. Here's the first time:

> **"Everything is permissible for me"—but not everything is beneficial. "Everything is permissible for me"—but I will not be mastered by anything.**
> **1 Corinthians 6:12**

Paul was quoting a popular phrase of some believers at the church: "Everything is permissible for me." This is the attitude of libertines in a nutshell. "I can do anything I want" is what they believe. Paul wasn't against freedom, of course, since he preached liberty to these very same believers when he said "the Lord is the Spirit and where the Spirit of the Lord is there is freedom" (2 Corinthians 3:17). Yet Paul adds some wise framework for freedom here:

While people have the power of volition and can essentially do whatever they want if they *decide* to do it, Paul points out that "not everything is beneficial." This is an obvious fact, of course, but he had to stress it because not everyone in Corinth realized it. Since following the deceitful desires of the sin nature is never beneficial, anything sinful is off-limits to the believer. Why? Because it's not beneficial; it's destructive. Say, for example, if a married man meets a pretty woman at work and entertains the idea of committing adultery with her, would this be beneficial to his life or destructive? Even if he's not a believer, it's a destructive course of action because it would hurt his wife and could harm his marriage, possibly even destroy it, not to mention the domino effect of hurting his children and losing the respect of the community. No sane person respects unfaithfulness, not even unbelievers.

Paul quotes the popular phase again in the second half of the verse and then adds "but I will *not* be mastered by *anything*." Here Paul isn't just talking about the corrupt desires of the flesh but rather anything neutral that has the capacity to master him and put him in bondage. Today, we see people mastered by many destructive addictions, like alcohol, drugs and various forms of sexual immorality. But millions are just as mastered by things that aren't considered bad, like food, computer games, watching or playing sports, TV, forms of recreation and even church activities. Of course none of these things are bad in and of themselves, but they can become bad if a person is *mastered* by them, in which case they become idols. We don't see many people in modern Western Civilization worshipping literal idols, but people can become so addicted to certain things that it becomes a form of idolatry because idolatry is the worship—the utter adoration—of something other than God. Christians are free, but we have to be careful to guard our hearts as the wellspring of life so that nothing takes us away from our devotion to the Lord (Proverbs 4:23).

Paul brought up the popular phrase again shortly later in his letter:

> **"Everything is permissible"—but not everything is beneficial. "Everything is permissible" —but not everything is constructive. [24] Nobody should seek his own good, but the good of others.**
>
> **1 Corinthians 10:23-24**

Paul again points out the obvious: Everything is permissible because we have been blessed with freewill and therefore have the power of decision. We have the power to *choose* to act or not act on any impulse, whether good or bad; but Paul stresses, once again, that not everything is beneficial. This is a repeat denouncement of the deceitful desires of the flesh, which are never beneficial. Christians are free in the Lord but the appetites of the sinful nature are off-limits because they are destructive. If there's any doubt, Paul cleared it up with his statement to the Roman believers: "What then? Shall we sin because we are not under law but under grace? By no means!" (Romans 6:15).

He repeats the phrase again, "everything is permissible" and this time adds "but not everything is constructive." This obviously refers to neutral things. The believer is free to do the neutral activity, but we have to ask ourselves if it's constructive. He then adds that "Nobody should seek his own good, but the good of others." For instance, if you've chosen to be a part of a certain church and are regularly late to the gatherings, is this constructive to the body of believers? Are you arriving late for your own good—to sleep in or whatever—or for the good of the fellowship? These are commons sense questions that we need to ask ourselves when it comes to the freedom we have in Christ.

Teachers and preachers can share these principles until they're blue in the face but some believers might never "get it" because they lack wisdom, which is the ability to distinguish difference. Anyone who wants wisdom must seek it as if it were a treasure; and God will give it to him or her (James 1:5).

The bottom line is this: Believers have freedom in Christ but it's not freedom to embrace the flesh, but rather freedom *from* the bondages of the flesh. We have true freedom in Christ, but we must be careful to not allow anything to master us, and we must use wisdom—common sense—in what we choose to do since not everything is constructive, for ourselves or others.

Sin Kills

This book is about legalism and we observed in the first nine chapters that "the letter kills," yet in this chapter we observe that sin kills just as well. This shouldn't be surprising since the Bible plainly declares that "the wages of sin is death" (Romans 6:23). Legalism and sinful license are two sides of the same bad coin. They *both* produce death. If anything, libertinism is worse. After all, what's the bigger problem in society today, legalism or fleshly license?

Neither legalism nor lawlessness is the answer. The bad coin must be thrown out altogether in favor of something that works; something that sets us totally free.

The answer is...

Chapter 11

Spirituality: The Fruit of Godliness

As noted last chapter, many people from legalistic homes or churches flee to libertinism for freedom but discover that fleshly license is its own bondage. Similarly, those from lawless backgrounds flee to religion for structure and respectability but then discover legalism is bondage as well. They swing from one extreme to another only to find that neither is the answer.

So what's the answer? Consider this parable…

Avoiding the Extremes of Legalism and Libertinism

Imagine, if you will, the earthly journey to spiritual maturity as a mountain. God is the mountain and the foothills are people "not far from the kingdom of God," which is what Jesus said about a wise Teacher of the Law in Mark 12:34. Since the mountain itself is the LORD the only way to get *on* the mountain is reconciliation with God, which comes through spiritual rebirth (John 3:3,6); consequently, there's only one path to get on the mountain and it's Jesus Christ (John 10:9). New believers are on the mountain, but they're at the bottom. As believers go up the mountain of spiritual growth they naturally get closer to the heart of God, which is the top. On each side of the mountain are dangerous cliffs, which aren't actually part of the peak. These cliffs represent legalism and lawlessness: Legalism is on the right while libertinism is on the left. It's impossible to get on the peak by these sides and those who are on the mountain—that is, believers—must avoid these dangerous cliffs or they'll risk falling off altogether.

Some believers get close to the dangerous cliffs on either side but, thankfully, they don't fall off, at least not yet. These are believers who flirt with legalism and libertinism and are therefore infected to some degree. Their flirtations are risky, but they're still on the mountain. They can't go any higher because the sides are so steep and dangerous. If they attempt to climb from that position they'll fall off. The only way they can go higher is to move away from the sides, which represents repentance from legalism or libertinism, depending on which side they're on.

The believers who wisely avoid both sides are free to go up the mountain closer and closer to the heart of God. Some may get to a certain level and decide they want to stay for one reason or another. Some of these may eventually stray to one edge or the other, even falling off. Those who keep going higher do so because they *want* to and the path is easy and enjoyable. Jesus said his yoke is easy and his burden is light (Matthew 11:28-30). Trying to move up on the edges, by contrast, is dangerous and very hard work, not to mention utterly fruitless.

The truths conveyed in this parable were understood by Solomon, the wisest man of his day:

> **Do not be <u>overrighteous</u>, neither be overwise—why destroy yourself? [17] Do not be <u>overwicked</u> and do not be a fool—why die before your time? [18] It is good to grasp the one and not let go of the other. The man who fears God will avoid all extremes.**
>
> **Ecclesiastes 7:16-18**

To be "overrighteous" or "overwise" refers to legalism whereas being "overwicked" or a "fool" refers to libertinism. Both are corrupt conditions and should be avoided at all costs. Solomon[51] says "it is good to grasp one and not let go of the other," which indicates that the truth is somewhere in between the two.

In the previous chapter I likened legalism and libertinism to the opposing sides of a bad coin and stressed that the coin needs tossed out altogether, but Carol shared an interesting variation today. She took a quarter and showed how it lies flat when it rests on one side or the other. The only way the coin can rise is by standing on its edge, which is the "middle ground" between heads or tails. She then illustrated that the coin can only be spun when it's in this position, to which she spun it. The coin spun round n' round and looked like it was having a blast! Likewise there's no genuine joy with legalism or libertinism. The former pleases religious pride while engaging the flesh in secret whereas the latter openly pleases the lusts of the flesh. In short, they both spring from the sinful nature and therefore can only please that nature (1 John 2:16). Any satisfaction experienced is shallow. Underneath is death, which is what the flesh produces.

Let's look at an even clearer parable on the extremes of legalism and licentiousness from Christ himself...

The Prodigal Son and His Brother

The Parable of the Prodigal Son isn't just about the prodigal son, as most think; it's also about his older brother. Let's give this story a fresh reading with the understanding that the prodigal son is a libertine and the older brother a legalist:

> **Jesus continued: "There was <u>a man</u> who had <u>two sons</u>. ¹² The younger one said to his father, 'Father, give me my share of the estate.' So he divided his property between them.**

---

[51] While some claim that Solomon wasn't the writer of Ecclesiastes, he's traditionally considered the author. I've always thought it was obvious.

[13] "Not long after that, the younger son got together all he had, set off for a distant country and there squandered his wealth in wild living. [14] After he had spent everything, there was a severe famine in that whole country, and he began to be in need. [15] So he went and hired himself out to a citizen of that country, who sent him to his fields to feed pigs. [16] He longed to fill his stomach with the pods that the pigs were eating, but no one gave him anything.

[17] "When he came to his senses, he said, 'How many of my father's hired men have food to spare, and here I am starving to death! [18] I will set out and go back to my father and say to him: Father, I have sinned against heaven and against you. [19] I am no longer worthy to be called your son; make me like one of your hired men.' [20] So he got up and went to his father.

"But while he was still a long way off, his father saw him and was filled with compassion for him; he ran to his son, threw his arms around him and kissed him.

[21] "The son said to him, 'Father, I have sinned against heaven and against you. I am no longer worthy to be called your son.'

[22] "But the father said to his servants, 'Quick! Bring the best robe and put it on him. Put a ring on his finger and sandals on his feet. [23] Bring the fattened calf and kill it. Let's have a feast and celebrate. [24] For this son of mine was dead and is alive; he was lost and is found.' So they began to celebrate.

[25] "Meanwhile, the older son was in the field. When he came near the house, he heard music and dancing. [26] So he called one of the servants and asked him what was going on. [27] 'Your brother has come,' he replied, 'and your father has killed the fattened calf because he has him back safe and sound.'

²⁸ "<u>The older brother became angry and refused to go in</u>. So his father went out and pleaded with him. ²⁹ But he answered his father, 'Look! <u>All these years I've been slaving for you</u> and never disobeyed your orders. <u>Yet you never gave me even a young goat so I could celebrate with my friends</u>. ³⁰But when this son of yours who has <u>squandered your property with prostitutes</u> comes home, you kill the fattened calf for him!'

³¹ " 'My son,' the father said, 'you are always with me, and <u>everything I have is yours</u>. ³² But we had to celebrate and be glad, because this brother of yours was dead and is alive again; he was lost and is found.' "

Luke 15:11-32

The opening verse shows that this parable is about three people: a man and his two sons. The story can be split into three basic parts: **The first third** is about the younger son who takes his inheritance and leaves home to waste it on foolish living. **The second third** is about the father and his joyous reaction to his repentant son. **The final third** is about the older son who's angry about his father's warm, celebratory reaction and complains about slaving for him for years; this third act closes with the father's response to the older son.

The younger son is an obvious type of carnal license. He disregards his father's will and indulges in sinful excess, which fails to bring him happiness. He ends up destitute and even "starving to death" (verse 17), which illustrates that "the wages of sin is death."

The good news is that this prodigal son ultimately realizes his error and repents. He genuinely humbles himself and goes back to his father. This shows that, while he was guilty of licentiousness, he wasn't so stubborn and stupid that he would rather die than give up his folly. In other words, he wasn't a dyed-in-the-wool libertine even though he functioned in that capacity for a season.

The father represents Father God, of course, and we observe his grace flowing to the humble. Indeed, the father literally runs to his repentant son, hugs him, kisses him and gives him the best apparel to don. He then throws a big party with loud music and joyous dancing. Surely "God gives his grace to the humble"! This is how our heavenly Father reacts when one of his children comes back to him after a season of folly.

But the older son doesn't share his father's joy (verses 25-30). Why? Because he's a legalist and this is a common trait of the disease of legalism. In fact, he gets angry! Can you believe it? His *only* brother has been missing for years[52] and when he finally has the sense to return he gets mad about it? This is absurd, but that's what legalism does to people. It's like when the Pharisees got angry at Jesus' mere intention of healing a man's shriveled hand on the Sabbath (Mark 3:1-6). Can you imagine being so clueless and deceived to the point of opposing a miraculous healing of God? No wonder Christ shot them a look of anger—he was righteously incensed by their stubbornness and idiocy.

Another indication of the older son's legalism can be seen in his works-orientation rather than relationship-orientation. He was so focused on toiling in the fields that the celebration started without him, which indicates that the partyers didn't even invite him! He evidently wasn't known for being a fun guy; hardcore legalists never are. When he finally discovers that his brother had returned he explodes and complains that he's been "slaving" for his father for years.

We know that the older brother didn't have a close relationship with his father for three reasons:

1. The father didn't even bother to send word to him that his brother had returned and there was going to be a big celebration.
2. The simple fact that the older brother didn't share his father's love and enthusiasm for his younger brother, which indicates that he didn't spend quality time with his father because you can only become like others if you actually spend time with them. It's the law of association (Proverbs 13:20). Simply put, he didn't have a real relationship with his father because he didn't have the heart of his father, not even a little bit. This is reminiscent of the Pharisees whom Jesus said did not have the love of the Father in their hearts (John 5:42). "God is love," the Scriptures teach, and

---

[52] Verse 29 implies that he was gone for years.

those who spend time with him will have the same heart of love, which includes tough love when appropriate.

3. The older brother complained that his father never gave him and his friends the means to throw a party to which his father replies, "Everything I have is yours." In other words, he didn't know his father enough to know that everything he had was already his! The father was essentially saying that the older son could've thrown a party anytime he wanted to, but he didn't because he didn't know his father and therefore didn't realize what was his. He was too focused on slaving for him in an effort to please him. He didn't have the attitude that he was a part of the family—the sole remaining heir—and that everything his father owned was essentially his. He had the mentality of a slave and slaves are property, not family members and heirs. The fact that everything of the father was still his shows that the older son does not represent a dyed-in-the-wool legalist, like the Pharisees, but rather a Christian legalist—saved (on the "mountain" of God), but faulty because he's hanging out on the right side of the mountain.

As you can see, neither son had the heart of their father. Both veered to opposite extremes, which are equally wrong. The younger son gave himself over to lawlessness for many years but, thankfully, had the sense to realize his error and repent. The older brother, on the other hand, gave himself over to legalism. He put on the airs of obedience, but he never knew the father and therefore didn't have his heart of love, freedom and joy.

Both lawlessness and legalism are extremes that must be avoided in favor of knowing the Father, which is the key to spirituality. Spirituality—in turn—is the key to godliness and true freedom.

Spirituality—The Spirit-Controlled Life

Both legalism and lawlessness must be discarded in favor of **spirituality**. This is a term that's thrown around a lot today, but it actually refers to the spirit-controlled life. This means being spirit-driven rather than flesh-driven; it means being controlled by your higher self as opposed to the lower self. To do this you simply have to learn to put off the old self and put on the new:

> **You were taught with regard to your former way of life, to <u>put off your old self</u>, which is being corrupted by its deceitful desires; ²³ to be made new in the attitude of your minds; ²⁴ and to <u>put on the new self</u>, created to be <u>like God</u> in <u>true righteousness</u> and <u>holiness</u>.   Ephesians 4:22-24**

I realize we've looked at this passage many times in this study, but that's because it contains the antidote to both legalism and libertinism. It's therefore imperative that we *get* it. The "old self" is the flesh or sin nature and we are instructed to put it off. Why? Because the old self is corrupted by "deceitful desires." Your flesh has desires, which means it has a voice, but these desires are deceitful. They promise happiness but they don't deliver. They can only ultimately bring death and all that goes with it. We are told to "put off" these fleshly desires. In the Greek this means to strip it off. We have to strip off the old way of thinking in favor of a new way. Verse 23 tells us how to do this: we must be made new in the attitude of our minds. What's the new attitude we should have? We are to count ourselves dead to the old self and alive to God in Christ Jesus (Romans 6:11). Counting ourselves alive to God includes accepting everything God says we are in Christ, that is, who we are in our new self, the spirit. We'll address this in the next section.

This results in what verse 24 calls putting "on the new self," which means living out of our spirits as led of the Holy Spirit. When we do this we'll be spirit-controlled and naturally produce the fruit thereof.

The New Testament describes this in different ways: When we are spirit-controlled we **"live by the spirit"** (Galatians 5:16), we **"clothe ourselves with the Lord Jesus Christ"** (Romans 13:14), we **"participate in the divine nature"** (2 Peter 1:4), we **"put on the new self"** (Colossians 3:10). How can putting on the new self be described as clothing ourselves with Christ or participating in the divine nature? Because the "new self" refers to our regenerated spirit which was "created to be *like God* in true righteousness and holiness" (verse 24).

If there's a *true* righteousness and holiness there's also a *false* righteousness and holiness, which is legalism. True righteousness and holiness can only be attained by, first, being born-again spiritually and, second, living out of your spirit rather than the flesh. The latter is a learning process, of course, and takes time, but the more you do it the easier it is and the more fruit you'll produce. The fruits of the spirit are the fruits of God's nature. Hence, those who live by their spirit, which is guided by the Holy Spirit, will be "like God" because the spirit naturally produces the fruits of his nature:

> **The acts of the sinful nature are obvious: sexual immorality, impurity and debauchery; [20]idolatry and witchcraft; hatred, discord, jealousy, fits of rage, selfish ambition, dissensions, factions [21]and envy; drunkenness, orgies, and the like. I warn you, as I did before, that those who live like this will not inherit the kingdom of God.**
>
> **[22] But the fruit of the spirit is love, joy, peace, patience, kindness, goodness, faithfulness, [23] gentleness and self-control. Against such things there is no law.   Galatians 5:19-23**

This list of the fruit of the spirit isn't exhaustive any more than the list of the works of the flesh is exhaustive. God has many other character traits, like righteousness (Philippians 1:11), truth (Ephesians 5:9), power (2 Timothy 1:7), righteous anger (Mark 3:1-6) and boldness (Mark 11:15-18).

The awesome news is that believers can walk free of the works of the flesh and the two ways they manifest in the Church—legalism and libertinism—simply by putting off the flesh in favor of participating in the divine nature. If this weren't possible Paul would never have instructed us to "**be imitators of God**" in Ephesians 5:1.

Speaking of that potent verse, Christians are usually blown away by it. They ask, "How can *I* possibly imitate God?" It's simple: Put off the flesh and learn to live out of your spirit with the guidance of the Holy Spirit and you'll automatically participate in the divine nature and produce the very fruit of God's character!

So how exactly do we walk in the spirit like this? There are three things that we have to do, all corresponding to the three parts of human nature—**mind**, **body** and **spirit**. These are the three keys to walking in the spirit. Let's look at each key, starting with **the mind**.

1. Count Yourself Dead to Sin and Alive to God

The first thing believers need to do in order to walk in the spirit has to do with **the mind**. Paul said that we are to be transformed by the renewing of our mind in Romans 12:2. The Greek word translated as "transformed" is where we get the English 'metamorphosis,' which means to be transformed as the result of a *process*. A great example of this process would be a lowly and not-particularly-good-looking caterpillar being transformed in its cocoon and emerging as a beautiful butterfly. Think about it, caterpillars crawl on the ground and are kind of ugly, whereas butterflies are beautiful and can fly. Believers can have just as stunning of a transformation, but it involves renewing the mind— we must let go of caterpillar-thinking (flesh-ruled thinking) in favor of butterfly-thinking (spirit-controlled thinking).

Here's a cornerstone passage on renewing the mind and being spirit-controlled:

> **The death he died, he died to sin once for all; but the life he lives, he lives to God.**
> **[11] In the same way, <u>count yourselves dead to sin</u> but <u>alive to God in Christ Jesus</u>. [12] Therefore do not let sin reign in your mortal body so that you obey its evil desires.**
>
> **Romans 6:10-12**

Verse 12 reveals the goal of this instruction—not letting sin reign in your body so that you obey its evil desires. In short, the goal is to *not* be flesh-ruled. Verse 11 shows us how to attain this goal: First, we must count ourselves dead to sin and, second, we must count ourselves alive to God in Christ Jesus.

Concerning the first part, counting ourselves dead to sin involves a new way of thinking. We must start counting ourselves as dead to the sins that normally tempt us if we want to experience freedom. For instance, if you have a weakness for lying, gossip, drunkenness or lust, you need to start making it your mindset that you are dead to these things. I used to have a problem with fits of rage so I had to start making it my mindset that I was dead to fits of rage in order to eventually walk in freedom. Making something your mindset includes making it your confession because words have the power of life and death (Proverbs 18:21). So I made this my regular confession: "I Dirk Waren am dead to fits of rage."

The second part of verse 11 is just as important. We need to count ourselves as "alive to God in Christ Jesus." Being alive to God in Christ Jesus is the opposite of being dead to God in the bondage of the flesh. So if you make it your mindset that you're dead to sin, be sure to also make it your mindset that you're alive to the opposite. For example, I made it my belief and confession that I'm dead to fits of rage, but I added that I'm alive to peace and self-control. Or say if a brother has a problem with lying or exaggerating, he would make it his mindset that he's dead to lying but alive to the truth. Or say if a sister has a problem with gossip & slander (which go hand-and-hand) she would make it her confession that she's dead to gossip & slander and alive to praying for others and speaking blessings over them.

Whatever your sin weakness is, count yourself dead to it and counteract it with the truth of *who you already are in your regenerated spirit*. You see, this whole instruction is geared toward getting the believer spirit-oriented instead of flesh-focused, spirit-controlled instead of flesh-ruled. For instance, the brother who has a problem with lying has a problem with lying because his flesh has a problem with lying. The only way for him to escape this condition is to stop being flesh-ruled because he'll continue to have a problem with lying as long as he's flesh-ruled. To walk free he'll have to learn to be spirit-controlled by changing his thinking so that it agrees with whom he is in his spirit rather than who he is in his flesh. Remember, our regenerated spirit was "created to be like God in true righteousness and holiness" (Ephesians 4:24). If you're a believer your spirit is *already* righteous and holy; it doesn't have a sin problem like your lower nature. It's whole and complete, which is what holiness is. The key to freedom is to line up your thinking with who you are in your spirit rather than who you are in your flesh.

This isn't merely a "mind over matter" principle, as some might think. If you're a believer, you can genuinely count yourself dead to sin because you *are* dead to sin in your spirit. Even if you don't *feel* like you're dead to sin, you *are* dead to sin. It's who you are in your spirit because *your spirit is righteous and holy like God!*

By the way, renewing your mind in this manner is tied to repentance since 'repent' literally means to change your mind for the better. Both the Greek words for 'repentance' and 'repent' are derived from the Greek for mind, which is *nous* (pronounced *noos*). To repent means to change your thinking, your mindset, your attitude. Any other type of "repentance" is incomplete and ineffective.

Who Are You "In Him"?

Notice that we are to count ourselves alive on to God *in Christ Jesus* (verse 11). Whenever you see phrases like "in Christ Jesus" or "in him" in the New Testament it's covenant phraseology. In other words, the passage is stating a fact about the believer who's in covenant with the Lord. Here's an example:

> **God made him who had no sin to be sin for us, so that
> in him we might become the righteousness of God.**
> **2 Corinthians 5:21**

Jesus didn't sin, of course, but the Father made him to *be* sin for us on the cross so that all those who enter into covenant with him would become the righteousness of God. As noted in **Chapter 3**, the word 'become' in the Greek means to come into being, that is, to be born. Hence, we "become" the righteousness of God through spiritual rebirth. If you're a believer this means that you are *already* righteous in your spirit and the more spirit-controlled you become the more righteous you will be.

So the key to walking in *practical* righteousness is to be spirit-focused rather than flesh-focused because, in your spirit, **you already**

are righteous. With this understanding, as you count yourself dead to sin make sure that you're also counting yourself alive to righteousness. It's the truth because it's who you already are in your spirit. Remember, Jesus said it's the truth that will set you free (John 8:31-32).

There are numerous ways the New Testament describes you in covenant with the LORD. Here are ten:

1. You're **holy** (Colossians 1:21-22).
2. You're a **child of God** (John 1:12-13).
3. You're a **new creation** (2 Corinthians 5:17).
4. You're the **righteousness of God** (2 Corinthians 5:21).
5. You're **dead to sin** (Romans 6:11,14,18).
6. You're **more than a conqueror** (Romans 8:37).
7. You're a **temple of the Holy Spirit** (1 Corinthians 6:19-20)
8. You're **rich** (2 Corinthians 8:9).
9. You're **healed** (1 Peter 2:24).
10. You're a **royal priest** or **priestess** of the Most High God (1 Peter 2:9)!

These are all "positional truths." A positional truth is any truth from the Scriptures that reveals your *position* in covenant with God and therefore *how God sees you* because of this position. For instance, Colossians 1:22 declares that we are "holy **in His sight**, without blemish and free from accusation." This is **how God sees you** because this is *who you are* in Christ. Just be wise to repent when you miss it so that God can faithfully purify you from all unrighteousness (1 John 1:8-9). This is "keeping with repentance" (Matthew & Luke 3:8). Don't allow the build-up of unconfessed sin to block the power and favor of God in your life. A side benefit of this is that it keeps your heart soft and malleable rather than hard and incorrigible.

For the New Testament believer, meaning YOU, these ten descriptions reveal *who you are* in your spirit, the "new self" (Ephesians 4:22-24).

How do you practice such positional truths? You practice them simply by *believing* them and not disagreeing with them. This shows that faith is key, which is the case with everything else in our covenant.

Remember, "The tongue has the power of life and death" so utilize this power accordingly. Never speak words that contradict who

God says you are. Never! This is tantamount to calling God a liar. Be sure to chew on these amazing positional truths and others as well. Make them your meditation and your confession. Take David, for example. He was diligent to "meditate" on God's Word, as shown in Psalm 119:15-16. The Hebrew word for 'meditate' is *siyach (SEE-akh)*, which means "to ponder and converse with oneself and, hence, out loud." As you do this with these positional truths, you'll grow in understanding and power. The more these truths become a part of you, the more you'll be set free of the flesh and the more you'll soar in the spirit free of the limitations of the fleshly plane.

Jesus said in John 8:31-32 that we must "continue" in his word if we are to "know the truth" and be set "free." Unlike your spiritual rebirth, which happened instantaneously, your metamorphosis from caterpillar-thinking to butterfly-thinking is a *process*; it may not happen overnight, but it will happen, so don't give up. If you miss it, be quick to repent and God will forgive you, and then keep moving forward. You don't drown by falling in the water; you drown by staying in the water!

If all you do is change your thinking to focus on who you already are in your spirit—dead to sin, righteous, holy—you'll be blessed, but there are two other keys to participating in the divine nature and they have to do with your **body** and your **spirit**…

2. Offering Your Body as a Living Sacrifice

Let's go back to Romans 6:11-12 and see what it goes on to say:

> **In the same way, count yourselves dead to sin but alive to God in Christ Jesus. [12] Therefore do not let sin reign in your mortal body so that you obey its evil desires. [13] Do not offer the parts of your body to sin, as instruments of wickedness, but rather <u>offer yourselves to God, as those who have been brought from death to life</u>; and <u>offer the parts of your body to him as instruments of righteousness</u>. [14] For sin shall not be your master, because you are not under law, but under grace.   Romans 6:11-14**

Since we are dead to sin and alive to God in our spirits, Paul says that we shouldn't offer the parts of our **bodies** to sin as instruments of wickedness, but rather to God as instruments of righteousness. We can do this because we've been brought from a condition of spiritual death to spiritual life, as verse 13 points out.

All unbelievers are spiritually dead. This doesn't mean that they don't have a spirit and the capacity for good, but rather that their spirit is dead to God. They're cut off from a relationship with their Creator because their spirit isn't in connection with him. Yet it's precisely because they have a spirit that they desperately want to connect with him, even though it's impossible. This, of course, gives birth to religion, which is the human attempt to connect with God. Authentic Christianity, by contrast, is God connecting with us through spiritual rebirth in Christ by the Holy Spirit.

In this passage Paul reasons that, since we've been brought from a condition of spiritual death to spiritual life, we are to offer the parts of our bodies to God's service as instruments of righteousness. This refers to two things:

1. Put into practice the truths you discover in God's Word, whether from your own studies or through receiving from others. In other words, line up your body with what God's Word teaches. This doesn't just include practical truths like "Husbands love your wives, just as Christ loved the church and gave himself up for her", but positional truths as well. How so? Because it takes your brain and your tongue to practice positional truth and both are parts of your body. If your brain and tongue aren't lining up with what God's Word says about you then you're not offering these parts of your body to Him as instruments of righteousness.

2. Put into practice whatever instruction God gives you, which includes serving in any role he calls you to or moving toward any objective he gives you. Seek the Lord in prayer concerning your purpose, both short-range and long-range. What are you inspired to do for God? What area of service really stirs you? Colossians 3:15 says to "let the peace of Christ rule in your hearts." What do you have a peace about doing? In other words, what do you have a good feeling about? Identify your strengths

and then major in them. Grasp the unique task God has called you to do in each season of your life. Whatever it is, start doing it and ask for God's strength and direction. A journey of a thousand miles starts with the first step.

When you begin utilizing the parts of your body as instruments of righteousness in God's service the law of displacement comes into play. Light displaces darkness, righteousness displaces wickedness, spirit replaces flesh. Sin shall not be your master for you are not under law (legalism) but under grace (God's favor in Christ), which is the root of spirituality (Titus 2:11-12)!

A Living Sacrifice in Worship

There's even more to offering yourself to God:

> **Therefore, I urge you, brothers, in view of God's mercy, to** <u>**offer your bodies as living sacrifices,**</u> **holy and pleasing to God –** <u>**this is your spiritual act of worship**</u>**.** [2] **Do not conform any longer to the pattern of this world, but** <u>**be transformed by the renewing of your mind**</u>**. Then you will be able to test and approve what God's will is – his good, pleasing and perfect will.**
>
> **Romans 12:1-2**

This passage plainly details the first two steps to spirituality; that is, being spirit-controlled. Verse 2 instructs us to be transformed by the renewing of our minds, which we've already addressed. Verse 1 tells us to offer our bodies to God as "living sacrifices" and adds "this is your spiritual act of *worship*." 'Worship' means to "reverently honor or adore." We can worship in two ways: **Through our actions** and **through our communion**. Actions have to do with *practice*. When we sincerely practice the truths of God's Word we are also honoring the LORD, which is worship. It's the same thing when we start lining up our lives with his assignment, big or small, we're worshipping him. Either way, our actions give glory to God. Communion, however, has to do with *communication*. Prayer is communion with God and we specifically honor him through the type of prayer known as praise & worship.

What exactly is praise & worship? The two go hand-and-hand. Praise is celebration and includes thanksgiving, raving and boasting; whereas worship is adoration. Praise naturally attracts God's presence and is in accordance with the law of respect: What you respect moves toward you while what you don't respect moves away from you. Worship, on the other hand, is adoration or awe, and is the response to being in his presence. See Psalm 95:1-7 and Psalm 100 for verification.

You'll see this principle at work in relationships all the time. Take, for instance, romantic relationships. Say if a woman is interested in a man and she praises his work, how will this make him feel? He'll feel important and respected. He'll feel like the "king of the world" and will naturally be more inclined to the woman, even if she's someone he might not have noticed otherwise. It's the same principle with God. When you start praising him and boasting of him he'll naturally be more inclined toward you. It's a simple principle.

We can further differentiate praise & worship as such: Praise celebrates God whereas worship humbly reveres him; praise lifts God up while worship bows when he is lifted; praise dances before God whereas worship pulls off his shoes; praise extols God for what he's done while worship adores him for who he is; praise says "Praise the Lord" whereas worship demonstrates that he is Lord; praise is thanksgiving for being a co-heir in Christ while worship lays the crown at His feet.

Many believers are more comfortable with worshipping God through what they do rather than through communion, but I encourage you to excel in both. I run across a lot of wives who complain that their husbands rarely tell them that they love them, if ever. They hardly even compliment them. When confronted, the husband typically argues that he loves his wife by *doing things* for her, including working hard to bring home the bread. This is wonderful, of course, but the wife *still* wants to hear him communicate it to her. Do you think it's any different with God?

Some men tend to veer away from praise & worship because they think it's somehow girly. But, let me tell you something, David is one of the most passionate praise & worship warriors recorded in the

Bible and he was wholly masculine. As a teenager he had the great faith and boldness to challenge the hulking Goliath with a slingshot when the entire army of Israel was shrinking back in terror (1 Samuel 17:24)! He went on to become one of the greatest kings of Israel, but God wouldn't allow him to build the Temple because he was a warrior king and had too much blood on his hands! See 1 Chronicles 28:3. Does this sound like a girly man? Or consider Moses' aide, Joshua. After Moses spoke with God in the Tent of Meeting, Joshua would stay and linger in God's presence (Exodus 33:11). Guess who God later chose to lead the Israelites in the conquest of Canaan? Joshua. There's clearly a link between those who choose to be mighty praise & worship warriors for God and those who are mighty warriors in his service. Those who are "ever praising" the LORD and who dwell in his presence "go from strength to strength" (Psalm 84:4-7). They are "transformed into his likeness with ever-increasing glory, which comes from the Lord, who is the Spirit" (2 Corinthians 3:18). In light of all this, anyone who claims that praise & worship is worthless or sissified is grossly ignorant.

Needless to say, every believer is called to deeper praise & worship. It will literally revolutionize your life, as it has mine and continues to do so.

If all we did was practice these first two keys to being spirit-controlled we'd be greatly blessed and experience freedom to a higher degree than ever. But there's one more step and it has to do with your **spirit**. It's what the Bible calls praying in the spirit.

3. Praying in the Spirit and Charging Yourself Up

Let's look at a couple of key passages about praying in **the spirit**:

> **But you, dear friends, <u>build yourselves up</u> in your most holy faith and <u>pray in the Holy Spirit</u>.**
> **Jude 1:20**

This verse shows that believers in general should "build themselves up" in faith by praying in the Holy Spirit. It gives the impression of charging up your faith like a battery. In the Greek "build yourselves up" means "to build upon." You see, every believer has a measure of faith at the time of salvation (Romans 12:3), but this measure can be built upon as the believer grows. In other words, believers *should* increase in faith as they mature. How do we do this? One way is through God's Word (Romans 10:17), another is by spending time in God's presence through praise & worship; after all, God is full of faith and therefore those who hang around him will develop the same faith he has. It's the law of association (Proverbs 13:20). Jude 1:20 (above) shows that praying in the Spirit is also essential for increasing in faith.

Here's another passage on praying in the spirit:

And <u>pray in the Spirit</u> <u>on all occasions</u> with all kinds of prayers and requests.

Ephesians 6:18

This verse appears right after Paul details the six pieces of the "armor of God," which shows that praying in the spirit is actually the seventh piece of the armor even though he doesn't analogize it like he does with the other six pieces (for instance, faith is a "shield" and the Word of God is a "sword" and so on). I liken praying in the spirit to *artillery* or a *missile* since you can pray in the spirit for people and situations a long distance away, even on the other side of the planet. This shows that praying in the spirit is actually a spiritual *weapon*, as is the sword of the spirit.

So we're clearly instructed in the Scriptures to charge our faith up by praying in the spirit and also to pray in the spirit on all occasions with all kinds of prayers and requests. The question now is, what is "praying in the Spirit"? After all, we can't very well pray in the spirit if we don't even know what it is. Thankfully, the Bible tells us exactly what it is:

> **For if I pray in a tongue, my spirit prays, but my mind is unfruitful. [15] So what shall I do? I will pray with my spirit, but I will also pray with my mind; I will sing with my spirit, but I will also sing with my mind.**
>
> **1 Corinthians 14:14-15**

By saying "if I pray in a tongue, my spirit prays" Paul was defining praying in the spirit. If he prayed in a tongue his spirit was praying, led of the Holy Spirit, and therefore he was praying in the spirit or praying in the Spirit (capitalized[53]). Praying in the spirit is synonymous with speaking in tongues, which is also known as glossolalia (*gloss-ah-LAY-lee-ah*). What is speaking in tongues? It's when a believer prays from his spirit rather than his mind and therefore speaks in a language unknown to him/her. We see this in verse 15 where Paul notes two types of prayer—praying with his spirit and praying with his mind, singing with his spirit and singing with his mind.

Praying with your mind is obvious: It's praying with a language you understand, which is typically the language you most often speak. For me it would be English. When I pray in English I'm praying with my mind because it's a language I know and understand. Praying with one's mind is wonderful and this is usually what people think of when they think of prayer, but when we pray in this manner we are limited to our own understanding. Whatever it is we're praying for—whether a person, people, place or situation—we're limited to our own understanding. This is where praying in the spirit comes into play. Praying in the spirit—speaking in tongues—bypasses the limitations of our understanding as led of the Holy Spirit. For instance, say if I'm praying for a believer who's struggling with a certain sin and has backslid to some degree. If I pray with my mind—my understanding—I am limited to what I know about the situation, but if I pray in the spirit for him I can address things beyond my understanding as led of the Holy Spirit.

---

[53] Since there is no capitalization in the original Greek text, translators have to determine if the word for spirit, *pneuma,* refers to the human spirit (un-capitalized) or the Holy Spirit (capitalized). Either/or works in this case since the human spirit prays as led of the Holy Spirit due to the fact that the believer's human spirit (un-capitalized) is birthed and indwelt by the Spirit (capitalized).

Or say if you're going to lose your job due to budget cuts or whatever in six months, but you don't know about it. You can't pray about this with your mind because you don't even know it's going to happen. However, the Holy Spirit knows everything because he's God and he indwells your spirit; he guides you. So when you pray in the spirit the Holy Spirit will likely guide your spirit to pray for your encouragement and a new job opportunity when you lose your current one in six months. You may not know about it, but the Holy Spirit does. As such, you were able to address something in prayer that your mind wasn't even cognizant of through praying in the spirit. You bypassed the limitations of your understanding.

This is why Paul encouraged us to "pray in the Spirit on all occasions" in Ephesians 6:18 and it's why he stressed that he would pray and sing with both his mind and his spirit. *Both* are important.

The gift of personal tongues is for *all believers,* which is why these passages on praying in the spirit refer to all believers and not just to some who have a special gift. Note how none of these passages say anything like "Now, *if* you have the gift of tongues, pray in the spirit on all occasions" or "*If* you can speak in tongues build yourself up in faith by praying in the Holy Spirit." Back when these passages were written it was assumed that all believers had the gift of personal tongues. Virtually every believer had it because leaders in the Church didn't shy away from emphasizing the importance of the baptism of the Holy Spirit, as they do today, unfortunately.

I describe praying in the spirit as "personal tongues" to distinguish it from the gift of tongues utilized in a church environment, which is followed by an interpretation in the common language. Not everyone has *this* gift, which Paul made clear in 1 Corinthians 12:30. The kind of speaking in tongues I'm talking about is different and refers to the believer praying *to God* with his or her spirit as led of the Holy Spirit. This is for *all* believers. Public tongues, on the other hand, isn't actually praying in the spirit because the believer who is functioning in this gift isn't praying *to God*, but is rather giving a message *from God* to the group of believers for their exhortation and encouragement. One refers to the believer praying to God with his/her spirit and the other refers to God speaking to the congregation. They're quite different. All believers can have the gift of personal tongues, but not all believers have the gift of public tongues. It's important to distinguish the two.

If every believer can have the gift of personal tongues, how do we get it? We receive it through…

The Baptism of the Holy Spirit

Many Christians are unaware of this, but there are six foundational doctrines—*teachings*—in Christianity; and "instructions about baptisms" is the third doctrine:

> **Therefore let us leave the elementary teachings about Christ and go on to maturity, not laying again the foundation of repentance from acts that lead to death, and of faith in God, [2] <u>instruction about baptisms</u>, the laying on of hands, the resurrection of the dead, and eternal judgment.**
>
> **Hebrews 6:1-2**

The word "baptisms" is plural because there's more than one baptism. When most people think of baptism they think of **water baptism**, but there are two other kinds of baptism for the believer, which are **baptism into Christ** and **the baptism of the Holy Spirit**. The word 'baptism' refers to "an immersion or washing." As such, water baptism refers to a believer's immersion into water symbolizing their death and resurrection in Christ; this is a testimony to the world and the Church, which is why it's done publicly. Although this is the most commonly understood form of baptism it's actually the least important, which isn't to say it's unimportant, of course.

It's not as important as the baptism into Christ because the baptism into Christ refers to entering into covenant with God through spiritual rebirth and the washing away of one's sins through the blood of Yeshua (Galatians 3:26-29). No one can be saved without this immersion into Christ. I'm sure you see why this baptism is more important than water baptism since water baptism is merely a symbolic testimony of *what has already taken place spiritually.* What's more important, the real inward baptism or the outward baptism that *represents* it?

Being baptized into Christ is essentially one-in-the-same as being "born of the Spirit" (John 3:3,6), but being born of the Spirit is distinct from the baptism of the Spirit, although they occasionally happen at the same time. When you're born of the Spirit the Spirit is *in* you (Romans 8:9 & 1 Corinthians 6:19), whereas when you're baptized in the Spirit the Spirit is *all over* you because you're immersed with the Spirit. It's the difference between drinking a glass of water and jumping into a pure, mountain lake.

Speaking in tongues is theoretically the *initial physical evidence* of the baptism in the Holy Spirit. While speaking in tongues is not the Holy Spirit and the Holy Spirit is not speaking in tongues, *they both go hand in hand.* Here are five scriptural examples of people receiving this baptism:

1. **The believers in Jerusalem, as shown in Acts 2:1-4.** All of them spoke in tongues.

2. **The Samaritans, as shown in Acts 8:12-19.** The Samaritans were part Jew and part Gentile. Verse 18 shows that Simon the sorcerer "saw" that the Spirit was given to the Samaritans when the apostles laid their hands on them. In other words, he *saw* evidence that they received the Holy Spirit. What did he see? We must interpret Scripture with Scripture, which is a hermeneutical rule. Since the rest of the New Testament shows that speaking in tongues is the initial evidence of the baptism of the Holy Spirit, this must've been what Simon saw—people speaking in languages they didn't know.

3. **Saul in Damascus, as shown in Acts 9:17-18.** Although speaking in tongues is not mentioned in this passage, the baptism of the Holy Spirit is, and we observe scriptural evidence elsewhere that Saul/Paul spoke in tongues on a regular basis, which is praying in the spirit (1 Corinthians 14:18-19).

4. **Cornelius' household in Caesarea, as shown in Acts 10:44-48.** This refers to the first Gentile believers. Verses 45-46 state that "The circumcised believers who had come with Peter were astonished that the gift of the Holy Spirit

had been poured out even on the Gentiles. *For they heard them speaking in tongues* and praising God." Since believers who are not baptized in the spirit can and do praise God, the evidence of the baptism is obviously speaking in tongues.

5. **The Ephesians, as shown in Acts 19:5-7.** This passage shows that all twelve spoke in tongues as a result of receiving the baptism, not just a select few.

As already noted *every* Christian can and should receive this baptism and pray in the spirit to supplement prayer in his or her native language. This can be observed in 1 Corinthians 14:14-15, 18-19 and Ephesians 6:18. I have to emphasize this because there's this idea rampant in the body of Christ that speaking in tongues was done away with once the biblical canon was completed, which is known as cessationism. Don't believe it. It's a colossal lie that has allowed the enemy to keep multitudes of sincere believers from the *full* empowerment and help of the Holy Spirit.

Praying in the spirit is important because it edifies us by building us up in faith and empowers us to minister, to love people and to walk free from sin.

Before we get into that, there are a few things about the baptism of the Spirit and speaking in tongues that need to be stressed and clarified:

- Just because a Christian is baptized in the Spirit and *can* speak in tongues, it does not mean that he or she *is* walking in the spirit and producing the fruit thereof, like love, joy, peace, kindness, faith, humility and self-control (Galatians 5:22-23). Putting it another way, to be spirit-controlled is synonymous with bearing fruit of the spirit but just because a believer is baptized in the Spirit and *can* speak in tongues it does not mean that he or she is participating in the divine nature by implementing one or more of the three keys as discussed in this chapter.
- With the above understanding, the baptism of the Holy Spirit and the corresponding gift of glossolalia should not be taken as a badge of superiority where the believer becomes condescending toward those who don't (yet) have it. To do this would be

arrogance and "God *opposes* the proud." Spirit-baptized believers who cop a pompous attitude will naturally slip into legalism. Speaking of which, there are plenty of tongues-talking legalists in the body of Christ—*too* many!

- Although the baptism of the Holy Spirit is wonderful and empowering—which is why I'm stressing it—it should *not* be viewed as a "cure all" or the all-and-end-all of Christianity.
- If a Christian can walk in the spirit to a good degree *without* the baptism of the Holy Spirit, how much more so if they *are* baptized in the Holy Spirit? In other words, just because you're doing well spiritually without speaking in tongues, don't let it rob you of this wonderful gift that God has provided for all believers!
- The baptism of the Holy Spirit is usually transferred through physical contact, that is, the ministry of laying on of hands, but not always. Although the gift can be received through someone who already has it, as shown in some of the above examples, a believer can also receive it simply through faith (Luke 11:9-13). In fact, everything in our covenant is by faith.
- If any believer has hands laid on him or her for this baptism and they don't speak in tongues it doesn't necessarily mean they didn't receive the baptism. They may have received it, but simply have yet to speak in tongues. We have to understand that speaking in tongues—praying in the spirit—is something that the believer does by his or her volition and is not something the Holy Spirit makes people do. Remember what Paul said: "So what shall *I* do? *I will* pray with my spirit, but *I will* also pray with my mind" (1 Corinthians 14:15). Just as praying in a language you understand is an act of your own will, so is praying in the spirit. With this understanding, if I so chose I could theoretically not pray in the spirit the rest of my life even though I am baptized in the Spirit. Are you following?
- On that note, there are too many Christians who are baptized in the Spirit and yet rarely, if ever, pray in the spirit. They therefore lack the empowerment the Holy Spirit wants to give them. Speaking of which…

The Empowerment and Help
of the Holy Spirit

The reason I'm going into so much detail about the baptism of the Spirit and praying in the spirit is because these are God-given sources of great empowerment for the believer to walk in newness of life and victory. Unfortunately, many believers settle for less than God's best and they go through life struggling with things they don't *have* to struggle with because God has provided the power and help they need—if only they knew of these truths and implemented them! It is for this purpose that God detailed these truths in his Word and it's why I'm stressing them here.

Notice the power that Paul said was available for his protégé Timothy:

> **For this reason I remind you to <u>fan into flame the gift of God</u>, which is in you through the <u>laying on of hands</u>. ⁷ For God did not give us a <u>spirit of timidity</u>, but a <u>spirit of power</u>, of <u>love</u> and of <u>self-discipline</u>.**
>
> **2 Timothy 1:6-7**

What gift was Paul talking about? He doesn't say, but there are clues: The gift was given through the laying on of hands and it is linked to the spirit or Spirit.[54] Since Scripture interprets Scripture we must conclude that Paul was referring to the baptism of the Holy Spirit because **1.** this gift involves the Spirit, **2.** there's repeated evidence that this gift is typically transferred through the laying on of hands, as detailed in the previous section, and **3.** this gift involves Spirit-given power. The baptism of the Spirit is the obvious answer.

By instructing Timothy to "fan into flame" this gift, Paul was simply encouraging Timothy to pray in the spirit more often, which is

---

[54] Remember, there's no capitalization in the original Greek and therefore translators have to discern whether "spirit" should be capitalized in reference to the Holy Spirit or *not* capitalized in reference to the human spirit. In this case, the NIV translators decided not to capitalize "spirit", nor did the KJV translators.

actually the seventh piece of the armor of God (Ephesians 6:18). What does he mean by fanning it into flame? Speaking from experience, when I first received the baptism of the Holy Spirit in 1986—two and a half years after my salvation—I'd generally keep saying the same phrase over and over in the spirit. It was just a handful of words and I had no idea what I was saying. Regardless, I put into practice this passage: I fanned the gift into flame by praying in the spirit whenever I had the opportunity, like driving to classes or to work or when I went off by myself to pray (Luke 5:16). In time my spiritual prayer language grew dramatically. How so? Because I fanned it into flame just as Paul instructed Timothy. This is the key to walking in the three blessings cited in verse 7: *power*, *love* and *self-discipline*. Let's take a look at each of these...

Power. One of the main purposes of the baptism of the Holy Spirit is for believers to be *empowered* to walk in newness of life and be witnesses to the world (Luke 24:49 & Acts 1:8). The Greek word for power is *dunamis*, which is where we get the English words dynamo and dynamite. 'Dynamo' bespeaks of electrical power or a really energetic, forceful person, and 'dynamite' suggests explosive power. These are earthly things. Imagine how much greater is God's *dunamis* power that's available to all believers through the baptism of the Holy Spirit! All we have to do is fan it into flame and keep fanning it into flame. When Paul said, "Do not get drunk on wine, which leads to debauchery. Instead, be filled with the Spirit" (Ephesians 5:18) he meant it in the sense of *keep being filled*. Praying in the spirit is an *ongoing* thing. Why do you think Jude said, "But you, dear friends, build yourselves up in your most holy faith and pray in the Holy Spirit" (Jude 1:20)? Why do you think Paul instructed, "And pray in the Spirit on *all occasions* with all kinds of prayers and requests" (Ephesians 6:18)? Because it's an ongoing activity. We don't pray in the spirit and then never do it again; that would be absurd. It's a daily thing.

If you have the baptism of the Holy Spirit,[55] I encourage you to pray in the spirit as soon as you get out of bed in the morning and as loud as possible; sing in the spirit as well, as Paul exemplified. Singing in the

---

[55] And, if you don't have it, please get it ASAP. It's available for *every* believer.

spirit, by the way, is merely praying in the spirit to a melody, like you're singing a song. Paul practiced this and he was a powerhouse for God, second only to Jesus Christ himself in the New Testament. If you want to be a powerhouse like him you'll have to do what he did. He's our example.

You can pray in the spirit or sing in the spirit while you're making coffee or taking a shower or driving. How long you do this is between you and God (I suggest at least 5-10 minutes), just do it and keep doing it—charge yourself up every morning and throughout the day. It's more powerful than strong coffee. In a sense, it's the ultimate drug because it's free and you don't have to deal with hangovers, not to mention the supply never runs out.

Think again about *dunamis* power—dynamite power. Does this sound like a boring thing? A deathly religious thing? No, it suggests the abundant life that the Messiah said he came to give us:

The thief comes only to steal and kill and destroy; I have come that they may have <u>life</u> and <u>have it to the full</u>.   John 10:10

The very reason Jesus came was to give us life and life to the full! When you get around Christians infected by legalism the last thing you'll discern is life to the full and all that comes with it—joy, excitement, energy, ideas, faith, strength, confidence, love, creativity, originality, etc. More likely you'll witness a stuffy, dead, dull, powerless, hackneyed religious spirit. It's a horrible shame. This is the image secular culture has of Christians, but it's a false image and, thankfully, we don't have to be like that. Praise God!

Do you want dynamite power at work in your life every day? Then pray in the spirit more and more! This is the very reason the LORD gave us the gift of speaking in tongues, not to argue with non-Charismatics!

Love. The type of love we're empowered to walk in by praying in the spirit is *agape* love, which is **purely practical love** or **love-in-action**, which isn't dependent on affinity or affection. It's important to distinguish this because there are four types of love observed in the Bible:

1. ***Storge* love** is family love, which includes the bond, affection and loyalty that develops between family members. Although the word itself, *storge (STOR-gay)*, is not found in the original text we see numerous examples of this type of love in the Bible, like Martha & Mary's love for their brother Lazarus in John 11.

   Of course, the opposite of *storge* love can develop between family members, which is when relatives develop hatred for each other. A couple of obvious examples are Cain & Abel (Genesis 4:1-11) and Joseph & his jealous brothers (Genesis 37).

2. ***Phileo* love** is friendship love or brotherly love, like the platonic affection/respect of David and Jonathan (2 Samuel 1:25-26). Philadelphia, "the city of brotherly love," was named after this type of love. You could say that *phileo* love is *storge* love applied to non-family members. There's an element of affection, respect or bond despite the fact that they're not kin. The word *phileo (fil-LAY-oh)* can be found some 25 times in the original Greek text of the New Testament whereas the noun form, *philia (fil-EE-ah)*, appears only once (which is why we're using *phileo* here and not *philia*).

   Jesus' *phileo* love for Martha, Mary and Lazarus is a good example of this form of love, as observed here:

   [5] **Now Jesus <u>loved</u>** *(phileo)* **Martha and her sister and Lazarus...**
   [35] **Jesus wept.**
   [36] **Then the Jews said, "See how he <u>loved</u>** *(phileo)* **him!"**

   John 11:5, 35-36

3. ***Eros* love** is *phileo* love between members of the opposite sex and includes a romantic element, but it doesn't refer to shallow sexual lust. Although the word *eros (eer-ROSS)* doesn't appear in the original manuscripts there are many examples of this type of love in the Scriptures. One overt example can be observed in the amazing Song of Songs. Here's a passionate expression of love from this book where the man is speaking to the woman:

> **show me your face,**
> **let me hear your voice;**
> **for your voice is sweet,**
> **and your face is lovely.**
> **Song of Songs 2:14**

4. *Agape* **love** is, again, purely practical love or love-in-action and is therefore not dependent on liking/respecting a person. It's usually described as divine love, which is true since "God is love," but it's really just **practical love** or **love-in-practice** *regardless of* **bond/respect/affection**. In other words, you can *agape* love someone for whom you have zero kinship (*storge* love), esteem/rapport (*phileo* love) or romantic fondness (*eros* love). Note the biblical definition:

> <u>Love</u> *(agape)* **is patient, love is kind. It does not envy. It does not boast, it is not proud. ⁵ It is not rude, it is not self-seeking, it is not easily angered, it keeps no record of wrongs. ⁶ Love does not delight in evil but rejoices with the truth. ⁷ It always protects, always trusts, always hopes, always perseveres.**
> **1 Corinthians 13:4-7**

Paul gave this definition of *agape* love by the Holy Spirit to encourage believers to practice *agape* love. Notice that he doesn't say anything about having warm feelings or respect toward the other person when applying *agape* love. Why? Because ***agape* love refers purely to *practical* love**, which is distinguished from *storge* love (familial love), *phileo* love (friendship love) and *eros* love (romantic love), each of which involve some type of connection, closeness or warm feelings. It's easy to walk in love toward people for whom you have kinship, respect or affection, but it's not so easy when you don't.

Think about it like this: The most famous passage of Scripture says "God so <u>loved</u> *(agape)* the world that he gave his one and only Son, that whoever believes in him shall not perish but have eternal life." Do you think this means that God has warm, fuzzy feelings for all the tyrants, warmongers, abusers, God-haters, rapists, murderers, molesters and perverts out there? Do you think he's up there with dreamy eyes saying, "Oh, I just so respect and love these wicked people!" Of course not. The passage is referring to *agape* love—purely practical love. The Father was *practicing* love when he had his one and only Son die for our sins; so did the Son when he willingly laid down his life. This opened the door for reconciliation and eternal life through spiritual rebirth. God made the first move, humanity didn't. The question is, how are we going to respond to his incredible example of *agape* love?

Those who respond positively to God's *agape* love and accept the gospel immediately enter into his *storge* love since they are born into God's family (1 John 3:9). These are candidates for becoming the Lord's friend, which has to do with *phileo* love and the favor that comes with it. As noted, *phileo* love refers to friendship love or brotherly love. Consider Jesus' statement to his disciples:

"You are my <u>friends</u> *if* you do what I command."
John 15:14

According to this verse not everyone is Jesus' friend, not even every believer, who is part of God's family and therefore possess his *storge* love. Christ's friends are limited to those who practice what he commands. This refers to believers who respect the Lord enough to know his Word and put it into practice, as well as obey the directions of the Spirit. God's grace (favor) for salvation is for all and is unmerited; it is simply received through humble repentance and faith (Acts 20:21), but this doesn't mean we can't increase in favor with God after we receive salvation. Why do you think the Scriptures say that Jesus—who is our example—*grew in favor with God* just as he grew in favor with people (Luke 2:52)? Why do you think Peter encouraged us to grow in the grace (favor) of our Lord and Savior Jesus Christ, just as we are to grow in knowledge (2 Peter 3:18)?

Sad to say, these simple truths are blasphemy in some circles of Christianity. It's both ignorant and shameful.

My point is that *agape* love is purely practical in nature and therefore you don't have to feel any warmth or respect toward the person or people with whom you share it. In short, *agape* is love-in-action and has little to do with affection, that is, *liking* the person. This explains how we can fulfill Jesus & Paul's instructions to love our enemies (Luke 6:27 & Romans 12:20-21). Do you *like* your enemies, that is, *phileo* love them? Do you respect them? Of course you don't. But this isn't a problem because we are **not** commanded to *phileo* love our enemies, but rather to *agape* love them. Are you following?

This shows why *agape* love is often defined as "unconditional love" since it is purely practical in nature and, again, not dependent upon liking an individual or on how well they treat you. Here's an example: I was at my desk in my den and had a few greeting cards ready to mail out on the side of my desk. Carol came in and noticed that one of the cards was made out to someone who's been known to treat us—particularly me—with contempt and slander. She said, "Oh, what a warmhearted soul you are!" I explained to her that it wasn't a big deal because I'm empowered by the spirit to love those who hate me without cause. It's been my regular practice for years. My flesh may not want to do it, but I strive to be spirit-controlled and not flesh-ruled. The main reason some believers have difficulty in doing this is because **1.** they're not walking in the spirit and therefore not producing the fruit thereof, the primary fruit being *agape* love (Galatians 5:19-23), **2.** they're not baptized in the Spirit or **3.** if they are, they're not praying in the spirit because praying in the spirit charges the believer up and empowers us to *agape* love our enemies and "overcome evil with good" (Romans 12:20-21).

By the way, when I refer to walking in love, I'm not referring to just the gentle variety. There's something called *tough love* because *agape* love "is kind" and "does not delight in evil." Sometimes the kindest thing you can do for people is to boldly confront the evil that has infected them, like Paul when he openly rebuked Peter for his legalism (Galatians 2:11-14) and Christ when he radically cleared the temple while yelling, pushing over tables and cracking a whip (Mark 11:15-18 & John 2:13-16). Some Christians think they're walking in *agape* love by being nicey-wicey doormats when, in fact, they're being cowardly and enabling evil to persist.[56] I should hastily add that this isn't an excuse to be a rash fool who's overly gung-ho with confronting and rebuking, which is abusive and usually results in unnecessary strife.

---

[56] For more information on this rarely-heard topic see the teaching *Gentle Love and Tough Love* at the FOL site.

Needless to say, if you want a more effective love walk, keep yourself filled with the Spirit by praying in the spirit and fanning into flame the *agape* love that's necessary to practice it.

Self-control. I've been in the Lord since 1984 and I've overcome certain struggles of the flesh as I've grown spiritually and continue to do so, but I know believers from the 1980s and 90s who are still struggling with the very same issues they had back then. I'm talking about things like alcoholism, drugs, depression, porn addiction and government idolatry. They never attained the self-control necessary to walk in victory in these areas. I don't mean fleshly self-control here, but rather the Spirit-empowered discipline necessary to strip off such bondages and walk according to the spirit, which naturally produces the fruit of the spirit, one of which is self-control.

If a believer is walking in spiritual self-control they'll have the power and discipline to walk free of fleshly bondages. This is something that develops over time, but praying in the spirit is key to producing this *dunamis* power and the necessary discipline, not to mention the other two keys to walking in the Spirit.

Notice what Jesus said about the purpose of the baptism of the Holy Spirit:

> **⁵ "but in a few days you will be <u>baptized with the Holy Spirit</u>…"**
> **⁸ "But <u>you will receive power</u> <u>when the Holy Spirit comes on you</u>; and you will be my <u>witnesses</u> in Jerusalem, and in all Judea and Samaria, and to the ends of the earth."** **Acts 1:5,8**

The purpose of the baptism of the Holy Spirit is to *empower* believers. Empowering believers to be witnesses means more than just the oomph it takes to share the gospel with people verbally, it includes the power to walk free of the flesh, including legalism and libertinism. After all, how effective is a witness who lacks the power to walk free of the bondages of the flesh?

The Messiah also said this about the Holy Spirit:

> **"But the <u>Counselor</u>, the Holy Spirit, whom the Father will send in my name, will <u>teach you all things</u> and will remind you of everything I have said to you."**   **John 14:26**

Here Christ describes the Holy Spirit as our "Counselor," which is translated as "Helper" in the King James Version. He goes on to say that the Counselor will teach us all things. Yeshua described this as guiding us "into all truth" in John 16:13. Needless to say, if you want more understanding and insight to the Scriptures and the will of God pray in the spirit more often.

As far as the Spirit being our helper, Paul said this:

> **In the same way, <u>the Spirit helps us in our weakness</u>. We do not know what we ought to pray for, but <u>the Spirit himself intercedes for us</u> with groans that words cannot express.**
> **Romans 8:26**

One of the purposes of the Holy Spirit—our "Helper"—is to help us in our weaknesses. He does this by interceding for us, which takes place when we pray in the spirit. When we speak in tongues the Spirit guides our spirit what to pray and, hence, intercedes for us. This can include "groans that words cannot express," which I've experienced on some occasions while praying in the spirit (Romans 8:26).

What we want to focus on here is that the Holy Spirit is our Helper who helps us in our weaknesses. As shared above, I've known believers who have problems in areas like alcohol, drugs, depression, porn addiction, lying and gossip/slander. In other words, they're weak in these areas. The good news is that one of the very purposes of the Holy Spirit is to *empower* believers to overcome in such areas, but we have to be baptized in the Spirit and fan into flame the gift—praying in the spirit on all occasions. As we do this, we'll cultivate the power *from within* to overcome in any area of weakness. This is *spiritual* power, not fleshly power. Let me give an example from my own life.

I used to have a huge problem with depression. Two professional Christian counselors said I needed to be on medication, but I *knew* that wasn't the route to go. If other believers choose to go on medication for a season, that's between them and the LORD, but—for me—it wasn't the way to go. I just knew it. So I kept following the Lord and growing in the Spirit. After a while, I noticed that the Spirit would lead my spirit to laugh uproariously sometimes while praying in the spirit. For example, there are times when I'm tempted to get blue, but instead I pray in the spirit and my spirit inspires me to laugh like crazy as led of the Holy Spirit. This has nothing to do with my mental state since laughing is the farthest thing from my mind on these occasions, but as my spirit prompts me to laugh uproariously with knee-slapping laughter I am naturally influenced by it—it rubs off. Needless to say, it keeps me out of depression! You see: The Holy Spirit helps me in my area of weakness and enables me to overcome.

If you have an area of weakness—and who doesn't?—charge yourself up regularly by praying in the spirit and the Holy Spirit will give you the power to overcome and walk in victory, I guarantee it. It may not happen overnight, but it will happen and one day you'll look back at your current struggle and laugh. Your weakness will come to mind and you'll just laugh about it!

Your weakness may not even be something of the flesh but simply a trait that's unique to you. For instance, you might have an extreme loathing for the punch-the-clock grind. The Holy Spirit will help you in this area of "weakness" as well. He'll give ideas, golden connections or open doors for you to make a living without the drudgery of punching a clock. Whatever your weakness or need is, the Holy Spirit is here and he's *in you* to help you!

Recapping the Three Keys

So the three keys to being spirit-controlled rather than flesh-ruled are as follows:

1. **Renew your mind.** Make it your mindset that you're dead to sin but alive to God in Christ Jesus. This includes making it your confession. Say: "I [state your name] am dead to sin and alive to God in Christ Jesus." Renewing your mind effectively includes

lining up your thoughts and words with who God's Word says you already are in Christ. For instance, the Bible says that you're dead to sin, holy, righteous and more than a conqueror in covenant with the Lord. These all describe who you are in your spirit as opposed to the flesh. You may not *feel* like you are these things, but you already are in your spirit. By accepting these positional truths by faith you're being spirit-focused rather than flesh-focused. Do it.

2. **Offer the parts of your body to God as instruments of righteousness.** This includes both serving the Lord—doing what God wants you to do (both general instructions from the Scriptures and specific instructions from the Spirit)—and praise & worship. Each puts into motion the law of displacement. By moving forward in the spirit you aren't slipping backwards in the flesh. By spending time in the light of God's presence through regular praise & worship darkness has no recourse but to flee. How do you get the darkness out of a room? You simple turn on the lights!

3. **Pray (and sing) in the spirit regularly.** This will keep you charged up and built-up in faith. It'll produce the power you need to walk in the full life Christ came to give us; it'll empower you to love people you don't have warm feelings toward, including your enemies who hate you without cause. It'll enable you to walk in tough love when necessary, including righteous radicalness, like when Paul radically rebuked an arrogant sorcerer and temporarily cursed him with blindness to humble him, as led of the Holy Spirit (Acts 13:8-12). It'll provide the self-discipline necessary to overcome personal weaknesses, including lack of confidence, depression and various sin problems, like alcoholism, drugs, lying, gossip and slander.

Practicing these three principles is simply a matter of wisdom and love. The first and greatest command is to **love God** with all your heart and the second is to **love people** as you **love yourself** (Matthew 22:34-39). As you can see, there are three applications to these two commands since we are commanded to love others *as* we love ourselves, which means you have to love yourself first. I mean that in a healthy sense, of course, and not a narcissistic one. If you genuinely love yourself you'll put these principles into practice on a regular basis. After all, if you fail to implement them you won't be intimate with God and you won't have a victorious Christian life. You'll be encumbered and limited by personal weaknesses or areas of the flesh. This will not bless you, it won't bless those linked to you, and it won't bless God.

Practicing these three principles is the key to walking in the spirit or participating in the divine nature. It's the key to producing the fruit of the spirit and, therefore, being *spiritual* rather than *carnal*. Simply put, it's the key to being spirit-controlled rather than flesh-ruled. The former gives life while the latter brings death.

24/7 "God-Consciousness"

This is the key to having a vital, active relationship with God, which is the antidote to all forms of legalism. By "active relationship" I don't mean thinking about God once or twice a day, but rather 24/7 God-consciousness where you're in constant connection and communion. This makes sense of Paul's instruction to "pray without ceasing" in 1 Thessalonians 5:17 (KJV). How can anyone possibly "pray without ceasing"? By participating in the divine nature and walking in 24/7 God-consciousness. A close relationship with your heavenly Father by the Holy Spirit through Christ involves the same time and attention that any close relationship requires. Like those relationships, it's not a chore, but a joy and an honor. It develops over time. David said, "Taste and see that the LORD is good" (Psalm 34:8). Once you've genuinely tasted of a relationship with God nothing else in life compares. It's the ultimate high!

It's your choice. You've been granted the awesome power of DECISION, which is volition. Whether you know it or not, you operated in this power to receive eternal salvation (Romans 10:9-10). Use this God-given gift to your advantage in your Christian walk. You're not a loser, you're a winner. Go forth and walk in the freedom and victory that God has bought for you at great cost! Rise up O man of God, rise up O woman of God, and soar on the heights in the spirit far above the limitations of the mental realm and the flesh! Amen.

"Put Off the Old Man"

It's imperative that you put off the "old man"—the flesh—for this to work. This is the very first thing we are instructed to do in Ephesians 4:22-24. We see the same instruction in this passage:

> **Do not lie to one another, since you have <u>put off the old man with his deeds</u>,** [10] **and have <u>put on the new man</u> who <u>is</u> renewed in knowledge according to the image of Him who created him,**[57]
>
> **Colossians 3:9-10** (NKJV)

Before you can put on the new man—that is, effectively walk in the spirit—you have to be willing to put off the old man and "his" fleshly deeds. This means repenting of any area of the flesh once it is revealed to you as sin. You see, God deals with his children according to the light we have. Once we have revelation of something we are responsible for living according to it. See John 9:39-41, 15:22 and 1 Timothy 1:13 for verification. And, no, this isn't an excuse to stay in ignorance.

Let me give a widespread example. In Westernized cultures today fornication is viewed as a normal lifestyle, but it's a sin according to God's Word. When the average male turns to the Lord he'll often come into the kingdom with the attitude that there's nothing wrong with fornication since it's such a prominent activity. Besides, "everyone does it," he might reason. As he grows spiritually, however (which would include learning from a wiser brother or sister in the Lord), he comes to realize that it's wrong and God has something better for him. Up until this point God may mercifully overlook transgressions in this area to a degree because the guy was corrupted by worldly culture and just didn't know any better. Once he *knows* the truth, however, he's obligated to walk according to it.

---

[57] Notice how verse 10 states that the "new man" *is* renewed in knowledge according to the image of the Creator. This refers to the regenerated human spirit and suggests that it's *already* renewed and complete (holy). Both the KJV and NKJV translate the passage as such and this corresponds to Ephesians 4:24. The New International Version wrongly translates this verse by saying that the new man "is *being* renewed in knowledge," which is why I didn't quote the NIV.

Additional examples abound: A Christian man who grew up in an Islamic culture where it was normal to subjugate and abuse women; believers raised in a society where racial prejudice is the status quo; youths in college and the drunken hedonism thereof. The LORD may condone transgressions in these areas for a season because of His compassion (sympathetic understanding) and mercy; once the believer knows better, however, s/he is obliged to walk according this new light.

This is simply a matter of loving God, the first and greatest command (1 John 2:15-17). It's also a matter of wisdom or common sense. Yet I'm surprised at how many people refuse to give up fornication after becoming believers and discovering it's a sin. Then they wonder why they don't feel close to the LORD and they're not blessed. I'll tell you why—they're not putting off the old man! They're being stubborn and stupid.

Think about it like this: Say you're a parent and have a baby who soiled her diaper. You take the old diaper off, clean her up, and then put on the new diaper. Wouldn't it be absurd to put the new diaper over the old diaper? Yet this is what many Christians do in effect when they refuse to put off the old self before putting on the new. They try to put the new man over the old man and it doesn't work. No wonder they're frustrated!

So please be sure to **put off** the deceitful desires of the flesh by keeping in repentance.

What about Holiness?

Holiness refers to absolute purity or wholeness and is an obvious trait of the *Holy* Spirit, who is God. It's also a trait of the human spirit in light of the fact that, when people believe the gospel, they are spiritually reborn by the *Holy* Spirit. Jesus put it in the clearest terms when he said, "The Spirit gives birth to spirit" (John 3:6). This is why Ephesians 4:24 instructs us to put on the new self since it was "created to be like God in true righteousness and *holiness*." My point? Holiness is a trait of your spirit, which is why the Bible says:

> **Once you were alienated from God and were
> enemies in your minds because of your evil behavior.
> ²² But now he has reconciled you by Christ's physical
> body through death to present you <u>holy in his sight</u>,
> <u>without blemish</u> and <u>free from accusation</u>—²³ if you
> continue in your faith, established and firm, not
> moved from the hope held out in the gospel.**
> **Colossians 1:21-23**

How is it that believers are holy in God's sight, without a
blemish and free from accusation? Because that's who we already are in
our spirit and God sees us according to our spirit and not our flesh. God
only sees our sin when we miss it, but he forgives us and cleanses us as
soon as we repent:

> **If we claim to be without sin, we deceive
> ourselves and the truth is not in us. ⁹ If we confess
> our sins, he is faithful and just and will forgive us our
> sins and <u>purify us from all unrighteousness</u>.**
> **1 John 1:8-9**

God forgives us as soon as we humbly confess and purifies us
from *all* unrighteousness. If God purifies us from all unrighteousness
what's that make us? Completely righteous in his sight. This is why it's
so important to keep your spiritual arteries free of the clogging of
unconfessed sin. When we stubbornly refuse to confess a transgression,
the LORD can't help but see that sin because we're not forgiven and
cleansed of it. The offense will stand between us and God and prevent
his grace from flowing in our lives to some degree. This is why the
psalmist said, "If I had cherished sin in my heart, the Lord would not
have listened" (Psalm 66:18). It's nothing deep.

Think about it like this: Say your spouse or close friend offends
you but stubbornly refuses to apologize (I'm not talking about something
petty). How will this affect your relationship? Warm feelings will cease
and it'll separate you to some degree. Only honest communication will
restore the fellowship or, more specifically, **repentance and
forgiveness**. When the offender humbly confesses, this releases you to

forgive and intimacy is restored. The repentance/forgiveness dynamic is awesome and keeps relationships *alive*. It keeps marriages, friendships and every other type of relationship *functioning*. Without the operation of these powerful principles—apologizing and forgiving—very few, if any, relationships would last.[58]

Getting back to holiness, some define holiness as avoiding sin and keeping undefiled by the world. While there's some truth to this definition, as far as human beings go, it doesn't wash as a full definition. After all, God is repeatedly described as holy in the Scriptures and, in fact, is worshipped for it (Isaiah 6:3 & Revelation 4:8), but God was holy eons before sin ever existed and needed avoided.

I define holiness as "absolute purity" because it's regularly cited in the Bible as the *opposite* of what is impure and indecent (see, for example, 1 Thessalonians 4:7, 2 Corinthians 7:1, Hebrews 7:26 & Deuteronomy 23:14).

"Wholeness" is another good definition. Wholeness is single-mindedness or integrity. It's the opposite of double-mindedness and inner conflict. God is holy—whole—because he has no inner conflict; he doesn't straddle the fence between good and evil.

Wholeness is the *whole* of the LORD's nature and therefore refers to all the fruits of the Spirit since the fruits of the Spirit are the very traits of the Creator. Charles Spurgeon put it like this: "Holiness is the harmony of all godly virtues." With this understanding, consider this passage:

> **As obedient children, <u>do not conform to the evil desires you had when you lived in ignorance</u>. [15]But just as he who called you is holy, so <u>be holy in all you do</u>; [16] for it is written, "Be holy, because I am holy."**
> **1 Peter 1:14-16**

As you can see, holiness is described as being the opposite of conforming to the evil desires of the flesh. What is the opposite of conforming to the evil desires of the flesh? Conforming to the good

---

[58] For important details on this and related subjects see my book *The Believer's Guide to FORGIVENESS & WARFARE.*

desires of the spirit, which are the fruits of the spirit. All the fruits of the Spirit combined refer to God's wholeness—the wholeness of his character—which is holiness. My point? Since holiness denotes all the fruits of the Spirit, the more believers put off the flesh and walk in the spirit the more holy they'll be! When you participate in the divine nature you'll produce the myriad fruits of the spirit. This is holiness, which is godliness or being like-God. It's spirituality, which is the spirit-controlled life as opposed to the flesh-ruled life. It's wholeness of being and purpose rather than double-mindedness. It's completeness.

In short, walking in the spirit is the key to holiness.

I bring holiness up because some great men of God say holiness is the answer to the extremes of legalism and libertinism, like Michael Brown. This is true. You could also say it's godliness. The reason I describe it as spirituality in this chapter is because it's the most fitting word to describe people who live out of their higher nature and produce the fruits of that nature, the fruit of the spirit.

Common Errors of "Holiness" Teachings

Holiness has unfortunately gotten a bad name over the years due to the infection of legalism in the Church and understandably so.

Legalists have enforced their pet rules under the guise of holiness when, actually, the rule in question often has nothing to do with holiness. For instance, playing card games isn't in-and-of-itself sinful; however, playing cards in a dubious atmosphere *can* lead to sin due to the **law of association** and other factors. See Proverbs 13:20 if you're not familiar with this 'law.' As the Bible says: "Bad company corrupts good character" (1 Corinthians 15:33). In other words, playing card games isn't wrong, it's the atmosphere you play the card games in that might corrupt you (e.g. gambling, greed, alcohol idolatry, whoredom and general hedonism). It would be for this reason that the Holy Spirit might move a believer to stop playing cards rather than because card games themselves are wrong. Please notice that I said it's the Holy Spirit who's supposed to move a person to stop doing something and not the enforcement of a rule by legalists. This means that the person has to have a relationship with God to some degree because otherwise he or she won't be able to discern the Holy Spirit's guidance. Focusing on relationship rather than rules is always the best protection against legalism.

The list of absurd "holiness" rules goes on and on—men can't have long hair, women can't have short hair, mandatory skirt length, sleeve length, such-and-such style of music is evil, viewing movies is worldly, etc.

Let's consider that last one. As pointed out in **Chapter 2**, legalists will typically denounce all R-rated films, as well as many PG and PG-13 ones, all in the name of holiness. They'll argue that there are too many sexually explicit (or implied) scenes, violence and cussing (etc.). Yet, consider the 1992 version of *Last of the Mohicans*. It's R-rated, but it's one of the most beautiful and moving films you'll likely ever watch. Yet staunch legalists will automatically denounce it because, after all, it's R-rated. It must therefore be evil or corrupting. While their motivations for doing this may be sincere, the issue isn't as black and white as they think. It never occurs to them, for instance, that the Bible is full of hard R-rated stories that are chock-full of incredible violence, sordidness and horror. When confronted with this fact they're either stunned to silence or will argue that these stories contain important themes or examples. If this is so, can't filmmakers do the same thing? Take *Star Trek: Nemesis*, for example. On the surface it's a serious sci-fi adventure, but the subtext explores the conflict of flesh & spirit and the story provides a sacrificial Christ-figure, an android no less!

So the message of the film in question must be considered. If the message is corrupt then I agree, avoid it like the plague. However, if the message is good and corresponds to the truths of human nature and the Bible, it may be worth checking out. Again, there are numerous R-rated stories in the Bible and they're worth one's time because they drive home an important lesson while, at the same time, entertain to some degree (and by "entertain" I simply mean capture your attention or amuse you). King David's lust over the bathing Bathsheba and his subsequent adultery and murder of her husband is an excellent example. Anyone who's been a believer for a number of years has read this story many times and visualized it in their minds each time. Many of us have even viewed film versions, like *King David* with Richard Gere. Is this sinful? No, it's the Word of God!

Furthermore, did you ever notice that God doesn't spell-out the messages in a lot of these stories? There's often an amount of ambiguity that requires reflection and further pursuit for answers. Those who have "ears to hear" will put in the effort while others won't. Take the story of Judah and his daughter-in-law Tamar from Genesis 38. Judah unjustly blamed the death of his two sons on Tamar and essentially condemned her to childless widowhood. Tamar understood her father-in-law's fleshly weaknesses and used it to her advantage in a story so sordid it'd be right at home next to any hard R-rated drama. Interestingly, God doesn't spell out the lessons in the story. Judah's hypocrisy is revealed but, at the same time, he should be commended for his honest repentance when confronted with the truth. Tamar's tactics to escape being a childless widow reveal shrewdness—it guaranteed her security for the future—but does this justify her insidious actions? The Bible doesn't spell-out the answers.

Or take Samson from Judges 13-16. Samson is honored in the New Testament's "Hall of Faith" chapter for his great faith,[59] but if you read his story it's clear that he was *not* an example of godliness or wisdom. Again, God refuses to spell everything out for the reader. These stories are fascinating, but they make you scratch your head. They provoke you to quarry them for gems of insight.

The best stories do this and so do the best films. *One Flew Over a Cockoo's Nest* is an excellent example. It's a subtle but ingenious denouncement of legalism and praise of the spirit of freedom.[60] Yet some Christians may find the pull-no-punches realities of a mental ward too unpleasant to watch, and that's perfectly okay. It *isn't* a pleasant film, but please don't take the legalistic attitude that it's an immoral film. Even though immorality is depicted, nothing could be further from the truth.

---

[59] That is, Hebrews 11.

[60] McMurphy (Nicholson), despite his obvious flaws, is the protagonist of the story. Although he's impulsive and has a weakness for the female gender (like Samson and King David), which got him into prison in the first place, he definitely has a spirit of freedom & life and inspires great love in the men of his ward. If there's any doubt, note how Chief (Will Sampson) dearly hugs him at the end. McMurphy's problem is that he needs to learn wisdom; then he can walk in his freedom without causing unnecessary harm to himself and others.

I said above that a movie may be worth checking out if the message is good. This shouldn't be interpreted to mean that a story has to have a happy ending in order to be worthwhile. The stories of Judas Iscariot and King Saul, as well as the prophecy of the Great White Throne Judgment in Revelation, don't have happy endings, but they each drive home a powerful truth—the wages of sin is death.

Also, I'm not saying that a film always has to have a deep moral to be watchable. What if you're in the mood for something light or amusing in the name of rest and recreation? Sloth is of the flesh, of course, but R&R is necessary and healthy, as long as it doesn't become an idol. The Bible teaches that there's "a time to weep and **a time to laugh**, a time to mourn and **a time to dance**" (Ecclesiastes 3:4).

These are just matters of common sense, but legalists will take the simplest of things and complicate them to no end.

Distinguishing Holiness and Worldliness

As pointed out in **Chapter 2**, religionists go awry with their "holiness" teachings because they lose sight of what the Bible itself calls worldly. Worldliness is any sin that springs from three things: **the lust of the eyes, the lust of the flesh** and **the pride of life** (1 John 2:15-17). With this understanding, a lot of activities or behaviors are only worldly depending upon the *intent* of the person's heart. For example, two females might wear the exact same scanty apparel, but one does it merely because it's the style she grew up with and the other does it to incite lust. I'm not saying that the former girl shouldn't learn to dress more modestly, which is a matter of wisdom, but she's not guilty of worldliness if her intentions are pure and she simply doesn't know any better. The intent of the heart makes all the difference. Even something considered good can be worldly if the intent of the heart is fleshly. Giving a sermon is good, but what if the pastor uses the occasion to brag on himself and tear down others? Ministering at a revival is good, but what if the evangelist's main interest is fleecing the flock and making a lot of moolah from the gig? Both the pastor and the evangelist are guilty of worldliness even though they're doing something good.

Another thing that should be stressed is that holiness is different for each believer depending on what their weaknesses are. For instance, one man can watch a TV show like *Survivor* where there are typically a few women in scanty apparel while another can't because he has a lust problem and can't risk stirring it up. One woman can enjoy a glass of wine but another can't because she's an alcoholic. One guy can listen to a certain style of music on occasion but another can't because he has no sense of balance. One woman can enjoy the shopping channel but another can't because she's a shopaholic. One man can go boating or play golf, but another can't because he idolizes the activity. Believers who decide not to do these activities do so because they know their weaknesses and are guarding their heart as the wellspring of life (Proverbs 4:23). With spiritual growth, however, these believers can become so strong that they eventually laugh at these kinds of temptations because they're no longer temptations at all. In other words, they *face* their fleshly weaknesses/fears and soar above them. But this takes time, wisdom and Holy Spirit guidance; otherwise it would be a case of foolishly placing temptation in one's path. Legalists would never advise facing one's fears/weaknesses; better to cloister yourself, they urge.

Holiness is also different for believers depending on where they're at spiritually and what the Holy Spirit has instructed them. For instance, one brother may have been instructed by the Lord to give up watching football on Sunday afternoon to use the time to draw closer to Him and serve in one capacity or another, but someone else hasn't been given this instruction.

One of my sisters is a very godly woman but she enjoys a glass of wine now and then. She told me last year that the Lord told her not to drink wine for three weeks and she complied. The Lord may have instructed her to do this just to stay freed-up and focus on him. After all, anything can become an addiction, which is a habit you can't live without. Of course I'm not talking about activities that are essential for living, like breathing; nor am I talking about wholly innocuous habits like going to bed early, but rather developed activities that are detrimental because they're either inherently wrong, like drug or porn addiction, or they're a neutral activity that's become harmful because the person has lost any sense of moderation. In short, the habit is robbing them of their time and preventing them from more fruitful pursuits/behaviors/pastimes. This is why it's good to periodically fast from certain things, particularly if you discern bondage setting in, however slight. Nip it in the bud and fast from it. Carol & I have taken long fasts from TV for this very reason. You can do this with any activity—computer games, fishing, golf, watching sports, going to certain establishments, movies, working out, etc.—*even* church-related activities (*gasp!*).

Be sensitive to the leading of the Spirit and periodically fast from anything you have an affinity for so that it doesn't become a bondage. Why? Because when something becomes a bondage you're no longer walking in freedom. It's being double-minded rather than single-minded or whole, which is holiness. As such, it's being *imbalanced* because you've lost self-control in this area. The spiritual man or woman, by contrast, is "temperate in *all things*" (1 Corinthians 9:25[61]), which means they maintain self-control in every area of their lives.

Holiness is also a matter of spiritual growth. What may be acceptable for one may not be acceptable for someone who's further on in the Lord. A brother recently encouraged me to view a certain movie about vigilantism which he claimed had a spiritual subtext. I viewed most of it, but couldn't finish it because it was so repugnant. I'm willing to watch a film that shows brutal reality if it drives home an important theme, like many stories in the Bible, but I didn't discern any depth to this particular movie and everything was just cartoony overkill—the style, the cussing, the violence. It just struck me as goofy, shallow and vile; a complete waste of my time. Perhaps it had a moral, but these negatives overshadowed any good, as far as I was concerned.

Everything shared in this section will rock the boat of legalists because they only think in terms of black and white. If something's wrong for brother Joe it must also be wrong for everyone else. If something's okay for sister Suzy it must also be okay for everyone else. This is true when it comes to black and white matters. For instance, adultery, murder, envy, slander and homosexuality are always wrong. But it's a different story when it comes to issues like the ones covered in this section. These things are right or wrong for the believer based on factors like the intent of the heart, the believer's weaknesses and

---

[61] KJV and NKJV.

strengths, their level of spiritual maturity, the counsel of the Holy Spirit and keeping free of potential bondages.

Spirituality Doesn't Mean
You Don't Have Natural Desires

We've discussed spirituality in this chapter, which is the spirit-controlled life, the opposite of the flesh-controlled life. It's wholeness of being rather than double-mindedness. It's walking in the freedom of the spirit rather than straddling the fence between the flesh and spirit. It's godliness. It's holiness.

Spirituality doesn't mean, however, that you don't have natural desires. It means that you're controlled by your spirit—your higher nature—rather than your flesh—your lower nature. As such, the desires of your natural self are submitted to your spiritual self. Your spirit has dominion over the flesh with the help of the Holy Spirit. Consequently, the body of flesh is put on the level of a slave and dominated. Take, for instance, sexual desire. There's nothing wrong with sexuality since God created our bodies with sex organs for the purpose of sex and reproduction, but he's given us wise parameters because sexuality is a fire that has the capacity for both good and bad. Consider natural fire: It can be a great blessing as long as you keep it under control—it can warm your body and cook your food—but it can also burn down your house or whole neighborhoods if let out of control. The sexual parameters that God has set are instinctive to our higher nature, which is why our conscience condemns us if we go out of bounds. These parameters are also recorded in the Bible. Within these boundaries our sexuality is positive and can bring a lot of good things, like intimacy, pleasure and children; outside of these parameters it can be a curse and yoke of bondage that causes all kinds of damage, like broken homes, broken hearts, diseases, illegitimate children, abortion, perversion and death. However, if we are spiritual—spirit-controlled—our sexuality will be a wonderful blessing.

Or take anger. Anger is an emotion and is neither good nor evil. It's neutral. It can be a positive force if we're spirit-controlled, but it can be a destructive force if we're flesh-ruled. In other words, anger becomes good or evil depending on whether you're spirit-controlled or flesh-ruled. For instance, when the Pharisees objected to Christ's mere intention of healing a man's deformed hand on the Sabbath in Mark 3:1-6, Jesus experienced righteous anger. These staunch legalists were so clueless and deceived that they objected to a miraculous healing of God! No wonder Yeshua was angry. If he were flesh-ruled, his anger could have provoked a foolish reaction, like having a fit of rage or even committing murder. At the very least he could've committed hateful gossip and slander. Instead he shot them all a glance of anger and healed the man despite their absurd resistance. The Messiah channeled his anger into something positive by giving these legalists a non-verbal public rebuke and healing the man's deformity. Because he was spirit-controlled and not flesh-ruled his anger was *good*.

My point is that the neutral desires of your natural self have the capacity for good or evil depending on if you're spirit-controlled or flesh-controlled.

Make it spirit-controlled and be blessed. Amen.

Being "Planted in the House of the LORD"

I have one last point on spirituality and it has to do with an article I read in a Christian magazine. The teacher cited these two passages to support regular church attendance:

> **The righteous will flourish like a palm tree,**
> **they will grow like a cedar of Lebanon;**
> ¹³ **planted in the house of the LORD,**
> **they will flourish in the courts of our God.**
> **Psalm 92:12-13**

> **Blessed are those who dwell in your house;**
> **they are ever praising you.**
> **Psalm 84:4**

The article was well-written and drove home the point that joining with believers at a healthy local church is an important key to proper spiritual growth. This is a good message, as verified by Hebrews 10:25, but it was wrong to cite these passages to support it. Why? Because using these passages to support attending Christian gatherings reflects an Old Testament mentality. In fact, it's a legalistic attitude. Let me explain...

Although the Holy Spirit was active among the Israelites in Old Testament times, it was much different than the way it is with believers in the New Testament. The Holy Spirit's work in that earlier era was limited and selective because the Israelites were spiritually un-regenerated. However, they did have a covenant with God and there are glimmerings of what the Spirit's function would be in the new covenant. David, for instance, was a type of the New Testament believer. Yet there was no spiritual rebirth, no indwelling and no baptism of the Spirit, at least not in the more thorough scale we enjoy today. The Israelites were *not* temples of the Holy Spirit as believers are in the new covenant because they weren't spiritually regenerated. The Temple of God was a literal temple—a building—and before that, a tent Tabernacle. Both the Tabernacle of Moses and the Temple of Solomon housed God's presence via the Ark of the Covenant. God therefore indwelled these structures and they were literally God's house.

Needless to say, to be "planted in the house of the LORD" or "dwell" there meant actually going to the Temple. Since the house of God was where God was, people had to go there to connect with him. Are you following?

Regardless of what some sincere pastors may say today, attending church gatherings is not the primary way to connect with God in the New Testament era, although it is *a way* due to the corporate anointing Jesus spoke of in Matthew 18:20, not to mention the anointing of fivefold ministry gifts, as detailed in Ephesians 4:11-13. Experiencing this "corporate anointing," however, doesn't require going to a specific *building*. It can take place wherever believers meet—a park, a street corner, the mall, someone's house, a vehicle, the workplace, etc.

The way believers dwell in God's house is simply by living out of their spirit rather than their flesh. Remember, our bodies are the temple of the Holy Spirit (1 Corinthians 6:19). The specific part of you that the Holy spirit inhabits is your spirit since the Spirit gave birth to your spirit—not your body—and your spirit was recreated as holy—not your body (John 3:6 & Ephesians 4:24). What I'm saying is that *the believer himself or herself* **is the house of God in the New Testament era and, more specifically, the believer's spirit**.

With this understanding, let's consider the two passages above. Psalm 92:12-13 says that those who are planted in the house of God will flourish. For believers in the New Testament era this actually means being planted in the spirit rather than planted in the flesh. How so? Because it's the believer's spirit that is the temple of God, not some building called a church! Believers who are planted in God's house—which is their spirit—participate in the divine nature and are spirit-controlled rather than flesh-ruled. They consequently escape the wages of flesh-rule, which is death. As such, they flourish.

Psalm 84:4 says that those who dwell in God's house are ever praising the LORD. For believers in the new covenant this means living out of their spirit as led of the Holy Spirit because their spirit is the temple of God, not some man-made structure. Those who live out of their spirit are spiritual and are ever-ready to offer the sacrifice of praise, as encouraged in Hebrews 13:15.

The idea that attending church gatherings is—by itself—the key to flourishing and a praise-giving spirit is absurd anyway. How many sourpuss legalists attend *every* church service? In fact, these people make a law out of it. By contrast, every believer who genuinely learns to put off the flesh, change their thinking, and put on the new self will indeed flourish spiritually and be a praise warrior. If going to a church service helps in accomplishing this then it can be included as *a way* believers are planted in God's house—that is, planted in their spirit rather than planted in their flesh—but going to a Christian gathering does not necessarily mean a person is planted in the house of the LORD. In fact, if you go to a gathering at a fellowship that's thoroughly infected by legalism—like the church of Laodicea in Revelation 3:14-20—the Lord *isn't even there*; he's knocking on the door wanting to come in!

Chapter 12

A License
to Live
FREE

Anytime this type of teaching is proclaimed some well-meaning believers will object on the grounds that it "gives people a license to sin." For some reason the notion of genuine freedom in Christ is unacceptable to them. They seem to think if believers are freed from the life-stifling confines of religious law they'll divert to the flesh, reveling in all the pent-up sins they weren't allowed to "enjoy" all those years under a system of rules and regulations. In other words, the dos & don'ts kept their flesh in check and releasing them from those confines would open up a Pandora's Box of carnal license.

As noted in the last two chapters, it is true that some believers who have been bound-up by religious law for years will swing toward the other extreme when they finally break free of the legalistic institution they were stuck in, whether family or church/sect or both. This is why youths who grow up in rigidly religious households suddenly become hellions when they go off to college. We've all seen it. They bask in their new-found sense of freedom, but they inevitably discover that the lifestyle of fleshliness doesn't grant them the happiness they crave. It's simply another form of bondage—bondage to the sinful nature rather than bondage to religious law. *Both* are slavery.

Even though some will swing like a pendulum from one extreme to the other, the idea that preaching freedom in Christ gives believers a license to sin is an erroneous understanding of Christian righteousness and responsibility. What the message of freedom really does is give believers a license to live free. Let's first look at...

Christian Righteousness and Responsibility

As far as righteousness goes, 2 Corinthians 5:21 says that God made him who had no sin, Jesus Christ, to become sin for us on the cross so that in him we might *become* the righteousness of God. As noted last chapter, 'become' in this text means "to come into existence, to be born." Hence, this passage is talking about spiritual rebirth where the believer's spirit is regenerated and reconciled to the LORD. As the Lord said, "Flesh gives birth to flesh, but the Spirit gives birth to spirit" (John 3:6). You see, the believer is *already righteous* in his or her spirit because s/he has been *born* that way. Thus the way to walk in *practical* righteousness is simply by learning to be spirit-controlled rather than flesh-ruled. This explains why Ephesians 4:22-24 instructs us to put off the old self—the flesh—in favor of putting on the new self—the spirit—because when we do this we'll literally "be like God in true righteousness and holiness."

This is how believers "participate in the divine nature and escape the corruption in the world caused by evil desires," as Peter put it (2 Peter 1:4). In short, this is how we successfully *imitate God*, which we are instructed to do in Ephesians 5:1. We imitate God because anyone who is spirit-controlled will naturally produce the fruits of the divine nature, which are the fruits of the spirit—love, joy, peace, patience, kindness, goodness, faith, faithfulness, gentleness, humility, self-control, dynamite power, vibrant life, righteousness and holiness (Galatians 5:22-

23).[62] 'Holiness' in this context refers to purity but, as we saw last chapter, holiness also refers to wholeness of being and therefore the harmony of all these virtues. *Agape* love could also be described as *the* fruit of the spirit because it binds all the fruits "together in perfect unity" (Colossians 3:14).

As far as Christian responsibility goes, every believer is responsible for himself or herself to recognize the desires of the flesh and put it off. Putting off the flesh includes being quick to repent when we miss it, which is "keeping with repentance" (1 John 1:8-9, Matthew & Luke 3:8). It's also the believer's responsibility to put on the new self and therefore be "clothed in Christ," as it is written:

Rather, clothe yourselves with the Lord Jesus Christ, and do not think about how to gratify the desires of the sinful nature.

Romans 13:14

If you put on the new self and are spirit-controlled rather than flesh-ruled you'll soar above the carnal desires of the flesh because the law of the spirit of life in Christ Jesus is greater than the law of sin and death (Romans 8:2). This is the only way a believer will conquer the flesh and be godly. The spirit of life in Christ renders the law of sin and death neutral and the only way it can be sparked to life is by thinking about fleshly inclinations, which feeds them and produces desire. Desire then gives birth to action (James 1:14-15).

Again, it's each Christian's *responsibility* to put off the flesh and put on the new self. A pastor can't do it for you, nor can any other minister or elder. Each believer must learn to do it for himself or herself. It's simply a matter of becoming spiritually mature and being a responsible individual.

Immature Christians, by contrast, are always struggling with the old man, which creates all kinds of problems in their lives and in the church. Some struggling is understandable because it comes with growth

---

[62] See also Acts 1:8, 2 Timothy 1:7, John 10:10, Ephesians 5:9, Philippians 1:11, 1 John 2:29 and Ephesians 4:24. Neither the list of works of the flesh in Galatians 5:19-21 nor the fruit of the spirit in 5:22-23 are comprehensive lists.

in the Lord, but those who keep struggling with the same areas of the flesh after five, ten, twenty or more years do so because either **1.** they're unaware of these truths, or **2.** they're evading their responsibility to put off the old self in favor of the new.

A License to Truly Live

Religious people just can't seem to accept that the LORD would set people totally free to live by their reborn spirit with the help & counsel of the Holy Spirit, but if God's people are not free to think, act and choose as they discern in their spirit and are shackled by a silly system of dos and don'ts then Christianity is no better than any other religion. In fact, it's no better than being a heathen in bondage to the flesh and a myriad of erroneous belief systems, like humanism, liberalism, Wicca or Sciencefictionology. Again, it would be a case of transferring from one kind of bondage to another. Why would God do that? What good would it do? All it would do is give the *appearance* of spirituality without the heart, the very definition of legal-ism. God doesn't want that! He wants his children free:

> **It is for freedom that Christ has set us free.**
> **Stand firm, then, and do not let yourselves be**
> **burdened again by a yoke of slavery.**
> **Galatians 5:1**

The grace of God is not a license to sin but rather a license to live:

> **"The thief comes only to steal and kill and destroy; I**
> **have come that they may have life, and have it to the**
> **full."**
> **John 10:10**

Does this sound like Jesus wants us to walk in more bondage after we come to him? He came to give us *life—life to the full*—not to put us into more bondage!

Churches and denominations that emphasize rules and regulations start to dry up because people instinctively sense that it's just more bondage, albeit a different kind. I'm here to tell you that the LORD is not a dictator, but a *liberator*. Why do you think Jesus quoted this passage from Isaiah when he started his public ministry:

> **"The Spirit of the Lord is on me, because <u>he has anointed me to preach good news</u> to the poor. <u>He has sent me to proclaim freedom for the prisoners</u> and recovery of sight for the blind, <u>to release the oppressed,</u>** [19] **to proclaim the year of the Lord's favor."**
>
> **Luke 4:18-19**

Christ was referring to himself and his mission. His purpose was *to set the captives free!* It's the devil who puts people into bondage— bondage to the flesh, bondage to sickness and disease, bondage to poverty, bondage to religion. But God wants us *free*—free to live, free to love, free to worship, free to serve, free to create and free to overcome. We believers will experience this wonderful freedom according to our level of understanding, our growth and our personal relationship with the Lord. Such freedom cannot be attained by following legalists and their elaborate systems of rules and regulations.

The Message of Freedom

The message of freedom is popular wherever you go. It attracts people because they naturally want to be free, not free to sin but to live, *really* live. That's what this book is all about—freedom from religion and freedom from the flesh to live free in Christ.

When I was in my late teens I was an unbeliever and didn't know anything about Christianity, but one thing I did know is that I was in bondage to the flesh. I was doing everything in *my* power to walk free of the flesh, but it was such a struggle. It was reminiscent of Paul's frustrating conflict in Romans 7:14-20: The very thing I didn't want to do is what I ended up doing, and what I wanted to do, I failed to do. I wanted free! And the message of Jesus Christ gave me that freedom, Praise God.

I thank the Lord I eventually found a local church that had a spirit of freedom during my formative years as a believer. When I found it, I camped out there for a whole decade, drinking in the freedom and learning of the things of God. As noted in previous chapters, I had visited other churches before settling into this one, but the air of deadness, authoritarianism or legalism sent me fleeing to the exit.

If, after reading this book, you sense the same things at your fellowship and your sincere efforts of spiritual warfare (as detailed in **Chapter 9**) haven't brought any change, it may be time to leave and find an assembly that has a spirit of freedom. As always, be led of the Holy Spirit. Make sure you have a peace and confirmation before leaving. Sometimes it's just a matter of common sense; for instance, if it's gotten to the point where you're turned-off by the very thought of going to a church service because it's such a useless drudgery or burden, that pretty much tells you everything you need to know—*leave*.

Getting back to the point, legitimate believers don't come to hear the message of grace in order to go out and have a sin party, they come to soak in the liberty and experience the abundant life that springs from the Fountain of Life, the liberty that was purchased for them at such great cost!

The people who are afraid of the message of freedom are the ones who don't trust the Church, which includes themselves. They don't trust themselves and this is why they don't think others can handle freedom. Actually, they're the very ones who need freedom the most. They need to be set free from the system of dos and don'ts they've shackled themselves to, a self-imposed state of bondage.

Once they're exposed to the message of freedom and get freed-up they can, in turn, spread the message of freedom and set others free. On and on until the Church universal is liberated from legalism.

Closing Blessing

May you walk free of legalism in all its ugly forms all the days of your spiritual journey on Earth. May you not just know *about* the LORD, but may you know Him personally, like Moses, David, Paul and John. May you continually increase in a spirit of **freedom**, **life**, **joy** **power**, **love**, **godliness** and **humility**.

Amen and amen.

Bibliography

NOTE: Just because a particular author appears in this bibliography—or in the main text—it doesn't automatically mean that I embrace every jot & tittle of what they teach (with the exception of the LORD, of course); it simply means I "ate the meat and spit out the bones" (1 Thessalonians 5:21). I encourage you to do the same with *any* teacher of God's Word.

Archer, Gleason, and Gary Hill. *Helps Word-Studies Lexicon.* Retrieved from http://biblehub.com/, 1987, 2011

Brown, Francis/Driver, S.R./Briggs, Charles A. *Brown-Driver-Briggs Lexicon.* Peabody: Hendrickson Publishers, 1994

Bullinger, Ethelbert W. *A Critical Lexicon and Concordance to the English and Greek New Testament.* Grand Rapids: Zondervan Publishing House, 1975

Cameneti, Michael. *The Missing Ingredient to Success.* Tulsa: Faith Library Publications, 2004

Cameneti, Joseph. *New Testament Prophets* (series). Believers Christian Fellowship, Warren, OH. September-October, 1990

Cameneti, Joseph. *Praise & Worship* (series). Believers Christian Fellowship, Warren, OH. May-July, 1987

Dake, Finis Jennings. *Dake's Annotated Reference Bible.* Lawrenceville: Dake Bible Sales, Inc., 1991

Houdmann, S. Michael. *Got Questions?* Retrieved from https://www.gotquestions.org/, 2002-2018

Lindsey, Hal. *The Liberation of Planet Earth.* New York: HarperCollins, 1974

Kirkwood, David. *Your Best Year Yet!* Pittsburgh: Ethnos Press, 1996

LORD, The. *Berean Study Bible.* Glassport: Bible Hub, 2016

LORD, The. *Douay-Rheims Bible.* Charlotte: Saint Benedict Press, 2000

LORD, The. *English Standard Version (ESV). Holy Bible.* Chicago: Crossway, 2001

LORD, The. *Holman Christian Standard Bible.* Nashville: Holman Bible Publishers, 2004

LORD, The. *King James Version. Holy Bible.* Iowa Falls: World Bible Publishers

LORD, The. *New American Standard Bible.* Nashville: Holman, 1977

LORD, The. *New International Version. Holy Bible.* Nashville: Holman, 1986

LORD, The. *New International Version (Revised). Holy Bible.* Nashville: Holman, 2011

LORD, The. *New King James Version Study Bible: Second Edition.* Nashville: Thomas Nelson, 2012

LORD, The. *New Living Translation. Holy Bible.* Carol Stream: Tyndale House Publishers, 2006

LORD, The. *The Amplified Bible.* Grand Rapids: Zondervan, 1987

LORD, The. *Quest Study Bible: New International Version.* Grand Rapids: Zondervan, 2003

LORD, The. *World English Bible (WEB).* Salt Lake City: Project Gutenberg, 2013

LORD, The. *Weymouth New Testament.* Ulan Press, 2012

LORD, The. *Young's Literal Translation (YLT). Holy Bible.* Grand Rapids: Baker Books, 1989

Servant, David. *The Baptism in the Holy Spirit.* Retrieved from http://www.davidservant.com/books/dmm/dmm_11/ 2018

Strong, James. *Strong's Exhaustive Concordance.* Grand Rapids: Baker, 1991

Vine, W.E. *Vine's Expository Dictionary of Biblical Words.* Cambridge: Nelson, 1985

Wiebe, Alan. *Praise and Worship* (series). Believers Christian Fellowship, Warren, OH.

Yandian, Bob. *Galatians—The Spirit-Controlled Life.* Tulsa: Harrison House, 1985

Fountain of Life

Teaching Ministry

(Psalm 36:9)

The mission of Fountain of Life is to **set the captives FREE** by **reaching the world** with the **life-changing truths of God's Word**, the **power of the Holy Spirit** and the **Awesome News of the message of the Mighty Christ**.

We're calling Spiritual Warriors all over the Earth to partner with us on this mission!

Books by Dirk Waren:

The Believer's Guide to Forgiveness & Warfare (2012)
Legalism Unmasked (2013/2018)
HELL KNOW! (2014/2016)
SHEOL KNOW! (2015)
The Four Stages of Spiritual Growth (2015)
ANGELS: Their Purpose and Your Responsibility (2017)
THE LAW and the Believer (2018)